MONTAGE
EISENSTEIN

Jacques Aumont

TRANSLATED BY ————
*Lee Hildreth,
Constance Penley, and
Andrew Ross*

BFI Publishing, London

INDIANA UNIVERSITY PRESS
Bloomington and Indianapolis

First published in the United States of America by
Indiana University Press
10th and Morton Streets
Bloomington, Indiana
and
Published in Great Britain by
The British Film Institute
127 Charing Cross Road
London WC2H OEA

Manufactured in the United States of America

This translation was made possible by a publication subvention grant from the Research Board of the University of Illinois at Urbana-Champaign.

Library of Congress Cataloging-in-Publication Data
Aumont, J. (Jacques)
    Montage Eisenstein.

    Translation of: Montage Eisenstein.
    Bibliography: p.
    Includes index.
    1. Eisenstein, Sergei, 1898–1948. I. Title.
PN1998.A3E533413 1985   791.43'0233'0924   85-45074
ISBN 0-253-33874-3
ISBN 0-253-20366-X (pbk.)
1 2 3 4 5 90 89 88 87

British Library Cataloguing in Publication Data
Aumont, Jacques
  Montage Eisenstein.
  1. Eïzenshteïn, Sergeï
  I. Title
  791.43'0233'0924   PN1998.A3ES/

ISBN 0-85170-187-6 (pbk.)

MONTAGE EISENSTEIN

THEORIES OF REPRESENTATION AND DIFFERENCE

General Editor: Teresa de Lauretis

CONTENTS

To Bertrand Augst

PREFACE

Appearances to the contrary, writing on Eisenstein is not an easy task. No other film director has been studied so exhaustively. Dozens of books have been devoted to almost every conceivable aspect of the Eisenstein "case," and few other filmmakers have achieved anything like the same kind of notoriety both during their lifetime and after. Indeed, there is no one else in film history who has so intricately combined filmmaking, film teaching, and film theorizing; no other director has written as much, has commented on his own work at such length, or has so obviously thought of himself as an aesthetician, a journalist, a philosopher, a semiotician, and a draughtsman (even if others have exhibited the same penchant for "mastery").

Far from facilitating the critic's task, this array of knowledge presents him or her with an awesome burden—the cloying impression that everything has already been said. While I certainly cannot claim to have read all that has been written in every language on "the greatest filmmaker of all time," I am acquainted with practically all the books of any importance—and a significant number of articles—on Eisenstein in English, French, German, Italian, and Russian, and I hope I will not sound too immodest if I say that this book is indebted to none of them. In fact, what I found in most, even the better ones, tended to obscure rather than illuminate my understanding of Eisenstein's work. Indeed, all these books and articles are more or less subtle illustrations of a given thesis about Eisenstein: to Marxist critics, Eisenstein can only be seen as the epitome of dialectical materialism as applied to film and film theory; to Bazinians, he is the malignant architect of a conception of cinema as montage which shatters the reflected order of a transparent world; to his established biographers, he is the true Leonardo of the twentieth century (pathologies and all); to film historians, he is a forbidding monument that cannot, however, be ignored. To each of them, he is a myth.

I wrote this book between 1976 and 1978, at a time when I was actively engaged in translating and editing Eisenstein's writings which had been discovered (or, in part, rediscovered) some five to ten years before. The more I familiarized myself with these writings (or, rather, the more I immersed myself in them), the more certain I grew that the Eisensteinian myth, like all myths, was a grave misrepresentation of the originality of Eisenstein's figure as a *thinker*. For I remain convinced that, in spite of the obvious aporias of his work, he is one of the great philosophers of art of our century.

Within its limitations (if only of size), this book attempts therefore to renovate the literature on Eisenstein in at least two respects. First, I have striven to be as thorough as possible in my knowledge of Eisenstein's work, notably his written and theoretical work; as far as I know, this is the first (and to date, still the only) book that is informed by a reading of all the available writings of Eisenstein: namely the six volumes of *Collected Works* published in Moscow in 1965–70, plus a few articles here and there. If I were to rewrite it now, I would, of course, have to take into consideration a few important texts that have been exhumed since 1978, most notably the major collection published (in French translation only) under the title *Cinématisme*: a collection that is highly representative of the art essayist in Eisenstein, and which, if it had been available to me then, would undoubtedly have helped to improve the balance of this book.

Second, I have tried to engage one of the main difficulties in dealing with Eisenstein, namely the extreme diversity of his work, his many different interests and talents, and above all, the ceaseless transformation of his conceptual system: in short, everything that might lead (and has often led) to the legitimate conclusion that there are *several Eisensteins*. One of the most basic assumptions of this book is that it is impossible to describe and evaluate Eisenstein's achievements—both in the domain of filmmaking and of theory—without taking into consideration the imbrication of his life (itself mediated by his autobiographical texts) with his cinematic production (including the innumerable unrealized projects, scripts, his drawings, his writings) and the less tangible space where theoretical production and elaboration takes place. Aside from a regrettable neglect of Eisenstein's drawings (which would deserve a study in its own right), the very structure of this book demonstrates, I hope, my concern for the complexities and the idiosyncrasies of the Eisensteinian opus.

My research began as a doctoral dissertation on "The Evolution of the Eisensteinian Concept of Montage," and so Eisenstein the theoretician remains central to the finished book. However, one of the results of my research was the recognition that there is no unitary "concept of montage" that comes to theoretical fruition over the course of his career—at least, not in the limited, rationally defined, and constant form by which one could characterize a true concept. Nevertheless, the *principle* of montage plays a crucial part in his writing as well as in his films, and occupies a central place in his philosophical and aesthetic system. Accordingly, I did not feel that I could expound my thesis without first probing and testing its consistency; that is why this book concludes with a chapter on montage, while the two preceding chapters attempt respectively to analyze the work of montage in Eisenstein's films (in two very different film sequences), and to describe the status of montage in the overall theoretical system elaborated by him (of which I have tried to provide a sketchy account). Finally, I had to account for the fact that Eisenstein's career as a filmmaker and as a thinker is absolutely inseparable from biographical (political, psychological) determinations: hence a first chapter that is entirely devoted to a few fragmentary reflections on Eisenstein's "character."

Written in deliberate intellectual isolation, this book, like any other, is a particular product of a personal history. Unlike most intellectuals of my generation, I discovered cinema rather late in life, and the period of this discovery was the true origin of this book. It is hardly an exaggeration to say that I owe most of its inspiration—not so much the knowledge as the passion—to my friends in *Cahiers du cinéma* around 1970; daily screenings and discussions were our unchanging diet, and I benefited more than words could say from years of work and friendship with Pierre Baudry, Pascal Bonitzer, Jean-Louis Comolli, Serge Daney, Pascal Kané, Jean Narboni, Bernard Eisenschitz, Jean-Pierre Oudart, Jacques Rivette, not to forget Sylvie Pierre, who was absolutely quintessential to my education in film.

During the later period of actual research and writing, help and encouragement came from other friends, colleagues, and students; I have been greatly stimulated by the cordial support of Michel Marie, Dominique Noguez, and Peter Schofer; Raymond Bellour was officially my advisor, but his role has been far more vital, intellectually and psychologically, than this official title indicates; with characteristic generosity, Christian Metz did much to hasten and facilitate the original publication of this book.

Finally, I would like to acknowledge the enormous debt I owe to Anne Faisandier for help, comfort, and the example she set.

Among my American colleagues, I owe special thanks to Rick Altman, Dudley Andrew, David Bordwell, Edwin Jahiel, Constance Penley, and Kristin Thompson, not only for what they did, directly and indirectly, to facilitate the publication of this translation, but also for the pleasure of their continued friendship.

In preparing this English edition, Lee Hildreth, Constance Penley, and Andrew Ross have been ideal translators; indeed, they have managed to substantially improve the book's style, without ever betraying its impulse.

Lee Hildreth's translation of Part II of "Eisenstein Taken at His Word" and "Eisensteinian Concepts" appeared originally in *Discourse*. I am grateful to the editors for allowing it to be reprinted here.

I did not need to think twice about the dedication of this English version of my book: to anyone who knows Bertrand Augst, it will come as no surprise.

Paris, April 1985

MONTAGE EISENSTEIN

Notes Towards a Biography

1

A Body of Memories

When he is almost forty-five, Eisenstein writes his memoirs in the form of an autobiography: "To write an autobiography is to write *about oneself*,"[1] writing with no other object than the self, or the making of its image.

More than anything else, however, autobiography is also about writing, the kind of serpentine writing that is devoted solely to the pleasure of the text, its vagrant spirit, or what he calls its *flânerie*. Two kinds of time, then, are spliced together throughout his writings: the diffuse and long-winded temporal pleasure of the imaginary, and the bodily, concrete present of writing. Writing the autobiography involves not only *jouissance* (of writing) and regression (symptomatic writing), but also the *jouissance* involved in this regression itself ("the warmish, rosy-hued haze of memories").[2] Thus, the uninterrupted pleasure of composition is heightened by the *jouissance* of pure memory, complete in itself: a meticulous labor of memory, sharply attuned to each and every detail, and a textual labor, devoted to the living, material body of anamnesis.

Irony

In his texts, Eisenstein is careful to eliminate any kind of affect whatsoever, and thus represses not just his desire but his very feelings.[3]

Consider the "maxim," which he took to heart in a formative way, by which philosophy represses the feeling of joy as well as sadness; his first defense, or mask, is always that of *nonfeeling*. There is no mention of friends or lovers in his texts,[4] and as for his childhood, it is invoked only in order to be able to deny, in a more objective way, whatever threatens to escape from his censored past.[5]

This, however, is still only a passive form of defense, and is seldom very successful, while his last resort is always irony, the famous Eisensteinian irony which helped him save his skin in real life and, in his texts, is consciously and explicitly assumed, even theorized (for example: "it looked as if my implacable irony had, very early on, killed off my taste for pathos for good . . ."). Reclaiming almost all of its old qualities as a rhetorical figure, irony becomes the only form of confidential discourse, the only way of expressing all the avowals of love addressed to the one soul whom Eisenstein worshipped above all others—Meyerhold.[6]

Indeed, the only comedy that he seriously tried to make, *M M M*, never materialized. And the irony we might have expected to see in his films is never there, except in a few sporadic moments scattered throughout his most explicitly erotic film, *The General Line.*

The Deviant Drive

His most prominent biographers insist that he categorically represses all impulses that would deviate from the norm of *homo Stalinus*, in other words, that he sublimates an awkward, homosexual desire—at any rate, it is clear that he was not a man of passion. Indeed, his greatest source of enjoyment involved the least personal intercourse; his *jouissance*, the art of putting body and desire to work, was always being pursued in the most discrete, obscure, but also deliberate, ways. There is an interesting passage in *Immoral Memories*[7] which describes two of the privileged sites of this *jouissance*, dancing and drawing, both of which "are, of course, nurtured from the same breast, and are but two different embodiments of the same drive." Using these two poles of the same drive as magnets, Eisenstein gathers together a host of memories in his touchingly ironic fashion: a string of "chained Prometheuses" which literally follow the path of the drive; one reference (solitary and fleeting) to his obscene, automatic drawings—repressed because destroyed; and a whole series of references to Mexico, his "paradise lost and regained" (a paradise of graphics, but of other things too, and here I shall not even mention Marie Seton's scurrilous tale of Eisenstein's brush with pederasty).

Many of his paradises that exist outside of Mexico or the womb are artificial paradises, or excuses for *trips* (Eisenstein's word). Hence, the encounters with religion, the blinding array of white churches laid out in the pages of "Novgorod—Los Remedios," the spell of the priestly vestments lovingly named in "Intellectual Cinema," or the act of swallowing the sacrament of "sweet opium" in Meyerhold's courses. It is as if he were addicted to a kind of imaginary drug (the drug of the imaginary), and perhaps this is one way of deciphering the long, involved, and obsessive anti-Freudian discourse that he offers in his desperate refusal to "restrict" the drives to the sexual. If the only *jouissance* is sexual (which he restricts in turn to the physiological), then what space is left for "his" drive to occupy? Hence his constant need to prove that this drive can also act as a kind of detour, that it not only works (he already knows this) but that it works legitimately.

The Mysticism of the Atheist

Whether it was repressed, concealed, or disavowed, his mysticism has long been accepted, or rather assumed. While in France, his greatest desire was to visit places like the Sainte Chapelle, Chartres, or Lourdes. In spite of Jean Mitry's unimpeachable claim (he accompanied Eisenstein) that Eisenstein's comments had no expressly religious overtones, and despite Eisenstein's own ironic remarks about Lourdes (which he never actually visited), Marie Seton's rumor about his "mystical" sensibility persists. The least that we can say is that if he was a mystic, then he was successful in hiding it, even to himself, the best reader of his own texts. The result of his trip to Novgorod, for example, where there is nothing else but "ecclesiasticism" (churches, pilgrimages, processions), is a text that barely alludes to spiritual matters, a text that is full of metaphorical variations on whiteness rather than flights of religious fancy.

There is something paradoxical, however, in his atheist's fascination for religious forms, especially those of his native, Orthodox Church. For he is clearly attracted not only by their association with irrationality (his scornful interest in superstitions, and his rejection, or denegation, of psychoanalysis), but also by their profound rationality—that of a power, a visible hierarchy, and a repressive apparatus. In other words, he is drawn towards the institution, the dogma, and the catechism, rather than to religion, faith, and prayer. As for his share of ecstasy, we know that he sought it elsewhere, and it had little to do with mysticism. He plays around with religious forms and rituals, using them as a kind of portable cloak for ironically covering over those affects that are a little too violent, or "implicating," as a kind of reservoir of signifiers, or metaphors, that is more closely guarded than elsewhere, and which is fed directly by the paradise of his childhood.

The Veiled Sex

Stereotypically, women, for him, are distant and inaccessible objects. An eponymous figure would indeed be the striptease which Eisenstein describes at length, and with a certain despondency; one never gets to see anything—and perhaps there is nothing to see anyway. The spotlight fades on cue, just as we are about to catch sight of the threatening absence. Clearly there is in this something of the archetypal scenario in which Freud describes the little boy's discovery of the mother's genitals.

Surely it is no surprise, then, when we encounter his somewhat abstracted attitude towards women? To cite only one example from *Immoral Memories*, he blithely confuses the Wenzel sisters with other sisters, who are themselves interchangeable, at least when they can be distinguished from the frilly clothes that they wear. This absent-mindedness is clearly a way of politely disguising his contempt.[8] It is no coincidence that he is so fascinated by the "ladies" of St. Petersburg station, by Parisian streetwalkers, and by pin-up girls.

The most extreme example of the genre, however, is the properly monstrous image of femininity presented by the ornamental "iron maidens" on the *fin de siècle* façade of a building constructed by Eisenstein's father. They are not only absurd and hideous, but also *deconstructible*; their infinitely fetishizable bodies break apart and disintegrate, to end up rusting in the drains. In addition, these monstrous iron bodies are hollow and so one can go in and walk about inside them, just like the Statue of Liberty which he mentions (it also possesses a body that is only a sum of its parts—chest, shoulders, neck, stomach, elbows, but no genitals). Hence the double symbolic revenge of the little boy terrified by feminine castration; the revenge of curiosity, since he can now stroll at will underneath the woman's skirts (*inside* these skirts, within her very body); and also the revenge of ignominiously vandalizing (the "last outrages" committed by the nasty, corrosive weather) these images of femininity.

Eisenstein's attitude towards sexuality has been examined often enough, above all, of course, because almost nothing is known about his sexual practices. Pera Atasheva, his wife, died without "revealing" anything, and those closest to him, like the Alexandrovs, the Strauchs, and the Tisses, have kept their peace on the subject. As for Eisenstein himself, there is only a fleeting mention here and there (like one unexplained allusion to "the unwholesome sexuality that was [his] lot"). Clearly, then, we should take with a grain of salt all the purely biographical conjectures about Eisenstein's "psychic make-up"—especially those (Seton, Fernandez) that rest shamelessly on dubious, even outrightly contrived, evidence.

Eisenstein shrinks from acknowledging that sexuality has any meaning in itself, and, indeed, will distance himself from any hint of interiority which is not intellectual.[9] Naturally, the repressed returns, either in the form of his obscene drawings, or in the all too transparent metaphors of *The General Line*. The conscious assertiveness of this attitude is quite unmistakable, however, and most of all when he is trying to rationalize his repression; one "theoretical" clue, for example, is his choice of Lawrence over Freud (if the paradigm has any meaning) as a sign of his refusal to recognize that the origin of all unconscious effects is "always in every case" a sexual one (which is to say, his refusal to recognize his desire never to recognize this). Sex is not really absent, then, it is present, but in its own allusive, hidden way.

Curiosity as Desire

No doubt prompted by an intellectual climate hostile to psychoanalysis, he frequently indulged in naively sweeping, anti-Freudian declarations. We know, however, that Eisenstein had read (quite closely) a number of books by and about Freud.[10] We could even say that he had assimilated the essential aspects of these texts, not, of course, their "extremist pansexualism," but at least the basics of the work on dreams, and, in particular, the Freudian conceptions of the symbolic. Of all Freud's texts, however, the one that had the greatest impact was *Leonardo da Vinci and a Memory of His Childhood*. Eisenstein, of course, was completely devoted to Leonardo. Moreover, Freud's portrait of the artist-engineer must have provided him with more than his share of self-recognition. Like Leonardo, the child Eisenstein was torn between mother and father; like Leonardo, he tried his hand at everything, and found it increasingly difficult to finish anything (films, books); and lastly, the description of Leonardo's "Platonic homosexuality" may also have struck a chord in him.

His identification with the personal genius of Leonardo is not, however, the only important factor in this. For Freud's text is one of his first attempts to deal with the question of the epistemophilic drive, and so it would not be implausible to expect Eisenstein to recognize, even if unconsciously, his own insatiable desire for knowledge as nothing more than a displacement of infantile sexual curiosity. If this parallel between the anxious curiosity of the child and the "mysteries of creation" is explicitly drawn out by Freud, it is also one of the central themes of Eisenstein's celebrated chapter entitled "Wie Sag' ich's meinem Kind?!" (besides, this is what the title means).[11]

In Eisenstein's opinion, this unquenchable curiosity is a compensation for the handicap of his "low-key sensibility"—just as an astronomical display of knowledge compensates for some kind of sexual "immaturity." This kind of curiosity, then, is the specific form of Eisensteinian desire, the kind that grows out of the desire to take watches apart, or to devote oneself to wanderlust or scholarship. If any more evidence were needed of the importance of this drive in Eisenstein, we could point to the ironic fatalism with which he refers, for example, to his "scrutinizing instinct," as "this unfortunate character trait of mine."

The Indiscriminate

His impressive cultural range is eclectic, to say the least: that of an autodidact who reads Maeterlinck, Kleist, and Schopenhauer during the civil war, devours volumes of history, and fearlessly takes on the classics of anthropological thought. There is no predetermined order to his reading, and it largely depends upon the direction his thought happens to take (his intellectual direction, which includes his work, and teaching). The result is an intellectual landscape littered with anything and everything, and arranged higgledy-piggledy, like a patchwork quilt—but also like a palimpsest, with various levels, the more recent barely covering the oldest. Perhaps this also accounts for the difficulty that he always seemed to have in truly assimilating (as opposed to understanding) Marxism, at first as a simple appendage, but increasingly in the form of a materialist metaphysic which was to orchestrate, justify, and if need be, exonerate everything else (this, at any rate, is how one is inclined to interpret the aims of *Nonindifferent Nature*).

The Mysteries of Mathematics

He loves mathematics and never passes up a chance to declare it. No doubt this is a boast about his own much celebrated "vanity," since it is this relatively unexpected trait which marks him out as a

Renaissance man, like Leonardo's artist-engineer. There is more to this, however; he "passed his exams with flying colors" in integral and differential calculus, for example, but "of course no longer remembers any of it," a fact which does not stop him from claiming that this was the source of his "tendency for discipline in thinking and [his] love of exactitude and precision." This is a fetishistic statement, which he repeats in a number of ways, but which, like all fetishes, is clearly only a disguise. Discipline in thinking? (what discipline?). Exactitude and precision? (maybe, if we look at his films and his theatrical work, but it is a different story altogether if we look for "exactitude," let alone "precision," in his theoretical work).

The fetish image, however, is not sealed off. Indeed he makes a point of declaring that he is especially fond of the theory of limits because of its inherent dynamism (a little further on, mathematics is cited as the very type of movement, of dialectics, and of the principle of becoming).

This imaginary mathematics, all done up in its Sunday best, is probably a new scientific guarantee brought in as methodological support for the philosophical guarantee already sought out in Marxism-Leninism. To go back even further still, we can point to the "very first pantomime" he ever wrote, a masterpiece of pure geometry, in his opinion, that attempts to dramatically assimilate the fact—that a straight line is a circle. What is most important, however, about this "array of geometrical displacements" is not so much the endless pleasure of repetitions that it provides, but rather the fact that, little by little, "the hero quietly loses his mind. . . ." The gist of this metaphor suggests something rather important about the place occupied in Eisenstein's imaginary by mathematics. Are the universal emblems or figures of reason (*ratio*, as he puts it) not themselves somehow marked by the sign of passion (madness), of mystery, and art, and also, on a contiguous plane, the *anti-ratio* of sex? This is not so paradoxical as it seems. Even though, in his writing, Eisenstein had exhaustively explored the antinomy between "mathematics" and the "mysteries of art," how could we ever forget that "his" mathematics is only the refracted image of a "true" mathematics that already belongs, like all objects of knowledge, on the side of desire?

Rational Teaching

The most interesting aspect of Eisenstein's teaching is what could be called its productive *double standard*. For the dynamics of his teaching stems from the tension between a curriculum that is so tightly crammed full that it has to be justified at great length (a syllabus more obsessed with universality than with coherence or practicality) and a practice which appeals to spontaneity, emotion, energy, and desire.[12] On the one hand, the oppressive austerity of his wide range of culture and scholarship, and on the other, the charismatic appeal of his little turns of thought, or redeeming gestures, that are so delightfully captured in the stenographic accounts of his courses.

These two sides are not, however, irreconcilable; the "granite-hard cine-science" on which his students are supposed to cut their teeth, is actually the hidden surface of Eisensteinian pedagogy. Remember the "discovery" of the student Nizhny, who had been naively gulled (or perhaps he was only pretending?) by Eisenstein's superb in-class attempt to act as if he were improvising. What was the response to this? "How can I take responsibility for appearing before students if I am not properly prepared?"; and in actual fact he had always obsessively, even manically, prepared and anticipated everything that was to happen in class.[13]

Whichever way you look at it, *mastery* is written all across his teaching, which is why teaching probably plays such an important part in his life, not only because it is "the true site of theoretical construction,"[14] as has been suggested, but also because his attitude to teaching is, in many respects, the model of his relation to the other: he wants only to be in the position of the Master, and at any cost.[15] The master is not, of course, the father, and so Eisenstein absolutely refuses to entertain the same relation with "his" students as he himself had enjoyed with Meyerhold; one of his favorite jokes about this consisted of repeatedly reminding them that he was not interested in producing "Eisenpups." On the other hand, he never passes up the opportunity to treat them, and everyone else, like subjects to be educated. Clearly, this is one of the keys to his conception of the spectator who must be educated, not only in the ordinary or general sense of acquiring culture, but at every single opportunity, and with every single film, sequence, and image. It is in this vein, then, that I shall be reading Eisenstein, even in the self-criticisms which marked his last years, beginning with the famous discourse of 1935, where his sovereign mastery is asserted with each sentence, dealing with problems as it suits him, mobilizing all the signs of his erudition, operating at the height of his irony—and finally leading everyone regally on to his own chosen ground.

Digressions

Another interesting thing about *Immoral Memories* is the secretive air which it affects. Eisenstein's "revelations" are always feigned. One remarkable example would be the long and important chapter "How I Learned to Draw," from which we learn many things, albeit indirectly, but not "how he learned to draw" (nor, even more important, how he perceived his relation to creativity). I cannot help thinking of Raymond Roussel's *How I Wrote Some of My Books,* or of the conjurer's trick of "revealing" his tricks. Eisenstein never says anything directly, either in the way of personal confessions or theoretical discoveries. Like everything else, his "revelations" are always being *postponed,* which is so typical of his writing; just as the signified is about to be offered up, the signifier is brought into play, and prevents its delivery. In "How I Learned to Draw," one passes through a complex and seemingly interminable maze of diverse characters and names, which leads only indirectly towards any final meaning. It is a good example of Eisenstein's tendency to employ proper names and particulars as a decoy, a way of avoiding the fatal moment when he has to say what he thinks.

This accounts for the double, or contradictory, aspect of his writing. It is both slow and ponderous, and abrupt and jerky; although there are no ellipses, and every nuance is explicitly articulated, each phrase, because of its own rigorous assertiveness, tends nonetheless to be a spare, incisive comment, like the "fragment" of montage. Don't be fooled by this strategic duplicity, for it actually involves two sides of the same response to enunciation; "take it or leave it"/"catch it if you can." Caught between these two invitations, the reader should at least know where he stands; and what is at stake is his position of mastery, one which Eisenstein challenges and steals for himself.

As a kind of self-analysis, Eisenstein made several attempts to define the significance of his digressions, in the course of which he almost always posits something like a *childhood memory* as the (mythical?) "origin" of the metonymic chain of signifiers, this endless chain which acts as an escape route, or as a camouflage for that struggle "with a specter" which was how he viewed the act of writing. Perhaps this accounts for his rigid, and even literally compulsive, side.

Restless

His writing, then, is a series of continual displacements or slippages. Sometimes, it is as if he were skidding along (perhaps even out of control: "As I begin this page, I don't know what will come next"). Confronted with things that "have to be committed to paper," he likes to think of himself as a mere scribe, an amused yet passive and disinterested witness, or as a neutral arena where issues can be addressed and fought over.

This endless displacement is what he saw as the very stuff of writing, the link between theory and practice. But it is also the mark of the delirious wanderings of an erudite desire, always wide of the mark, but which justifies itself as a form of the true "will to pleasure," a truly sensual pleasure stripped of aggressivity (one is reminded of what Barthes says about color)[16]—its emblem might be the "foetal happiness" that he describes, rather lucidly, at the end of "How I Learned to Draw."

Here are several images, then, of Eisenstein: the traveller (Europe, America, and the Japan he would like to have had the chance to see); the great *bricoleur* of meaning, of all sorts of meaning; the explorer of many different systems of thought; and last but not least, the Fregoli of writing. What links all of these together is his restlessness, the true sign of his distaste for fixity and resolution (Eisenstein is always on the move, and always just passing through).[17]

Like

It was Fontanier, I think, who ridiculed the kind of poetry that gets carried away with its metaphors. He would have had plenty to say about Eisenstein's habit of heaping up strange and often arbitrary "images," a practice which results in a kind of literary effect that is not unlike Gongorism. The body or the letter of the text is never allowed to retain its shape; it is forced not only to keep up with these perpetual displacements, but also to respond to the excessive demands of Eisenstein's metaphors.

What is the effect of this veritable "curtain" of signifiers superimposed upon the "virgin" text (a notion which has no real significance for our author)? First, to make out of the whole Text a kind of new global signified. For the structural *like* of the metaphor is an open sesame, because it sanctions any and every kind of substitution. Everything can be compared, everything can be said figuratively, and everything can be represented. This, in effect, is what lies behind the theory of "intellectual cinema," and we can also see the same fetishizing of metaphorization in the concept of figuration (could we suggest that this is also the source of the very idea that nature is not "indifferent," and that culture must be "organic"?).

Second, and in a much more limited biographical sense, I would say that this "curtain" of signifiers does actually function as a kind of curtain, because the metaphors are always at their most diffuse and gratuitous when a real emotion is somewhere involved. One could cite, for example, the protracted density of the metaphors which smother the conversation (undoubtedly a crucial one) with his father. Metaphors, in a very real sense, are all the reader *is allowed to know* (which, of course, is not worthless).[18] There is something in this use of metaphor which smacks of Freud's "censorship," and from this perspective, *Immoral Memories*, if no other of Eisenstein's works, would warrant a full-scale "interpretation." It would be unwise, however, to confuse this, as has been done so often recently, with a psychoanalysis.

The Graphics of Writing

"What is a line?—a line speaks of movement."[19] This is how Eisenstein defines drawing, but his statement is equally relevant to the visual "line" of his texts (the incessant typographical indentations, the pseudo-versified look of many of the pages, the compact character, by contrast, of so many of the paragraphs); this also speaks of the kind of movement which connects sentences together (and, if necessary, sets them off against each other). There are densely interwoven paragraphs (one thinks of Cocteau's "caterpillars"), finely clipped fragments, meandering pages: in short, he draws his texts.

Citation as Escape

Just as obligatory is Eisenstein's penchant for citations. There is something compulsive about this, not only in the case of certain names (Pushkin, Joyce, Daumier, Zola) which obsessively crop up in his discourse, but also in more contingent contexts, like those rambling digressions which we have discussed. As with the metaphors, it is as if they occur only when he wants to avoid, even for the mere time-span of a sentence, something that would be very "heavy" to him personally. Eisenstein would insist, and not without justification, that this glut of citations is just one more manifestation of the principle of montage,[20] but this would not alter the fact that the citations always constitute a practical way of purging the text of anything that threatens to implicate him too directly or intimately. And lastly, we should note that this essentially scholarly practice allows knowledge to triumph once again (the "epistemophilic drive") in its disavowal of all evidence of self-recognition.

Citation as Reference

This scholarly practice also points, however, to his love for references (a taste that is far from indiscriminate: only the best will do). His seemingly endless roll-call of proper names betrays a desire to be included, himself, in that infinite and imaginary list—the "cream" of creation's host of intellects. On the one hand, these references act as a simple discursive support (and often as a kind of *garde-fou*, especially in the case of some of the allusions to the Marxist doxa), and on the other hand, they serve as an endorsement of Eisenstein's *status*, his place in the hit-parade of artistic geniuses.[21] (A secondary effect is that these references protect, or absolve him of certain "faults," which can then be freely acknowledged. Since Tchaikovsky was superstitious, Chaplin vain, and Meyerhold jealous and vindictive, then my own little peccadilloes are hardly worth noticing. . . .)

The Name of the Author

He thinks of his films, his texts, and his drawings in terms of a whole *oeuvre*, where everything is interrelated in some way, and where the balance or structure of these relations is governed by a proprietary subject-author. Ideas about "unity," or the "author" and his "theme," for example, are a recurrent feature of the later texts (especially the unfinished *Method*).[22]

Since this authorial status is not a given, the next best guarantee would be the signature, or the trace, of the Author under the various forms of his Name (the Name which his father carefully writes out while his children respectfully look on in silence [IM, p. 23]): the extensive reference to his publications and works, or the intense self-congratulation which greeted the appearance and mercurial success of *The Film Sense*. Many (unsuccessful) attempts to publish other collections were to follow, and his last years were devoted to his passion for large synthesizing projects like *Nonindifferent Nature* or *Method*. What lies behind this is the idea of a developing *system* which would be the ineluctable creation of one person, and with respect to which the work itself is only a visible trace of the overall authorial system.[23] Clearly, there is something idealistic about the notion of a predetermined author, an author that is always a more or less privileged, judging subject.

"Predetermined" is not too strong a term to describe the teleological way in which Eisenstein conceives of his own subjective history. Everything is decided by the first throw of the dice (if not before), and the first impression is often quite final (how "determining," then, are the "moving lines" of his childhood, or the pontoon bridge near Izhorsk, so often cited?). The upshot is that our author never really has to learn anything (except, perhaps, mathematics, which proves useless to him anyway). Although he has "never learned how to draw," he draws nonetheless (and how!), and although he "recognizes" art, it is like a lover recognizing his beloved, or a murderer recognizing his victim. His relations with art are almost too good to be true.

"I was unlucky with my fathers"

The emblem for this section is the thick red pencil lines that "someone" drew across the beginning of *Sergei Eisenstein*, or the black marks, not from Eisenstein's hand, which fortuitously cut short the script of *Alexander Nevsky* after his victory over the Germans, but before his humiliation at the hands of the Tartars. Also, in a similar, though parallel vein, are the heavy self-criticisms of *Bezhin Meadow*, and of the second part of *Ivan the Terrible*.

The first manifestation of "bad luck," however, particularly with respect to his father figures (Mikhail Osipovich Eisenstein, Meyerhold, and also Stalin, not to mention the Soviet state itself), is that all of them exacted their respective censures on him. It begins with silence: Meyerhold's "tight lip" about artistic matters, his father's silence about sex, the buffoonery of the "fathers" who "smothered his faith," and the "doctors of the law" who will fail to cure him of dialectical thinking (IM, p. 214)—and to crown it all, the most awesome silence, the deafening lie of the Stalinist era. Confronted with such lies and such silence, Sergei Mikhailovich Eisenstein's almost religious response is simply to obey ("I always modelled myself on papa"; "I was so insanely docile and obedient," etc.).

The result of this (a structural rather than a chronological consequence, since he was always engaged in some filial struggle) was the inevitable revolt which engenders repression. His "disrespect," for example, affirmed from an early age in the flippant liberties he took with stately gentlemen visitors; and later in the "flawed" play by Ostrovsky in which the space of classical theater is invaded by the lower theatrical orders of circus and music hall; the way in which he savors at length the destruction of the Czar's statue in *October*; or the cutting irony of some of his responses to critics at the congress of 1935. In each instance, and in so many others, a sacrosanct father-figure is being mocked, and with increasing vigor as he felt the tightening of its grip.

Psychoanalysis, of course, should be allowed to have its say (indeed, a "psychoanalytical" study of the Eisenstein case remains to be done).[24] Of the little we know about his childhood, failure seems to have been a persistent feature: a childhood fraught with anxiety, parental misunderstandings, and, as all his biographers emphasize, with the pangs of solitude, shot through by some awful apprehension of his irreducible *difference*. If we can see how this difference is manifest in a whole series of "shortcomings," the most serious being his extraordinary difficulty at communicating, which fact came to define his official personality,[25] then we should also be able to see how these difficulties are more than compensated for by the ostentatious posturing which permeates all his texts, and which grants him the expedient privilege of mastery (on this last point, the most important father-figure was undoubtedly Meyerhold. From what we know, it was probably towards him that Eisenstein experienced the most intense range of Oedipal passions, from infatuation and identification to jealousy and parricidal desire. And it is probably from Meyerhold more than from his "biological" father that he had inherited his Donjuanism—the lists, the performances, the compulsion to seduce—which characterizes his attitude to his work and his various projects).[26]

Mama

"Like every society lady, Mama had her Thursdays." Not only did she have "her Thursdays," but she was also well endowed with a substantial *trousseau* (after she left, the house had barely any furniture), a throng of lovers, and, to crown it all, "a lively mind of her own." Eisenstein's description of his mother is quite perfunctory. Aside from her bourgeois wealth (mercantile bourgeoisie), she functions, in his discourse, as a metonym for sex; when he talks about her affairs, and her quarrels with his father, she is crudely represented as being *over-sexed*, and it is from her worldly books that he learns "the facts of life," as if by accident, and undoubtedly in a shameful and secretive way (from his father, or from his opposition to him, Eisenstein learned the more upright arts of politics and thinking). His last word on her is a throw-away (in describing the nightmarish scene which led to his parents' divorce): she is *hysterical*—a cliché which was bandied about with impunity in his day.

This portrait, even if it is quite clearcut, is somewhat ambivalent. Here is this hysteric who cuckolds, insults, and humiliates poor Mikhail Osipovich, but when it comes down to it, for Eisenstein, it could just as well be any woman. Finally, however, the only image of his mother that this "boy from Riga" will retain is that of an everloving mother who, before she becomes Sex, is the womb where his foetus peacefully lies, the paradise lost which haunts his memories. (This clearly is the source of his ambiguous relations with Julia Ivanovna in real life, and the contradictions of his biographers on the subject: Seton, for example, paints a dreadful picture of a dragon-mother who hounds him right up until the end of a lifetime of persecution; at the other extreme, Shklovsky assures us that "at his mother's slightest bidding he would come running, abandoning everything he was working on at the time." But what if they are both correct?)

Dual Nationality

It is France that he discovers first: a *History of the French Revolution* (by Mignet), books on the Commune ("banned" books found in his father's library), and *Les Misérables.* He knew all about the history of nineteenth-century France and its revolutions long before he knew the history of Russia. France would always be Eisenstein's truly nurturing maternal figure, his first motherland. In terms of the logic of misogyny, however, France will also come to be the great whore, the New Babylon, overrun by all sorts of "loose" women, not to mention the very home of scandal, of snobbism, and of Parisian frivolity (he took a rather dim, moralistic view, for example, of Cocteau and the Surrealists).

His attitude to Russian culture and history (Lenin's "heritage,") is quite different. Certainly it is a point of reference for him, but a much more *belated* one. Not only the trinity of Pushkin-Gogol-Dostoyevsky, but many other names (painters: Repin, Serov, Surikov; musicians: Scriabin; and writers . . .) less well known to us, constantly crop up in the great aesthetic syntheses of the period 1937–47 (and also in his own lecture courses), while the great names of official Russian history increasingly figure too. This is all undertaken in a very serious vein, however. For, in his ponderously meditated acceptance of this "heritage," there is very little (Pushkin is the exception) of the spontaneity or youthful exuberance that is visible in his relation to France.

Sade's Way

The young Eisenstein hardly had any time for breaking open watches to see what was inside, for he was too busy with the incessant quarrelling of his parents, and his own nightmares about them. If he did little more in the way of tearing apart dolls, this was all "reversed"—as he put it—in a later analytic passion which is not without its share of sadism (his mania for taxonomy included). So too can we suggest some relation between the daily and nightly spectacle of terrifying parental "scenes" and the components of mise-en-scène in sadism itself. Hence his perpetual apprehensiveness about the very nature of all spectacle, but especially theatrical spectacle.

This relation to sadism is complex, since it is never played out in the real, but we can trace its effects almost everywhere in his work and his relation to art.

1) LOOKING

"The barest features of the most fleeting images are cast in molten iron within my spectator's memory." He is also intensely alert to the spectator's point of view, and his dream is of being able to see himself "from outside," as an "external observer." Seeing, for him, is apprehending, and not simply because his profession is a "visual" one. Vision (the scopic), to begin with, is the privileged vehicle of understanding. One chapter in particular, which is almost entirely devoted to the scopic drive, illustrates this specifically. He is describing the effect of the rehearsals in *A Doll's House*, which he watched at Meyerhold's: "Lost in thought, between the uprights and the wall, back towards the window, holding my breath, I look dead ahead." A little earlier, he tells us that he was "shivering," not from the cold, but from the effect of these rehearsals; and he concludes the little scenario thus: "Perhaps it is from this that my tendency stems . . . to dig down into every crevice of the problem myself, to penetrate into it, trying to understand it ever more deeply, to get ever nearer to the core" (IM, p. 79). Here, then, are the lineaments of the Freudian schema of the primal scene: the furtive look, the fearful trembling, the desire to know, and, above all, the subsequent passion for analysis, for fragmentation (*démontage*), and for montage itself.

2) SCENARIO, PLOT, AND FANTASY

Always in search of origins, he claims that nineteenth-century postcards were the source of his "hostility towards 'the plot' and 'stories' that marks the beginning of [his] film career" (IM, p. 20). This distaste for the anecdotal (concretely confirmed by all his work in the twenties) hardly seems consistent with the rather foolish little skits portrayed by these postcards, for their mawkishness would surely induce boredom rather than anger. Indeed, I would be inclined to interpret this

strong "hostility" in terms of fear, or repression. Perhaps the truly
original sin of the "plot" (the story line, or scenario) is that it is the
site, or at least the possible site, of an excessive imaginary investment.

This is all the more plausible if one considers the violence which
is crudely and systematically displayed in Eisenstein's anecdotes. Those
which populate *Immoral Memories* range from the women "who poke
out the eyes of the Communard prisoners with their umbrellas" to the
gallant knight of Persian legend, forced (but helped along by some
internal will) to wallow in the mire, and from the kind of amused
anxiety provoked by the bombing of Moscow to his wild story about
the pilgrimage to Novgorod, a story that is intensely impersonal but
also involves "suffering the torments of hell." He can always find
excuses for *articulating* these frail shudders of sadistic delight. His
stories are never innocent, and have more to do with fantasy, night-
mare, and desire than with the anecdotes themselves. In this context,
some of his scenarios are worth mentioning: the epic account of blood,
fire, and iron in *Moscow*; the desert of *Fergana Canal*, tortured by
dryness, and flayed by the hooves of Tamerlane's horses; the martyrs
of Vitia, the young hero of *Bezhin Meadow*; the humiliation of the
Potemkin's sailors, and the horrors of civil war (in *Red Cavalry*), etc.
So too with the films and drawings (especially the series of bullfights,
so reminiscent of Bataille). My response to this endless repetition of
the same perverse fascination in a thousand "plots" would be that,
when all is said and done, it is just as well that he mistrusted narra-
tivity.

3) THE MURDERED BODY

Look, for example, at the beginning of "How I Learned to Draw":
"Who in Moscow didn't know Kogan? . . . Let us take Karl Ivanovich.
Let us make him very thin. If his nose doesn't stick out enough, lengthen
it a little [etc.]" This radical alteration imposed on poor Kogan's body
will be repeated in *Nonindifferent Nature* on a painting by El Greco
and an engraving by Piranesi. *Every Wise Man* is nothing but a long
series of insults aimed at a stereotypical Ostrovsky. Each of the Odessa
steps is a moment of fracture, punishing and breaking apart the bodies,
and in his treatment of the murder in *Crime and Punishment*, he insists
on using the distorted images produced by wide-angle lens.[27] The last
example would be the extraordinary attention devoted to physical discipline in *Ivan the Terrible*: the long punishing hours of makeup for
Cherkasov, his body contorted to its very limits for Anastasia's mourning, the constricting doorway, the oppressively low ceilings, the break-
ing-up of perspective.

It is as if the body (and its forms: the letter, the text, matter) is only there to be murdered, blown up, cut open, broken down, and put together again. Everything goes through an imaginary reshaping, from the pursuit of the "organic," in mythical conformity to the "laws of nature," through the "figurations" that he has to twist into the shape of true "images," to the pursuit of the ecstatic.[28] Montage (and *démontage*, the definitive sadistic operation) is more than a systematic, syntagmatic activity, like playing with an erector set, it is concerned with the very body of things. And every body only exists to be cut up.

Alexander Nevsky

There is something at stake in Eisenstein's relation to this young and beautiful hero (the colorless perfection of Nevsky's beauty is set off by the rustic look of his companions), something below the surface that is not readily noticeable in the conventional pattern of its plot and imagery, and something which is left unresolved about the ephebophiliac blondness of Alexander's young page.

Alexander Nevsky. The name is irrevocably associated with Eisenstein's childhood (as for many Russian schoolboys): the Alexander Nevsky monastery, which Eisenstein, along with his grandmother, explored on foot (perhaps he visited his grandfather Konetsky's tomb there). His parents lived in Riga, the city of Bishop Albert, founder of the Livonian order of knights, and, as an adolescent, he will imagine the ghost of this warrior saint flitting across the Volkhov in the moonlight, surrounded by the white churches of Novgorod. There is a whole bundle of associations which links the saintly heroism of Nevsky with a pious and dutiful childhood devoted to the cult of great men. Furthermore, beneath the smooth surface of the filmic images, one can make out his recreation of an infant's world, in heroic battles between toy soldiers, the sadism (Pskov) of adolescent fantasies, and the mawkish sentimentalism of "rosewater" novels. The net effect is like making a nostalgic film about one's childhood. (The only problem with dealing with this, the very worst film in Eisenstein's oeuvre, lies in determining how all of this—Saint-Sulpice, the toy soldiers, and the rosewater—could fit in, one day, with an official, doxical view of history).

Mexico, the Home of Metaphor

In "Intellectual Cinema," the most beautiful chapter in *Immoral Memories*, there is a magnificent page about Mexico that is all the more revealing since the trip to Mexico, despite its staggering effect on Eisenstein, is usually only mentioned indirectly, as if it were a scar of some old wound. He is recounting his arrival in Mexico, and the fact that he is reading (an ordinary enough thing for him to do) a rather popular Soviet novel called *The Golden Calf* which mentions Popocatepetl, this "unreal" name which, by a simple turn of his head, is transformed into the reality of the mountain itself, within which simmers a volcano so real that one day he will narrowly miss falling into it (IM, pp. 210-11).

Otherwise, Mexico is always a country of romance and dreams, or to be more precise, everything related to it is romanticized. The "real" Mexico—where interesting little scenarios develop in trains, police stations, cafés, and haciendas—never really goes beyond the improbable actuality of the imaginary country which is the setting for *The Mexican*, his first play (the scenario of *Que Viva Mexico!* is particularly significant in this context; even with the best "historical" intentions, and "ideological" guarantees, it offers a veritable array of episodes, each one more fantastic and spellbinding than the one before).

Mexico is also an inexhaustible mine of metaphors (the most poetic ones, because they are, quite literally, the most far-fetched), and formal shapes, not only in its painting and architecture, but also its most simple, and archaic, or natural, human forms. It is no surprise to find that Eisenstein compares this vast image-repertoire to a star which guides the navigator. A land of gods, and a heaven of men, Mexico, like all paradises, is a place which belongs by right to Eisenstein's childhood, and to which he can return at will.[29]

The Far East

Japanese imperialism, the civil war and the revolution in China, Mao's Long March, these are burning historical issues, and it is odd to find that he alludes to them so little. All we have on record are two film projects, one in 1926, after the success of *Potemkin*, which touches on the "events in Canton," and the other, almost a decade later, based on Malraux's *La Condition humaine*, neither of which came to anything. If he was at all obsessed by the East, then it was in a totally different context.

The biggest attraction (responsible for so many of his theoretical adventures) is ideogrammatic writing—which he calls, curiously enough, "hieroglyphics"—writing that is still full of the traces of its figurative origins; but he is also attracted to a calligraphic tradition of drawing as writing and rewriting, and to a highly codified kind of theater that is a language in itself. For Eisenstein, the true stars of China and Japan were the kings of kabuki, with whom he had his photograph taken, or Mei Lan-fang, about whom he planned to make a film, or Hokusai, whose engravings he complained about not being able to buy.

In his last years, as he began to stray even further from everyday realities, his discovery of Chinese philosophy (through the books of Lin Yutang and the classic studies of Marcel Granet) came to color his understanding of the dialectical science of contradiction, and of the endless transformation and dualism of all things—for which process he makes copious use of the emblem of yin-and-yang. (Just as Mexico was a privileged geography of pleasure, China and Japan constitute a theoretico-philosophical image-repertoire, a kind of referent that is even more imaginary yet, and ought not to be scrutinized too closely.)

The Circus: A Decentered Arena

It is not by chance that the circus is a privileged space for Eisenstein. It is a circular enclosure where everything is focused on the actor. And it is an arena (he loved bullfights): the same circularity, the same stepped seating, the same intense spectacle. When the Proletkult was established in Moscow, it called its theater the Central Arena. Even if it is a sheer coincidence, the theater was always seen by him in terms of a contest, a violent and dangerous ritual, and also a virtuoso event.

It is a focal set-up, but it is also a de-centered space, and thus *eccentric*. The spectacle is concentrated in such a way that it will have its most explosive effect. And if ever this was the case, then it was Eisenstein's production of *Enough Simplicity in Every Wise Man*, the shock waves from which inspired his first theory of montage, the famous Montage of Attractions.

This notion of the theater as a circus appeals to a profoundly imaginary logic on Eisenstein's part. One thinks of the passage in *Immoral Memories* where he confesses that his greatest love was for the clowns (the most eccentric feature of the circus; his greatest pleasure was to be compared to a clown), and this was primarily as a reaction against his uptight, bourgeois father, who only liked the dancing horses.

"Enough simplicity in every wise man"

There are at least two reasons for the repeated references, especially towards the end of his life, to his famous adaptation of Ostrovsky's play. First, it remained the high point of a theatrical career which spanned all of his work as a set designer, painter, director, and producer of drama. It brought together all of his experiences, and influences, from his first amateur work to the later, wild ferment of futurism and eccentrism, including his love of circus for its cranky, undisciplined, and whimsical side.[30] And second, it has a contextual, metonymic importance as a sign of its times: the Proletkult adventure, and other passionate experiments of the day.

In either case, the play is associated with some sort of liberating impulse: the freedom of "artistic license," certainly, but also another, more general, or fundamental, freedom. "How free directors were in those days!"—Eisenstein's comment is both a confession and an expression of regret, and he immediately qualifies it by adding specifically erotic details which bear witness to this ambivalence. These lost liberties, then, were once enjoyed not only by the young artist of genius who could do anything he wanted, or the young man barely escaped from the paternal prohibition, but also, though this is more discreetly invoked, by the whole revolutionary period.

Classes and Class Struggle

He is conscious of his bourgeois background, and he shows it. At times, he regards it as a kind of original sin, when his class origins, for example, threaten to stand in the way of his attempts to strike up friendships with other pupils at his elementary school. However, he never feels like an intellectual who has been called to the Marxist, socialist, or revolutionary cause on the basis of a class alliance—a story which has been the fate, ever since Marx and Engels, of all those bourgeois intellectuals who were led into taking up "proletarian" positions on the strength of logical thinking alone (of Eisenstein's contemporaries, one thinks of Brecht and Lu-Sin, who both shared some of his own intellectual parentage).

Although there is no doubt that his commitment to revolution was totally sincere and unreserved (albeit rather belated, as a whole), his attachment was basically a sentimental one. We need not entirely accept his claim that if he "enlists in the cause of social protest" it is because "of this irreducible prototype of all social tyranny that is the tyranny of the father within the family." We should, however, point out that the revolution gave him the timely opportunity to substitute one father (Meyerhold) for another, and also that he never did pay anything but lip service to the idea of class struggle, preferring instead the Manichean abstraction of the Stalinist version of historical materialism, and, even more arcane, the endless speculations provoked, in his final years, by his application of "dialectical" materialism.

History, 1: The Narrow View

"I have lived through an epoch without parallel. But it is not of the epoch that I want to write. I want to describe how, like a completely unforeseen counterpoint, the average man passes through an age of greatness."

He is, as Marxism demands, "subject to" History. But, for Eisenstein, history is conceived, at least within the subjective criteria of *Immoral Memories*, as a timely series of points of reference for his memories: "the dacha by the sea" and also, let me see, ah yes, the year of Mukden, that was in 1904. . . . History is a list of dates, unproblematically described in terms of a shared chronology.

These dates, however, are lived, even if they are often lived "at a tangent" to what was really happening (the most obvious example is his account of how he spent his time on 25 October 1917). And whenever he was directly and actively involved—that is, during the civil war—it was always in a completely incidental way.

This profoundly passive relation to history-as-it-is-being-made is evidence of his flexible attitude to politics, one which I have described as opportunist[31] (a term that is not entirely accurate, however, since it implies at least some articulation of an actual position—one that will always bend to the will of the doxa). If he conceives at all of history in terms of class struggle, it is only as an abstract, and generally convenient, idea.

History, 2: Fiction Is Stranger than Fact

History is also nothing but *stories*, the contents of a series of narrative representations. Take, for example, the endless catalogue of proper names at the end of "Wie sag' ich's meinem Kind?!" where stars from show-business figure side by side with stars from history, a different kind of spectacle altogether. The latter, moreover, are always *seen* in some kind of scenario (Lloyd George seen in Parliament, a Mexican bishop shown being filmed, Brusilov at his trial, etc.). Even the Moscow air raids of 1941 are described as a symphony of sounds, a concert of impressions. And lastly: "None of these vivid impressions could wipe out Mignet's descriptions of the social hell of pre-Revolutionary France" (IM, p. 15). Etc.

When it comes to the crunch, however, Eisenstein's appropriation of history (one that includes the present—two world wars and the Revolution) on the level of representation and narrative, is anything but innocent. First, because it allows him to include history on the grand scale of global narratives; everyone knows that stories can be told differently the second time around. Since history is nothing but narrative, then one can rewrite it with impunity. Eisenstein, however, took this idea to its extreme. Even if we stick to the films that he actually finished, we can think of the way in which he misrepresented the reign of Ivan IV, the last years of Nevsky, and the storming of the Winter Palace.

And second, because this inclusion of history within an imaginary treasury of stories makes it into a kind of inert material, stripped of its dynamism and its contradictions. Eisenstein's conception of history as a petrified teleology is quite strikingly complicit with the Stalinist version, which fixes all individuals, groups, and concrete forces according to their place within history as a whole (but subject to "revision" every so often). The problem with these later texts is that they pride themselves on a facile monothematism, which lumps together in a rather unsatisfactory way the insurrections of *Strike* and *Potemkin* and the reincarnated czars of holy Russia. (The irony of this is that Eisenstein himself was to become one of these embalmed heroes after his death, labelled for eternity as the "painter of the revolution," but this reputation, of course, conveniently serves as an official smokescreen.)

The Conformist

His master, Meyerhold, for whom he confessed his love, was arrested in 1938, and died while being deported in 1942. Eisenstein has this to say in 1946: "Although his faults as a person have probably erased the traces of his influence as a master from the pages of the history of our theatrical art. . . ." What faults? And how could they have been responsible for changing (or rather "erasing") one of the faces of history? (Eisenstein, however, was perfectly aware of the absurdity of this claim, since he was deferring to the mood of the moment at the same time as he was discreetly preserving the literary heritage of Meyerhold.)

In those days, of course, there was nothing unusual about being in favor one day and out the next. Between 1935 and 1938, Eisenstein himself was constantly walking the tightrope of official opinion. Indeed, if he had not had the chance to make *Nevsky*, he might very well have been arrested, deported, and assassinated, like Tretyakov in 1937, Meyerhold in 1938, Babel in 1939, and others. There is nothing surprising, then, about the sheer compromises which obliged him, for example, to make two broadcasts on Radio Moscow (during, and after, the German-Russian nonaggression pact, respectively): one, celebrating the German alliance, and the other "to brother Jews of the whole world," celebrating the resistance to Nazism[32]—not to mention the many laudatory addresses to the government, or the wonderful Soviet constitution, etc., throughout the thirties.

Beyond these more obvious consequences, however, this conformism, or acceptance, of explicit directives as well as more implicit forms of ideological pressure, is a constant feature of his work. We need only think of the "modification" of *October* after Trotsky's disgrace, of *The General Line* (and the extraordinary "investigation" which preceded the film, in which Eisenstein was solely interested in measuring the prevailing winds of official opinion [see FW 1, pp. 51-52]), of *Bezhin Meadow*, and *Ivan the Terrible: Part Two*, for which he had prepared himself. There was always something of the little "boy from Riga," "so insanely docile and obedient" in Eisenstein, and it was a particular form of irresponsibility which he himself later theorized as his "supreme fortune" in his having seen his "personal theme" correspond so closely to the watchwords of the day.

In this context, it is all the more remarkable that his theoretical work should display, as we shall see, the kind of dogged resolution that it does. Against all the elements, in the darkest days of the "anti-formalist" attacks, and in the face of the total lack of understanding of colleagues and bureaucrats alike, Eisenstein stood unflinchingly by the basic principles of intellectual montage (and its extension in the "interior monologue"). The thirties and, to a lesser extent, the forties, are littered with polemical texts that are more critical than defensive, in which he vehemently expresses both his contempt for any compromise on the matter of "cinematographic language," and the necessity for rigorous, formal work. Clearly, there is quite a disparity between the obedient little boy-cum-cinéaste, who is prepared to forget history as required, and the theoretician who, for example, from the manifesto of 1928 right up to his very last works, was insistent that the "talking pictures" were a mistake, because he perceived them as an illegitimate form of the true audio-visual counterpoint. Eisenstein's absolute priority, the only practice he would not renounce, was that of his theory (in fact, he even went so far as to endorse Luther's "I cannot do otherwise"!).

Theorizing

It has frequently been remarked that there is never any applied theory in Eisenstein. Indeed, it often seems as if the reverse were the case, that the theory and its successive formulations are only there to provide rationalist ballast for what the filmic practice has achieved through the extemporaneous or the impulsive. But Eisenstein was well aware of this. According to Marie Seton, he professed that his theories were not made to be applied. Obviously, this is not what he had to say on more official occasions (the Soviet Cinematography Congress of 1935, for example), but here is at least one instance: "To be more precise would amount to purely dogmatic charlatanry, and a mere play on words. The solution can only come from something new, which is to say, from a material that is suitably chosen from a correct theoretical point of view . . . and from the intuition necessary to its elaboration" (FW 1, p. 39). Everything is there, and his prescription for a correct practice is: always make it new, choose your materials "well," use lots of intuition—but also, make sure you have a sound theoretical foundation.

This, of course, is not the last word on the lack of coherence which his theoretical reflections display. We shall see (especially in the last chapter) that these reflections underwent many changes and alterations, and that Eisenstein's theoretical method was clearly not as scientific as he would have it believed (see, for example, what we said earlier about the place of mathematics in his imaginary). Indeed, it seems that he is almost incapable of working through a concept in a logical manner, always preferring to invent another one instead.

Similarly, if we were to look for theoretical coherence, continuity, and what could be called tenacity (Leonardo's *ostinato rigore*) in Eisenstein's work, it would not be in the constancy or feasibility of his concepts. For these concepts are not tools; they are completely inseparable from the very way in which they are formulated.[33]

Eisensteinian Concepts

2

" . . . when I myself am creating,
I recall Goethe's remark, 'grau ist
die Theorie,' and I plunge headlong
into creative spontaneity."

"Poor Salieri!" 1940 (RW 3, pp. 33-34)

打松·追射   辩论

Eisenstein's watchword is this clearcut refusal of a theory "cut off from life," and of anything that might resemble a theory for theory's sake, as in the expression "Art for Art's sake." In the introduction to this work we spoke of the diffuse, ubiquitous presence of theory in all of his writings. (And in the preceding chapter we have seen how he even manages to theorize his biography.) But, on the other hand, and by way of compensation, it would be impossible to overemphasize the permanent infiltration, the contamination of his theoretical system(s) by all the "accidents" of life.

A theory that is "not cut off from life"—that is the very least that can be said about Eisenstein's theoretical writings. But if this symbiosis of production, creation, subjective experience, and theoretical reflection was absolutely indispensable to Eisenstein (and, moreover, one of the most remarkable manifestations we have of the extraordinary force at work within him), it does not make things easier for anyone wishing to submit his purely theoretical work to an orderly, scientific examination. Despite his efforts and his frequently stated desire, Eisenstein did not finish—much less publish—any of the great theoretical syntheses upon which he embarked. The major texts—*Nonindifferent Nature, Montage, Regissura*, and *Method* (which is almost completely unknown)—are no more than outlines, drafts, or rough sketches in which his thoughts sometimes (often) go off in all directions.

These difficulties persist upon closer scrutiny, particularly if one examines, as I will do, the consistency or the coherence of these theories, and tries to find in them concepts which are fairly identifiable, fixed, clearly defined. It is just as well to state at the outset that this goal will certainly not be achieved.

Eisenstein is a most curious theoretician. As unscientific as possible, in a way, and yet his thought was not without rigor. There is much to suggest that the close connection between his theory's development—its vitality—and Eisenstein's own life story induced in him a dual and fairly contradictory need:

—The process in which he engages—a remodeling, a transformation, a dynamiting of the cultural "heritage"—has as its equivalent and accompaniment the almost permanent *invention* of new concepts, often based on others of his own invention which are themselves transformed or "outgrown." Eisenstein himself rather aptly dubbed this aspect of his work a "theoretical self-service cafeteria" (FW 3, p. 227; an unpublished fragment dated 1944, not in RW).

—At the same time there is a will in him to anchor his sometimes very risky concepts in the most solid referential grounds—hence all those sketches of "systems" intended to patch the whole thing together; hence the lavish display of culture, the paraphernalia of citations which flow from his pen; hence, finally and above all, his concern to attach himself expressly to the best of all referents—Marxist-Leninist dogma.

Let there be no misunderstanding—I have no intention of adding my voice to the chorus of those who proclaim that Eisenstein, while an author of very fine films, is not a "valid" theoretician. On the contrary, my entire undertaking is intended to bring out the great rigor and the fabulous persistence of Eisenstein the theoretician. If I make a point of highlighting what may appear to be limitations or defects, it is rather to explain and excuse in advance the nearly inevitable insufficiency of the simple description, let alone classification, which I am now going to offer.

Thus with no illusions about the theoretical value of this distinction, I propose, purely for practical purposes, to define two major "categories" of Eisensteinian concepts, each of which, besides being linked organically to the other, is informed diachronically (in particular by what has often been considered the parenthesis of the 1930s—a decade which, as we shall demonstrate in the following chapter, was far from being a simple theoretical "gap").

1. Thus, first of all, there are what might be called the "technical" concepts—those concerned with photography, composition, filming,

montage, sound, acting, style, etc. In a word, everything that corresponds most immediately to the notion of the "self-service cafeteria" and is aimed more or less explicitly at producing a theory directed at cinematic practice.

These concepts themselves are scarcely homogeneous. Some are quite directly the result of reflections on certain specific films. That is essentially the case with *montage* (of which little will be said here since a chapter will be devoted to it at the end of this study), the *frame*, and also the final form taken by the reflections on this topic, namely, the notion of *audio-visual counterpoint*. Other concepts in this first category, while equally important, are from the outset more general, more "purely" theoretical, namely, the *fragment* and its corollary, *conflict*.

2. Then, by way of differentiation, there are all the "general" concepts, those which are concerned with the social function of art, its subjective effects, its general history, and which are the main subject of all of Eisenstein's efforts at synthesis during the 1930s and 40s.

The central idea here, covering the social and ideological role of the cinema as well as the problem of the spectator's response, is incontestably that of efficacy (Eisenstein says "influence"), whether it takes specific form in the "scientific" mode of stimulus and effect, as it does in the twenties—or whether, abandoning the Pavlovian mode for more "philosophical" regions, it is materialized in the famous concept of *ecstasy* and in the search for organicism (we shall see how these two concepts incorporate the idea of *pathos*, which, in any case, is not peculiar to Eisenstein).

The problem with such a summary, of course, is that entire sections of Eisenstein's work are conspicuously missing, and precisely those which would raise questions about the very simplified classification proposed. The most glaring omission here is the absence of the double concept of *figuration/image*, which is *both* practical ("technical") in origin and "general" in its scope. (And, if one had to choose, this notion could very well be taken to represent the culminating point of all Eisenstein's reflections—see chapter 4.)

In this chapter then, we shall content ourselves with attempting to fill in another gap (almost as blatant) by saying a few words about the idea of *attraction*, and by devoting two rather brief notes, first to "the question of form," and second to that of "dialectics."

One final point. In the main, my work remains very deliberately, *inside* the framework of the Eisensteinian problematic, and that will no doubt appear to be a limitation. There are other theoreticians of the cinema, some of them as important as Eisenstein (even if few of them have been as fecund and as inventive). Moreover, after several decades of groping experiment, outlines of something resembling "a" theory of the cinema—or at least a certain space, an area of film theory— are beginning to take shape. I am aware of all of this, and I realize, therefore, that what is perhaps the most important issue ("Eisenstein's place in a general theory of cinema") will still remain unbroached at the end of this book.

Having said this, I am just that much freer to call for an approach which does not seek to situate Eisenstein in relation to theory in general (as people have always done until now, when they were not using him to oppose other theories), but aims, on the contrary, to *describe* the Eisensteinian system as closely as possible in all its complexities. I am firmly convinced that Eisenstein's reputation as a lax, even a fuzzy, theoretician will not stand up even under an examination as incomplete and imperfect as the following one. Here the slowness and haphazard character which has marked the history of the publication of Eistenstein's writings should be taken into account. Since they have been published in an extremely fragmentary and incomplete manner, and given his propensity for defining the words and concepts he uses only by an implicit allusion to the whole of his system, how could that system have been perceived as anything but vague, nebulous, and contradictory? (To cite an example we shall return to, it seems just about impossible to measure correctly the impact of the important essay "Vertical Montage," which, in its English version in *The Film Sense* ["Synchronization of Senses," "Color and Meaning," and "Form and Content: Practice"], appears very shaky, unless it is read as an application and popularization of "Montage 1937," an essay that remained unpublished until 1965, and even today is still almost unknown in the West.)

One of the ambitions of my work is thus to promote the *reading* of Eisenstein as an indispensable prerequisite to any evaluation (other than one which would be lazy and "fuzzy" itself) of his place in the history of film theory.

I. Fragment/Frame/Conflict

Taking even a very broad overview of the tortured landscape of the "history of cinema," there is something which never fails to emerge around the twenties, even if, when it does appear, it looks a bit like a forgotten continent. I mean, of course, what has often been called "montage-roi" (not by just anybody, but by the likes of Bazin, Mitry, Metz). The notion and the very expression "montage-roi" are certainly more than subject to critical scrutiny (some elements of a critique will be offered in passing). However, they show distinctly (and Metz brought this out very clearly in his famous text "Le Cinéma, langue ou langage?") that everything of any significance that was produced in the Russian cinema of the twenties, owes its importance to montage, or more precisely to a certain conception of montage as *fragmentation* (or *chopping,* as it has sometimes been termed pejoratively).

There can be no question of attributing this central idea of fragmentation to Eisenstein alone. The historical and theoretical importance of Kuleshov's famous experiments, for example, is well known. Nor is it unknown that a whole section of Vertov's work (it too only very recently examined) revolves around this very same epicenter, along with the concepts of *interval* and *uninterrupted montage.*

However, it is in Eisenstein's work that one finds by far the most systematic attempt to connect and organize on the theoretical plane all the problems connected with the idea of fragmentation. Hence our use of the term *fragment*; but, before stating why and how it seems possible to articulate a first grouping around that term, we must deal with two objections which will not fail to be made and which both have to do with the history of the word.

(1) First, it must not be forgotten that we are referring to a body of texts written in Russian. In that language, the word in question, *kusok,* is very commonly used, and not only in writings on cinema (by Pudovkin or Chukhrai, for whom it has no specific meaning, as well as by Kuleshov or Eisenstein). The Oxford Russian-English dictionary gives as its equivalents "lump," "piece," "bit," and "slice" (as used in phrases like "go to pieces," "bit of luck," or "slice of cake"). Even if we confine ourselves to the vocabulary of cinema, it is a common term—*kusok fil'ma,* a "piece of film," a "bit of film," is the expression normally used in editing rooms.

The Eisensteinian *fragment,* as I hope to demonstrate, is not just any piece, not just any *kusok.* (No more than it is just any "fragment" in French or in English.) Therefore, there can be no question of concealing the definitely arbitrary character of the French (or English) translation; above all, there can be no question of considering the content of this word as given or known in advance.

(2) Matters are further complicated by the fact that Eisenstein says very little, and then only from time to time, about this concept which is so central to his theory (that, at least, is what I postulate). Here we

are caught in the middle of that typically Eisensteinian configuration of a notion which is defined only by its context, by association, or by its causes and effects.

It is not a taste for paradox that prompts me to open this "catalogue" with a concept impossible to locate. For if its definition is never given, it is nonetheless central to the whole Eisensteinian theory. Very nearly on a par with the concept of montage, it is, I believe, the word most often used by Eisenstein. Still more important, of all the concepts developed and/or used during the twenties, it is the only one, again along with montage, to have survived all the successive (uninterrupted) waves of theoretical updating and remodeling; it is the only one that is applicable to Eisenstein's attitude toward film material right up to the very end.

For the sake of convenience, and also in order not to depart completely from the letter of the Eisensteinian text, I shall allow myself a metaphor in the reconstruction of this concept, a metaphor suggested by the title and the method of the famous essay "Vertical Montage" (1940) (RW 2, p. 189). That essay is in part concerned with the analysis of a sequence of *Alexander Nevsky* (and it is this part that concerns me here). In the analysis, the idea of "verticality" refers to an intention to break down and sort out the various elements which compose each piece, each fragment of the filmic chain (which is implicitly conceived of as being "horizontal"). The very least that this breakdown would accomplish is the separation of image and sound.

Thus, we shall first define a vertical dimension of the fragment where the analytic breakdown (and our inspiration here is provided by the famous diagrams in which the *Nevsky* sequence is described in "symphonic" terms) of the fragment parallels the musical line. But, more than in "Vertical Montage" and its famous diagrams, it is in a text of 1929, "The Filmic Fourth Dimension," that this verticality was defined and described without being named. In fact, in the course of a history/typology of the different categories of montage (which we shall have occasion to mention again), this text insists at great length on the possibility and the necessity of inventorying and mastering the constitutive parameters of the image (and, first of all, the physical parameters—luminosity, sharpness of focus, contrast, camera angle, length, graphic "sonority," etc.).

Without sticking too closely to the letter of a text whose terms Eisenstein himself reconsidered many times, I think it can be said that there are two essential points here.

1) First, there is the insistence on the "physical," or the "phys-iological" (to use Eisenstein's term) characteristics of each fragment, which focuses precisely on the individualization of every fragment as a *film image*,[1] on the specificity of that image as compared to other types of figurative representation, but also on the fact that it is an image, something constructed, composed, which does not obey any spontaneous "laws" of analogy. To put it in completely anachronistic terms, Eisenstein "discovered" that the image is not reducible to the analogon, but the so-called "analogical" image already supposes the simultaneous operation of numerous and diverse *codes*. An exhaustive inventory of these constitutive parameters of the image is probably impossible. (Or, to be more precise, no matter how far it is carried, by its very nature, it always remains strictly limited by the empiricism of the procedure, as Noel Burch's effort in *Theory of Film Practice* will suffice to convince anyone.) And thus, for Eisenstein, the impor-tant thing at this point would seem to have been, not the inventory itself, but the affirmation of the existence of these parameters—in the name of a fundamentally materialist attitude for which it was in prin-ciple inadmissible that the image could not be broken down into con-stitutive elements or explained in terms of a "molecular" model. As proof of his relative indifference to the precise concepts of the supposed list of parameters, we shall point only to the haste with which, shortly after setting it up, Eisenstein abandons the category of *tonal* montage, the category in which:

> the montage is placed under the sign of the *emotional tone* of the frag-ment. And what's more, the dominant tone. The general *tone* of the fragment. ("The Filmic Fourth Dimension," 1929, RW 2, p. 53)

—and where, therefore, one must eventually say what this "tone" is, i.e., define its "basic unit." That is a dangerously exacting requirement, which Eisenstein satisfies only in a very evasive manner, and for good reason. No doubt the notion of *harmonic* montage served this purpose, among others. It is a much less compromising, because infinitely more fluid, notion—at least as far as its definition is concerned.[2] Harmonic montage "is distinguished [from tonal montage] . . . by the fact that it takes into consideration all of the stimuli of a fragment" (ibid., RW 2, p. 56). To consider all the stimuli (all the parameters) of a fragment in the aggregate, to relate them to those of another fragment, also taken as a totality, does not really require that they be named (except in the convenient form of a series of specific cases, apropos of the examination of given sequences of particular films—which Eisenstein does in the balance of the text).

2) However, despite this hasty eschewal of the ambition to name and describe things exhaustively, one can still discern traces of a lingering temptation to absolutely master the fragment, or the image, by breaking it down analytically into "stimuli." It is the temptation, if you will, to claim to be able to *calculate* each fragment (its composition, and therefore, its effect). It is no accident that in the 1929 text Eisenstein uses a musical metaphor to provide names for his montage categories. In music, the tones are submitted to rules which are fixed, canonical, mathematically determinable (mathematics reappear in their role of fetish of precision); even the overtones, despite their perhaps more uncertain nature, are of the order, if not of the calculable, at least of the predictable.

In what has by now become the canonical mode of "I know very well, but just the same . . ." Eisenstein continues to deny from beginning to end that he is tempted by mastery. In a contradiction which is never resolved, Eisenstein will always simultaneously affirm *and* reject this desire for mastery. Countless examples of this could be given to demonstrate that Eisenstein never stopped pursuing control of every detail—from *Ivan the Terrible* ("I achieved exactly what I had set out to do," he told his students in 1947) to *Nevsky* (the quite "delirious" analysis of the correspondence between image and sound in the famous sequence on Lake Chudskoy); from the extension of his calculation to include the style and gestures of the actor (the subject of one of his last essays) to his analysis of the "Stanislavsky system," praised (in 1937) for the minute analysis of style and emotions which it requires the actor to produce. Etc. (We cannot quote everything.)[3]

(Perhaps this essential contradiction originates basically from the fact that out of everything Eisenstein wrote on the subject of the fragment, his notion of vertical breakdown is the most closely related to his own filmmaking practices. Eisenstein is famous for the minute attention to detail with which he prepared, and worked out the details of, even the most inconsequential of his film projects, just as he did with the least of his classroom exercises. And lest that be forgotten, the stenographic record of his courses at the VGIK is there to remind us. His penchant for considering his editing room as an experimental laboratory is also well known. It required but a single step to move from these practices to the theorizing, the legalizing of this *personal experience* of mastery.)

To expand on the metaphor introduced by this inconceivable "verticality," let us now define two other "dimensions" of the fragment, both of them abundantly attested to in the Eisensteinian text (even if never in these terms). First of all, there would be what we shall term the *horizontal* dimension of the film diachrony, according to which the fragment would come to be inscribed as a fragment of discourse, defined by its total relationship with the other fragments which precede and follow it. Here we are touching upon the question of the syntagmatic axis of film and the possibility of a syntax.

Syntax. Eisenstein never believed much in the utopia of cine-language, or of cine-grammar, even if, on occasion, in the twenties, he allowed the idea of it to emerge:

> When the elements of montage are selected from the filmed fragments in the course of the process of construction, of filming, and of giving things form, the peculiarities of the influence of cinema must not be forgotten. . . . They define the concept of montage as the indispensable language, charged with meaning, and the only possible one for cinema, offering a perfect parallelism with the role of the word in verbal material. ("Montage of Cine-Attractions," published in 1925 in *Sevodniachaye Kino [Cinema Today]*, A. Belenson, ed. Never reprinted since in Russian. Not included in RW; FW 1, p. 138)

Such a formulation would seem to place him unequivocally on the side of that "erector-set cinema" which Metz, in his already cited text, sees as a "sumptuous impasse." However, it is necessary (as Metz himself has since agreed) to temper these trenchant formulations.

This necessity is imposed on us, first of all, for historical reasons that arise from what might be called the "general background" in linguistics of the filmmakers of the twenties. In his critique, Metz makes an important distinction between *langue*, or the so-called "cine-language system" (the utopian fruit of an overestimation of the grammatical possibilities of montage) and *langage*, or cinematic language (the "normal" metaphor to designate the semiotic processes at work in film). Now it seems to me very unlikely that this conceptual distinction between the language-system and language could have been made by filmmakers in any case. It is all the more unlikely because the Russian term *yazyk*, which means *langue*, can also, in many cases, be translated as *langage* (and designate, in fact, a language situation in general). When Eisenstein, or Vertov, uses the term "cine-language," he should not necessarily be taken at his linguistic word.

For, on the other hand, each time he abandons the metaphor of *langue* (that is, almost all the time), Eisenstein is very explicit on this point. Never does he confuse the film image, the fragment (the "shot"), with a word; nor does he ever confuse any assembly of fragments with a verbal type of statement. Thus, the insistence with which he describes and analyzes the fragment in specifically iconic (or rather, filmic) terms, as well as the importance he attaches (as we shall see) to the specific effectiveness of this fragment, separates him irrevocably from the mechanistic conception of a "cine-grammar" of montage. Eisenstein never thought that "the film was understood because of its syntax," and I believe he would have agreed with Metz that "the syntax of a film is understood because the film has been understood, and only when it has been understood." Suffice it to refer the reader to the rest of the text cited earlier, in which the "parallel with the word" is spelled out, and, above all, expressed in purely *cinematic* terms, such as the necessity for the filmmaker to treat each fragment like a "new point of view, differentiated from that of the [preceding] fragment" ("Montage of Cine-Attractions," 1925); that is, to construct each fragment like a new image of the material filmed, possessing its own definition in terms of "parameters."

Syntagm. On the other hand, and within the chain of film discourse, it is certain that Eisenstein is deeply preoccupied with this value of the fragment as a *unit* of composition. The essential meaning of the concept of montage (to which the "horizontal" nature of the fragment is obviously related) is that, for Eisenstein, meaning is communicated by putting *each* fragment into relationship with those that surround it:

a) at the moment of "matching" (the word is obviously completely inappropriate, since it has come to designate precisely everything against which Eisenstein is struggling—the illusion of continuity and homogeneity, transparency), or rather, at the moment of the "jump" from one fragment to another. As for the productivity of the relationship of one fragment to another, perhaps it is enough for the moment to remember the famous and often repeated motto, "the juxtaposition of two fragments resembles their product more than it does their sum" ("Off-Frame," 1929, RW 2, pp. 283 ff. [translated in *Film Form* as "The Cinematographic Principle and the Ideogram"]; "Montage 1938," RW 2, pp. 156 ff.).

b) but also, through less immediate, more systematized relationships. In all of Eisenstein's films, there is a *system* of fragments, and all the considerations on the analytic breakdown of the fragment (as well as the related ones on "harmonic" montage) serve precisely, and first of all, to affirm the existence of that system. Following this out to its logical conclusion, it could almost be said that the fragment does not exist outside of this system of its relations to the other fragments (to the whole of the text). The idea that it could be autonomized and extracted as a unit of meaning is completely contrary to that constant preoccupation with the systematic, of which *The General Line* is an example, and whose culmination will be seen in *Ivan*, with the notion of organicism.

It remains to be pointed out (aiming here at the connotations which the word "fragment" itself fortunately has [in French and in English] of the notion of "fracture" or "infraction") that the fragment is again defined according to a dimension which could be called cross-sectional. The metaphor of perpendicularity is meant to indicate that, if the horizontal and vertical dimensions refer us to the space of the film, to the film text, it remains to account for the production of the film, or more precisely, its relationship to what it is made out of (what is sometimes called the "profilmic").[4] Here it is a question of shooting (*prise de vue*)—and the characteristic of the Eisensteinian fragment here demands that we read the expression "*prise de vue*" ("shooting") as active, to take it actively.[5] *Filming* first of all provides a *broken, fragmented* image of the profilmic material, and second, it extracts something from the image. (It extracts meaning—at least potential meaning and, at the very least, representation.)

Eisenstein, who did not shy away from plays on words, on several occasions connected the Russian word *obraz* (image)—more punningly than etymologically, it should be noted—to the root *otrez* (which also evokes the idea of a cut, adding to it the idea that something has been removed, or amputated).[6] Despite their undeniably illogical basis, these associations seem to me quite symptomatic of the importance, in the definition of the fragment, of this function of "cut-out," of "slice," of "extraction," functions which compose, I believe, the essential meaning that Eisenstein attached to the word "frame."

Frame. The word, taken as is from French (*cadre*), did not exist in Russian before its introduction into the film vocabulary. There is therefore nothing pictorial in the word *kadr*, the film frame. At least there is nothing etymologically pictorial in the word, for insofar as the thing it designates is concerned, Soviet commercial cinema and also a large part of the "avant-garde" cinema had sought and found their compositional models during the twenties precisely in painting.

Insofar as the theory of framing is concerned, we are muddling about between the Tretiakova, the Shchukin Museum, and the geometric styl-

izations of which everyone has had more than enough. ("Off-Frame,"
1929, RW 2, pp. 292 ff.)

And it is precisely in protest against this muddling that Eisenstein
proposes his conception of the frame, for which it is no longer a question of "cramming" so many elements inside a pre-established frame
("the worn-out method of the spatial organization of the phenomenon
before the camera"), but rather a case of "cutting out" its "compositional unit": "The other method, apprehension by the camera, organization by it. A piece of reality is sliced off with the camera lens"
(ibid., RW 2, pp. 294 ff).

What does that mean? In fact, this idea of refusing to arrange what
is in front of the camera may well appear a bit hazy, especially when
one thinks of the minute attention to detail that is characteristic of
Eisenstein's directing style. And what is this magical "organization,"
this "slicing" of reality by the camera? Obviously, what must be sought
here is not an indication of some practical method of filming, but the
indication of an attitude with respect to the process of filming. Perhaps
nothing can elucidate it better than the comparison Eisenstein himself
made a few years later between framing and the work of selecting
significant elements in the theater:

> the playing upon the changes of dimension and camera angles . . . has
> already established itself in the theater. And every theater director, if
> he is not slipshod, masters it and uses it to some degree. It is true that
> he does it less perfectly than the film director does, although in a more
> refined way, but at the same time less consciously, for the stage director
> is not constrained to "frame," each time taking into the frame only
> what is necessary for the given phase of the movement of the scene.
> But this sorting out of the sole elements necessary . . . is also obligatory
> for its construction on the stage. It is true that there he is deprived of
> the possibility of physically cutting off all the rest, which the edge of
> the frame does in cinema. ("Montage 1937")

Framing is therefore the specific translation, into the cinematic vocabulary, of a general operation of all representation, according to
Eisenstein—the choosing, the selecting and the foregrounding of the
significant elements alone.

This is obviously the way to read the famous and slightly provocative aphorism "The frame is a *cell* of montage" (and the whole
development of this biological metaphor).[7] The frame has to do with
editing, and with montage, because it is an aspect of the fragment.
Frame/fragment—of course, the two terms are not equivalent. And if

we had to differentiate between them, the former would doubtless be related to filming, the latter to montage. Now, not only does Eisenstein never employ that dichotomy (in fact, the two words are often inter-changeable in his writings), but, even more important, he constantly insists on the necessity of considering the question of framing and that of montage at the same time and on the same basis (from "Off-Frame," where he says he is "smashing the frame-montage dualism," to "Mon-tage 1937," in which he states twenty times over that the whole study of the question of framing is only a part of that of montage).

This definition of the fragment as including the frame (or, what amounts to the same thing, of montage as including framing as a special case), is obviously not without consequences for Eisensteinian con-cepts in the area of editing and shooting. In particular, so far as mon-tage is concerned, we are still far from being liberated from the long-prevalent image of "Eisenstein-the-editor," the erector-set freak, etc. It seems to me very symptomatic in this regard that someone like Pascal Bonitzer, who in other respects is very careful to oppose the concept of fragment to the vague notion of shot (and who, moreover, has written one of the most pertinent articles on the Eisensteinian use of the close-up),[8] refuses to envisage the fragment also as shooting:

> The term *fragment* presupposes *only* montage, and not at all the actual *prise de vue* [*Translator's Note:* which means: (a) shooting (this is the usual meaning assigned to this term); (b) the *taking* of a view (if one takes apart the expression)] (that is why the effect is so strange when Eisenstein, intending to speak of the composition of elements in the shot speaks of "montage within the fragment").[9]

I know, of course, that Bonitzer posits a definition of shooting which is very special, since it designates at the same time the institution of a point of view and the fading out of that point of view, i.e., what produces that fixed place, characteristic of the "classic" cinema, which has been called the "Absent One."[10] It nonetheless seems to me that Eisenstein's attitude with respect to framing could be linked easily enough to this idea of *prise de vue* (which the same Bonitzer defines, in a very apt phrase, as "productive power and a trap for the look"). Eisensteinian "manipulation," in effect, is very far from being limited to his propensity for breaking the discourse up into pieces. It continues (it begins) with the statement, repeated a hundred times over, of the necessity for a choice of point of view, for a carving out of the profilmic ("shooting," "taking" a view)—and of the organization of the latter (the "calculation" of parameters). That has already been demonstrated earlier in this study, and consequently I shall content myself with providing three new pieces of evidence, from different periods and diverse in nature, without commenting on them at length. The first is a significant passage from a text written in 1926:

> The image is nothing but the extension of the choice. Of the choice of precisely such and such an object and no other—of an object precisely from this point of view with this "framing" (*Ausschnitt*, as the Germans say), and not another. And the cinematic conditions create the "image-figure" from the putting together of these "framings." ("Béla Forgets the Scissors," RW 2, p. 277; FW 1, p. 162)

It could not be clearer (if we bear in mind the German word, *Ausschnitt*, just about the literal equivalent of *otrez*); framing, image, and montage are three moments in the same treatment of the objects.

The second piece of evidence is the course on *Crime and Punishment* given in 1934, as it is reported by Nizhny, a kind of *tour de force* of teaching in which Eisenstein insisted that the entire scene be shot from a single camera position, and with a single wide-angle lens. What happens there, in defining and affecting a frame, is a distortion, a disarticulation of the space and the characters, which is aimed at making the frame a point of view on the action, constantly changing and constantly imposed on the spectator. (Once again, I quite agree that the effect sought and produced is not the same as in the classic cinema. The spectator's gaze is however no less "trapped"—quite the contrary.)

Finally, all the work on the duration of shots and depth of field in *Ivan the Terrible* (a real depth of field, even if it occasionally operates as a denial of depth, as in the very example Bonitzer has chosen—we shall return to this point); this work, moreover, is very often combined with that of perspective effects, such as the wide-angle lens, mentioned above.

This will to manipulate, this desire to produce *consciously*, right down to the very last detail of the image (knowing how it was made, and, why not [see below], what effect it will produce)—all of this is obviously the clearest expression, in the theoretical realm, of the status of author, of creator, explicitly claimed by Eisenstein. Or more precisely, in view of his lifelong demand for a vision of creation as "spontaneity overflowing with *joie de vivre*," it is the expression of his absolute *mastery*. He is the Mozart of the cinema, he is the one who "sends all the rules—those crutches—to hell and gone." But he is equally the cinema's Salieri, who knows exactly what he is doing, and skillfully dissects the music.

> But at the same time, I am always aware of this extremely important
> fact—besides moments of creative transport, all of us and I, more than
> anyone, need ever more precise scrutiny of what it is we are engaged
> in doing. ("Poor Salieri!" 1940, RW 2, p. 26)

The master is the one who is capable of dissecting, describing
precisely—hence the attempt to provide a "vertical" account of the
multiple parameters of the image. But the master is also one who sees
the root of the problem, the essence of things—whence the insistent
emphasis on the coherence of all the images linked to the fragment
(montage/framing/image). Whence, more broadly, the ceaseless attempts to place concepts like that of the fragment on philosophical
and theoretical "solid ground."

This is the very role assigned to that "metaphorical," or "special
transfiguration" ("Off-Frame") of the dialectic (or, to put things more
crudely, that wild application of the theory of contradiction)[11] which
Eisenstein calls *conflict*. Conflict is, indeed, his master-word during
the twenties, and it will continue to haunt all of his subsequent theoretical production. Here again, the examples and quotations would
be countless, and a few phrases will have to suffice to indicate the tone
and the substance:

> In the realm of art, this dialectical principle of the dynamic is embodied
> in
>
> CONFLICT
>
> as a fundamental, essential principle of the constitution of any work of
> art and of any kind of art.[12]

and this one, more specifically concerned with the fragment:

> By what then are montage and its embryo—the frame—characterized?
> By collision. By the conflict of two fragments placed side by side. By
> conflict. By collision. ("Off-Frame," 1929, RW 2, p. 290)

Naturally, these quotations come from texts which themselves provide
examples of conflicts; in "Dramaturgie der Film-Form" there is even
a taxonomy. There are conflicts "inside the frame" (conflicts of graphic
directions, of different "planes," of volumes, of masses), conflicts between two successive fragments, between the object filmed and its
space, between the event and the time of its unfolding, etc. Of course,
like all Eisensteinian classifications, this one is vertiginous, and one
would be hard put to grant it a functional value. (But conflict obviously
never sufficed to define all the filmic elements for which it served as

a general rubric; some ten years after these shattering declarations of principle, Eisenstein felt the need to devote a long study to the question of the frame.)[13] The important thing, at this point in our study, is therefore to show how conflict or, rather, its utilization in subsuming all individual problems (montage, internal organization of shots, scenography, handling of time and space) is, at the very least, the symptom of a will to unity and mastery of which the concept of the fragment is the sign.

II. Attraction/Stimulus/Influence

The idea of attraction and, even more, the expression "montage of attractions" always tend to come up when Eisenstein is spoken of (at the price, moreover, of a fairly constant contradiction in meaning with respect to the second of these two terms, which is very frequently misrepresented as "montage by attractions" or some such other distortion, for example, "attraction-montage"). The expression itself is of course quite a fascinating one, and still retains an air of mystery, not least because Eisenstein himself did not refrain from participating in the veritable mythologizing of the "attraction," among other places in this passage from a very well-known text:

> So then, let us go back to our books and our notebooks . . . Laboratory analyses and diagrams . . . Mendeleev's Periodic Table and the laws of Gay-Lussac and Boyle Mariotte in the realm of art! . . . Let us not forget that the man who has saddled himself with this task of a scientific study of the mysteries and secrets (of art) is a young engineer.
> From all the disciplines he has explored, he has retained this first rule, that, properly speaking, a procedure becomes scientific from the moment the field of investigation acquires a unit of measure.
> Let us therefore search for the unit which will measure the influence exerted by art!
> Science has its "ions," its "electrons," its "neutrons." Art will have— attractions! ("How I Became a Film Director," 1945, RW 3, pp. 241 ff.)

There can be no mistaking the massive irony of this fragment. Affectionately lampooning a certain scientistic atmosphere of the twenties (which he had been among the first to embrace), here Eisenstein nonetheless reintroduces and elaborates upon a "scientific" notion of attraction—which certainly does not make it any easier to understand what he means by this term.

Let us therefore briefly recall how "attractions" actually appeared in Eisenstein's writings. It was in a *theater* manifesto, published in 1923 by *Lef*, the journal of "Left-wing Art." Of course (and for once all of Eisenstein's biographers are in agreement), the idea of attraction does not suddenly appear out of the blue in the article in *Lef*. Traces of it are to be found in Eisenstein's very first "professional" production, that of *The Mexican* (in particular, the famous boxing match that was included "life size" in the show); it can even be traced further back, and can be seen taking shape in Meyerhold's direction of *Mystery-Bouffe*, by Mayakovsky (a play which Eisenstein was very familiar with). But more than anything, I believe that the premises for it are to be found in Eisenstein's precocious taste for the circus, above all for its "eccentric" side. Thus the attraction is originally the music hall number or sketch, a peak moment in the show, relatively autonomous, and calling upon techniques of representation which are not those of dramatic illusion, drawing upon more aggressive forms of the performing arts (the circus, the music hall, the sideshow).

The point cannot be emphasized too much. While they may not account for everything, the "circus" origins of the notion of attraction already imply the essential characteristics of that notion as it will be developed subsequently, and more specifically, in thinking of the cinema. Thus, I repeat:

(a) The attraction is an "aggressive" and sufficiently autonomous peak moment in the performance:

> On the level of form, I situate the attraction as the first and autonomous element of the construction of the show. ("Montage of Attractions," RW 2, p. 271; FW 1, p. 117)

From this point of view, the most fully developed example of it is the "trick," that is, any kind of special performance, such as those demonstrations of physical prowess peppered throughout *Every Wise Man*. It is even an especially well "sold" attraction, says Eisenstein (although it has the major defect of not really taking the spectator into account).

(b) The attraction is thus from its inception (before becoming a method) a highly commendable means of escaping from something of which Eisenstein has a holy terror, namely naturalism, the theatrical illusion, Aristotelian verisimilitude (and, to anticipate somewhat, what the history of cinema will call "transparency"):

> Without letting ourselves be tied down by pious devotion to the logic of everyday life and literary tradition, let us make this procedure a method of production. (Ibid., RW 2, p. 27; FW 1, pp. 117 ff.)

Thus in cinema, the concept of attraction (which, it hardly need be said, will never really be "applied") will be what is opposed to any static "reflection" of events, and therefore it escapes from the corollary obligation to treat the theme by means of actions "logically" connected to that event (according to the "logic of everyday life").

It is in this direction that we must look for the sole strict equivalent of the theatrical attraction in cinema (even if, as will be seen, the posterity of the idea of attraction is not limited to these cases of "pure" attractions). To give an example, I would readily agree with Amengual in considering that, in *Potemkin*, the attractions are:

> the close-up of vermin which precedes the medical officer's dive into the sea, the allegorical monument which serves as an introduction to the Odessa of the tyrants, and the awakening of the lion-people, for their metaphorical character. (*S. M. Eisenstein*, p. 27)

(However, the notion of metaphor is in no way included in the idea of attraction, but only in what will subsequently be defined as "intellectual montage," based, of course, on the attraction.) The attraction in cinema as well as elsewhere, thus supposes, first, a strong degree of autonomy (which will be expressed, in terms of montage, by the requirement of a high degree of heterogeneity)[14] and, second, a visually striking existence (a requirement of effectiveness, as we shall see, but also a desire to be "anti-literary" that was characteristic of the entire period).

But the passage from the "original" attraction, that of *The Mexican* and *Every Wise Man*, in which a plot which could be summarized in a few sentences serves as a base onto which no fewer than twenty-five attractions are grafted (among them, let us remember, the famous *Glumov's Diary*, which was Eisenstein's first film, and which was itself an attraction in which the "principle of attraction" was again at work, in the transformations of the character Glumov—immediate visual representations of a weak and servile will—simple metaphors for Glumov's cringing personality). In cinema, and insofar as it has existed there, the attraction retains this same character: "In fact, it is not phenomena that are confronted, but chains of associations" ("Montage of Cine-Attractions," 1924, RW 2, p. 275; FW 1, p. 130). In cinema the attraction is defined by its "associative" relationship to the theme—and by its concatenation with other attractions, the whole of the chain being what makes it possible to transmit this "theme" to the spectator: "free montage of selected and autonomous actions (attractions), but having for their specific goal a certain final thematic effect" ("Montage of Attractions," RW 2, p. 271; FW 1, p. 118).

Naturally, the question of "association" (including the connotations which psychoanalysis has accustomed us to attribute to the word) is in no way exhausted by the concept of attraction. Long after he had all but eliminated the word "attraction" from his vocabulary, Eisenstein returned in an even more insistent and often more precise manner to this problem. He did so first of all with the theory of intellectual montage (which, at the time of its first appearance, was called "intellectual attraction")[15]; then, in the thirties, in his fascination with "interior monologue." And it took the trauma of *Bezhin Meadow* (largely based on both interior monologue and association) to cause this theme to disappear from Eisenstein's reflections (at least from what we know of it, for it seems that the essay *Method*, as far as we can tell, again gave space—around 1943–44—to these preoccupations). We shall have occasion to speak again about intellectual montage and interior monologue. Therefore, I shall not insist on the point and will merely note here the extreme limit of the reflection on this subject, reached, I believe, in a text of 1934, "Torito" (which is part of the *Regissura* cycle), in which Eisenstein, striving "to unravel the skein of associations" which determined the composition of a frame of *Que Viva Mexico!*, unravels in fact a whole series of visual reminiscences, symbolic transcriptions, but also childhood memories and personal feelings. In the face of such a piece of analysis (it goes on for pages), the protestations of anti-Freudianism carry very little weight.

But let us return to the "first version" of the attraction. The double definition of it just given (as a performance and as an association of ideas) still remains, in effect, insufficient. It runs the risk, among other things, of giving the impression—despite the clarity of such historico-ideological determinations as the rejection of naturalism, "disrespect" for the cultural heritage, a preoccupation with scientificity—that the concept of the attraction is concerned only with the issue of the *form* of the work of art. It will be seen in any case that for Eisenstein the question of form is never reducible to a purely formal problem, so it is clearly not a matter of devalorizing this aspect of things. However, the essential feature of the idea of attraction might be missed if we were to neglect what could be called its third definition (inseparable, of course, from the first two), namely, everything in this idea that implies an effort *to attract* the spectator's attention.

This question of the spectator, and, more broadly, of the ideological efficacy of art, is far from being specific to Eisenstein. Indeed it is one of the great dominant ideas of the whole immediate post-revolutionary period, in the form of agitprop (a double notion of agitation and propaganda, developed by Trotsky, among others—perhaps more than by Lenin). In Eisenstein, this need for propaganda work through artistic means is manifested very explicitly with trenchant slogans:

> Outside of agitation, the cinema does not exist. ("Montage of Cine-Attractions," RW 2, p. 275; FW 1, p. 135)

or this more vivid one:

> It is the duty of the cinema to grab the stunned spectator by the hair and, with an imperious gesture, bring him face to face with the problems of today. ("Days of Enthusiasm," 1929, RW 1, p. 141; FW 1, p. 52)

In other passages dealing with the spectator, it is a question of "plowing up his psyche," of "shaping him in the desired mould," even of "obliging him to like dull, everyday work."[16] All of this, once again, belongs largely to the style of the period, to the party and government chiefs, but also to all the intellectual trends which, like the Proletkult, extolled the advent of "proletarian culture," or which, like *Lef*, called for the shaping of a "new spectator."[17]

But much more than this ideological determination, there is another determination, much more specific to Eisenstein (even though it too is largely marked by the period), which colors this aspect of the attraction. I am referring, of course, to "reflexology," that theory which believed it possible to account for all the activity of the human brain (thought and also "feelings") in terms of reflexes, by the repeated use of the diagram action → reaction. Like Pavlovianism, which comes directly out of it, this theory holds that all human behavior can be considered as the response, more or less complex, more or less "conditioned," to a series of stimuli. Its essential thesis consists in stating that it is theoretically conceivable (and that one day it will be practically possible) to determine, or to calculate those processes of response to stimuli (and, consequently, to determine the stimuli necessary to obtain a given desired response).

It is obviously this last "scientific" proposition which Eisenstein appropriated most readily, and in an abundantly overdetermined gesture. While if not out of real scientific necessity (as he takes pleasure in letting it be understood), at least out of an authentic desire to "be scientific," the whole Eisensteinian reflection on the theme of "influence" (what we would nowadays call "efficacy")[18] borrows the methods, the theses, and the terminology used by the "reflexologists," in particular, Bekhterev's. The most visible manifestation of this borrowing will no doubt be in his writings of the twenties, in the simple translation of the whole problem of efficacy into a question of *stimuli* (of "excitants," as they are called in Russian)—How many stimuli? Which stimuli? What is the effect produced by given stimuli? etc., etc. These are the questions Eisenstein asks, and by which he always implies, on the horizon, the possibility of a calculation, however complex and uncertain it might be, of efficacy.

Naturally, Eisenstein does not fail to notice that, even if reflexology were indeed able to "calculate" a spectator, we would still be very far from the mark. The receptor with which the filmmaker deals is not a spectator-subject, it is the audience, the public. It is, Eisenstein tells us, because this public was incorrectly calculated that certain stimuli failed, even though they had been carefully determined, produced, and edited with a view to obtaining a particular effect. Example: the conclusion of *Strike*, which:

> *did not have* that blood-curdling effect on the working class public for the simple reason that in the mind of the worker beef blood is associated first of all with the blood recuperation plant of the slaughterhouses! As for the effect on the peasant accustomed to slaughtering cattle himself, it was absolutely nil.[19]

Conclusion: In order to calculate stimuli effectively, the nature of the public being addressed must first be determined. And the means of this determination will be provided by another "science," Marxism-Leninism. It is with reference to the Marxist class analysis that such a knowledge of the public (the real public?) is determined and, therefore, that a film is calculated. Of course, the reference to Marxism-Leninism is not specific to Eisenstein—there is scarcely a revolutionary artist, especially in the twenties, who did not attempt to envisage his work and those to whom it was addressed in terms of class. What is more original in Eisenstein is the combination of Marxism and reflexology, in which there is a kind of impression that each term "rubs off" on the other (reflexology, in particular, provided the young Eisenstein's Marxism with what we might call a somewhat rigid feel). Class spirit, for example, is manifested:

> 1) *In the definition of the orientation of the film*—in the socially useful effect which an emotional and psychic charge communicates to the spectators and which is formed by a chain of stimuli directed towards them in a proper manner.

2) *In the choice of excitants themselves.* In two directions. In a correct evaluation of their inevitable class efficacy. . . . The second factor in the choice of excitants [stimuli] is class acceptance of one excitant or another. ("The Method for Making a Workers' Film," 1925, RW 1, p. 117; FW 1, p. 25)

The idea of attraction is obviously bound up with this whole idea of efficacy. The feature of attraction which causes it to lend itself so well to the purposes of the calculation of efficacy is first of all its isolatable nature, the fact that it can be autonomized, separated out. It is clear that if one wants to calculate efficacy (even "class" efficacy), it is better to be dealing with material composed of discrete, commutable elements, and, as Eisenstein said, with a material that is actually measurable. That is the very thing he has in mind when he speaks of the attraction as the "molecular unit . . . of the efficacy of the theater" (RW 2, p. 271; FW 1, p. 118).

This is basically what is said in the famous definition of attraction, as stated in the *Lef* manifesto, which synthesizes all the aspects of that term that have been outlined in succession:

Attraction (from the point of view of the theater) is every aggressive moment of the theater performance, that is, every element subjecting the spectator to a sensory or psychic action verified by means of experiment and mathematically calculated to produce in the spectator certain emotional shocks which, in turn, once they have been united, alone determine the possibility of perceiving the ideological aspect of the performance given, its final ideological conclusion. (RW 2, p. 270; FW, p. 117)

Everything is here—the attraction as a show, but also as a violence done to the spectator (which will allow Shklovsky to speak, most aptly, of "montage of surprises"), the attraction as ultimately effective due to the calculation that is made, and even the "associative" relationship between the central theme (conceived here solely in terms of its ideological aspect) and the attractions that carry it.

The problem at this stage (an immediately *practical* problem, which was expressed in the films) resides in the tension, not to say the contradiction, between its aggressiveness, its surprise aspect (its Proletkult aspect), and its efficacy, its utilitarianism (its Leninist aspect, so to speak). This is a tension which, at the level of Soviet society as a whole, quickly turned, as we know, into absolute incompatibility. Let us recall Lenin's diatribes against the "tabula rasa" policy of the Proletkult, which he considered implicitly leftist, and to which he preferred more traditional methods of educating and influencing the spectator.

In Eisenstein, the contradiction is resolved, with scarcely any time lag at all, in the same spirit. First of all, with the practically total disappearance, as early as *Potemkin*, of the word "attraction" and its immediate replacement with another terminology, that of "pathos," to which we shall return shortly.

This sudden abandonment of a term, and of a concept, so violently defended up to that point, is probably much less unequivocal and much more tactical than it seems to be. First of all, even though it is clearly not the most important point, it can be remarked that the word "attraction," which was brutally rejected in 1926 (*Potemkin* is "an absolute revision of the attractions of *Strike*" ["Constantza," a text written in 1926, first published in *Bronenosets Potemkin*, ed. N. Kleiman & K. Levina, Moscow, 1968; FW 1, p. 35]), was to make new appearances, furtively but constantly, in certain later writings (the mythical "IA 28," "Intellectual Attraction 1928," introducing the idea of "intellectual montage," or, for example, certain theses on color put forward in 1946, which especially stress the "autonomizable" aspect of the attraction).[20] But above all, despite all the apparent abruptness and radicalness of his reversal, Eisenstein does not in fact give up much of the content of the concept of attraction. At the very most, he gives up the "eccentricity" that had been so irritating to some viewers of *Strike*. All the rest, certainly the essential, is immediately reinvested; the idea of "association," in the premises of intellectual montage (see below), and that of efficacy in a "new look" version of efficacy:

> Because in *Potemkin* there is an absolute revision of attractions (at least from *Strike*) and a positive effect (pathos)—a pressing appeal to activity—obtained by means which are all "negative." . . . after the battle, our contemporaries . . . need a page of sentiment. And I believe that it is only through sentiment that they can be led to the necessary and correct, *left-wing*, active "pumping-up." . . . For the term "stimulus," in reflexology, applies both to the rap of the stick on the skull and the luminous tenderness of the blue sky as well. ("Constantza," FW 1, pp. 35-36)

Eisenstein's apparent about-face is therefore, on this essential point, neither a conversion nor a renunciation. The idea of efficacy remains, with the same double determination: politico-ideological considerations, shaped by the necessities of the present moment (the present moment of the government authorities exclusively, see *Potemkin*, presented as "NEP-style" work!); and psychological considerations aiming at the spectator as a subject (as potential psychic energy, and always in terms of conditioned reflexes).

Naturally, over the years, this idea was to be profoundly reworked. More precisely, and perhaps a bit schematically, it might be said that the center of the idea of efficacy over the next twenty years amounts to a more and more pronounced demonstration of the dichotomy between its politico-ideological aspect and its psychological aspect.

Concerning the first determination, the political one, it must first of all be said that it will always be present. Tirelessly, and no doubt with the greatest sincerity, Eisenstein reaffirms the submission of all artistic activity to a final goal—the building of socialism. The conception of cinema he defends is unambiguously *utilitarian*:

> Our cinema is above all a tool insofar as its fundamental activity is concerned—a tool to exert an influence on people, and to reeducate. ("Sergei Eisenstein," 1944, RW 1, p. 86; FW 3, p. 52)

Of course, the formulations of utilitarianism will change, shaped as they are by the transformations of Soviet government policy. Eisenstein's written production includes countless pages written "for the occasion," in which he proclaims, in terms adapted to the needs of the moment, his attachment to the "thematic" and utilitarian aspect of Soviet cinema.[21] While his sincerity is, as I have said, undeniable, one might question the interest of the more and more stereotyped language in which his approbation is expressed. Many of the texts of the thirties (and even more in the forties, a period when he was overwhelmed with official responsibilities) are nothing more than accumulations of conformist expressions, reflecting the wasting away of political thought which marked the Stalin era, far more than it does any weakness specific to Eisenstein. Thus it is that this aspect of efficacy as agitprop has a tendency (like all the political concepts of that period) not to stand for much, for it is little more than an inscription on a prayer roll.

With respect to the other determination of efficacy, that which aims at acting upon (playing with) the spectator, it is an entirely different matter.

The somewhat mechanical "fashioning" of this "raw material" of all utilitarian art which the spectator is before he or she is anything else, gives way (at a rate almost equivalent to the speed with which the political formulations are hollowed out) to considerations marked by more subtle differentiations in which the model of the action exerted on the spectator, i.e., of the influence, ceases, among other things to be something along the lines of hammering, and is metaphorized into more refined energetic terms.

I will not go into details of all the steps involved in this transformation now. They will be dealt with again later on. They lead us from a text like "Montage of Cine-Attractions" (1925), in which the notion of "psychic energy" appears (in a still very rudimentary, Pavlovian form), that energy which will have to be devoted entirely to action by the man of the future, no longer to be diverted into fiction cinema; to the stage, the "resting-place," to use Eisenstein's term,[22] which "interior monologue" represents. It is a stage of capital importance, which moves the psycho-energetic model from the strictly utilitarian field to a real consideration of the spectator as a desiring subject. The final step in this series will involve coming to terms with the very special spectatorial process called "ecstasy," and a search for laws of the "organicism" of works of art capable of producing (or of reproducing, of mimicking) that ecstasy.

Here it would be necessary to study in greater detail the evolution of a terminology in which the notions of "energy profit," "savings of expenditure of energy," etc., certainly do not cover merely the concern, often expressed in the twenties, to "pump up," or to "recharge" the spectator so that he or she will be in a fit (psychological) condition to work at building socialism. Indeed, the theoretical space of these formulations, despite their haziness, is probably closer, at least in part, to Freud than to Pavlov. In any case, it is clear that the double register here by which the spectator was "calculated" has been entirely abandoned. The utilitarian (politico-ideological) end-goal, expressed in what are finally tame slogans, gives way to the end-goal of ecstasy—and the determination of effective stimuli is submerged in a much more ambitious calculation—that of organicism.

(Having just written these words, I must temper them on two counts. First of all, because the question of the "expenditure of [psychic] energy" is quite often, at least as a guarantee, related to another kind of energy, that used by the subject-citizen in his productive work. Thus, in 1937, Eisenstein explains that an improperly calculated composition of the frame leads to an expenditure of superfluous energy at the time of reception, and prevents the correct reception of the work, and finally has an effect on work capacity [sic—this is in "Montage 1937," RW 2, p. 335]. Second, and above all, because of the constant ideological preoccupation, which this time is not merely a guarantee or a rhetorical precaution. As will be seen in the third section of this chapter, throughout various investigations Eisenstein always places an ideological aim at the center of the task of the Soviet artist, an ideological aim which moreover is diversely evaluated according to the moment, and which would be among other things the final justification of ecstasy.)

III. A Parenthesis on the Question of Form

The "question" of form is far more than a question. For Eisenstein it marks the boundaries of a real battlefield, a struggle, and not merely a verbal one, between "work on the form of the work of art" and "formalism." On one side you have what he never stopped calling for; on the other, what was thrown in his face, constantly and violently. Like so many milestones in this war, the titles of certain articles are very revealing: "On the Problem of a Materialist Approach to Form" (1925); "Dramaturgie der Film-Form" (1929); "In the Interests of Form" (1932); "Film Language" (1934); "The Structure of the Film" (1939); "A Close-Up View" (1945)—and we could go on and on.

Indeed, here as elsewhere, Eisenstein's approach to this problem is largely dependent on the circumstances (even if only the theoretical ones of its elaboration), and one can only agree with François Albéra when he observes that "it is not possible to give a systematic account of the content-form relationship in Eisenstein's theoretical writings."[23] We shall therefore content ourselves with a few very brief observations about the place of this question of form in the Eisensteinian conceptual system.

No accusation has been leveled at Eisenstein so often as that of "formalism." This began as early as his first film, as is reported in particular by the Soviet historian Lebedev (nonetheless, a declared partisan of Eisenstein's inquiries into the question of form).[24] As soon as that film was released, it was criticized for its "disconnected" quality—a direct consequence of the application of the principle of "montage of cine-attractions"—and for his abuse of metaphors.

As we know, that was nothing compared to what he was yet to endure. During a ten-year period, from about 1927 to 1937, Eisenstein never ceased to be in total and ever more manifest opposition to an official doctrine which, from "vital man" to "socialist realism," proved to be as aggressive as it was regressive. This began with *October* and *The General Line*, which, after a perfunctory tip of the hat to the artist of *Potemkin*, were unanimously charged with "coldness," "artificiality," "lack of realism," and, if we read between the lines, formalism. This continued and increased with the "administrative" harassments, which, from the time of his return to Moscow in 1932 until the 1935

Congress of Filmmakers, prevented him, among other things, from completing no fewer than five projects, some of them very far advanced. And this all culminates of course, in the affronts suffered by *Bezhin Meadow*, a film that was completed twice and twice sent into oblivion.

All of this is well known, and if I mention it, it is not so much to move the reader to shed tears over the persecution of Eisenstein (all things considered, he came through it all quite well) as to point out the veritable ideological "mountain" he had to move in his stubborn work on form, which was never so intense as it was during those years. And, I am doing so above all in order to explain the central role he assigned in this work to a point which might reasonably have been assumed to be taken for granted, if only in the light of the "classics of Marxism," that of the "form/content" dichotomy.

It is around this point that all of Eisenstein's tactical and defensive positions crystallized, in response to the general "critique of formalism." He never makes that "dichotomy" his own. For him, "form" is not opposed to "content," it is opposed to *formlessness.*

> Whereas some are ready to persecute work in the area of form so fanatically by stigmatizing it with the label of "formalism," and by preferring to it . . . the totally formless. ("On the Problem of a Materialist Approach to Form," 1925, RW 1, p. 109; FW 1, p. 145)

Thus all of the formulations of the thirties, in the style of "form must be elevated to the level of content" with which he was so often reproached as regressive manifestations of an Hegelian conception ("form as perceptible representation of content, the latter always foremost") are to be read above all as *concessive* definitions, by which Eisenstein agrees to go over to the enemy's side for a moment only in order to enjoy a greater triumph there. The temporary borrowing of such terminology (however threadbare, however "idealist" it may be) should not cause us to forget that in the same movement (in the same interventions) Eisenstein actually denies any validity to the form/content distinction, in particular by his violent opposition to the stereotype of the "sound idea poorly expressed," which served as a justification for so many sloppy films. To be convinced of this, one has only to recall the mischievous little observations with which he favors Yutkevich (who had been among his severest critics). Among others he hurled at him this remark about Yutkevich's film, *Counter-Shot*: "A formal imperfection is an indication of a lack of precision in the apprehension of the idea" ("Final Speech at the 1935 Conference," RW 2, p. 127).

I cannot give here a detailed demonstration of this (which would be long and drawn out), but it seems to me that in Eisenstein's whole attitude in response to accusations of formalism (i.e., of autonomizing "form" and neglecting "content"), there is nothing which goes beyond rhetorical precautions, and these are, after all, quite understandable.[25]

From this point of view, the thirties look a bit like a period of relative withdrawal (in his public statements, for it is an entirely different matter in the unpublished texts of the period, from *Regissura* to "Montage 1937"), between the conception, for example, expressed in 1929:

> The organizing principle of the idea constitutes, in fact, the real "content" of the work. A principle materialized by the whole of the sociopsychological stimuli for which the form is the means of manifestation. ("Perspectives," 1929, RW 2, p. 38; FW 1, p. 190)

—and the broader conception, which, in the forties, would express the preoccupation with "form" in the concern with the "organicism" of the works. And it is in the points these two conceptions have in common that one should look for the definition of Eisenstein's attitude with respect to the question of form. Beyond obvious differences in wording, the constant feature is always a determination to make the form adequate not so much to a supposed "content" from which it is in any case indissociable, but rather to the very movement of the *influence* exerted on the spectator.

Therefore, above and beyond superficial variations in the Eisensteinian discourse on form, there would remain a central assertion, taken up again in different . . . forms—namely, that form is the vector of ideology. There is not so much a coincidence as a very clear concordance between statements like these:

> *Strike* [is] not only a revolutionary victory in itself, but also *an ideological victory in the realm* of form.

and further:

> revolutionary form is the product of technically correct methods of giving concrete form to a new vision and a new approach to things and phenomena—the new class ideology. ("On the Problem of a Materialist Approach to Form," 1925, RW 1, pp. 109-111; FW 1, pp. 145-148)

and this assertion:

> We reach the conclusion that every apparently abstract process of composition and every method express an ideological and political concep-

tion referring to the subject in question. ("Problems of Composition," 1946, RW 4, pp. 675-709)

This is a statement of principle which is obviously directed against all those who, in the name of sacrosanct "content," accuse him of formalism, but it is also a statement of principle *against formalism.*[26]

Thus all of Eisenstein's work on the problem of form is contained in what he called "revolutionary form" in 1925. However, here again we must reiterate what has been said or will be said about efficacy and montage, i.e., that these concepts, or rather, very general principles, are presented in terminologies which radically differ from period to period.

During nearly the whole silent period, this "revolutionary form" remains closely linked to the preoccupation with the "calculation" of the spectator—then founded, as has been seen, on the dual determination of physiological reflexes and class reflexes. In the text on *Strike,* which has already been quoted extensively, we find a fairly complete description of what this "form" implies:

> Tearing fragments loose from the surrounding milieu, according to a conscious and deliberate calculation, predetermined for the purpose of conquering the spectator, after having unleashed these fragments upon him in an appropriate confrontation, while associating him in the appropriate way with the proposed final ideal motif. ("On the Problem of a Materialist Approach to Form," RW 1, p. 115; FW 1, p. 153)

Everything is here—fragment and frame, the calculation of stimuli, montage as "confrontation" (conflict), the ideological goal and even the mechanistic temptation (no longer to see form as anything other than the assembly of stimuli, as an equation or chemical reaction).

This vocabulary of 1925 is of course going to be modified (discarding, in particular, all the jargon of reflexology), and even the words which will be retained (conflict, frame, montage . . .) will be redefined and reinvested in new systems. But the ideological aim, at each moment of this evolution, will remain at the center of the requirement with respect to form from which Eisenstein never departs. It is not possible to follow step by step all of this work, which, as I said at the outset, is full of wanderings and apparent contradictions. But I insist once more on the persistence of the link established by Eisenstein between "form" and "ideology"; I would even say, once and once only, the *dialectical* link between these two dimensions, for if Eisenstein has shown himself to be a dialectician (in the pre-Marxist sense of the term as well), it is certainly in this respect. One only need see, for example, the way in which, in 1932, and *in the interest of form* (that is the title of his article), he reverses the official slogan of "ideological plenitude," "recall[ing] once again the genetic indissociability of the *idea*, the *manner of expression*, and . . . the aspect, the appearance" ("In the Interest of Form," 1932, RW 5, p. 43; FW 1, p. 234). And after that, as will be seen, the greater project, related to "organicism," will imply the maintenance and the expansion (at the cost of what is certainly a very considerable displacement) of this concept of form as a vector of ideology.

I should like to take up again here some points already raised, in order to show (schematically) how the question of form comes into play. It has been seen in particular that, in the whole problem of efficacy (= effectiveness of the actualizations of the ideological aim), the idea of a calculation, of the possibility of a science of this efficacy, is always implied. And it is this will to science (or, if you prefer, this belief of Eisenstein's in the possibility of being scientific) in the realization of a certain ideological aim, which contaminates Eisenstein's whole attitude towards form. What he is striving to define, basically, in his great theoretical essays (*Montage, Nonindifferent Nature*) as well as in his teaching at the VGIK (see *Regissura*) are formal laws —and this perhaps is the stumbling block of his whole system of thought.

Not that this thought leads to nothing. Quite the contrary—anything might be said about the work on form in his films except that it is incoherent or haphazard (cf. the following chapter); and, above all, one must reread the stenographic record of Eisenstein's courses on film directing, in which, if not laws, at the very least a real method of formal invention (of the "calculation" of forms) is set forth with staggering clarity.

But if the reader compares the successes of the films and the professorial eloquence with the texts in which Eisenstein analyzes his own productions (after the fact, in that situation of "outside observer" which he so readily fantasized)—he or she will be struck by how much the analysis cedes in ideological rigor, to the advantage of a great formal finesse (and almost a formalism) of description. This appears quite flagrantly, for example, in the analysis of a sequence of *Potemkin* dating from 1934 and, what is more, in a context in which Eisenstein is seeking precisely to defend himself once again against the charge of formalism ("Film Language"). What do we find in this minute description and in these diagrams? Of course, some indications of the overall "meaning" of the piece (union between the shore and the ship by means of yawls)—but these indications are locked in, and swamped by a mass of graphic, pictorial "themes," contrasting odd with even, dark with light, vertical with horizontal, circular with angular, etc., in a skillful intertwining pattern, to such a degree that the overall impression derived from this text is very much the one Eisenstein wishes to avoid—the impression of an incredible formal science (and it is quite probable that such an analysis actually reproduces at least a part of something that took place at the time of the editing of the film), but also and especially the impression of a machine whose motor is racing, of a calculation that is overwrought, of a gratuitous performance.

Of course, it is not at all the sequence of *Potemkin* itself that appears ineffective or gratuitous to me (far from it), but the frenzied demonstration, the kind of parametric saturation in which Eisenstein indulges. Of what importance, after all, is this game of substitutions—of a group of three characters for a group of two, of a parasol for an arcade? Such an analysis only provokes incredulousness in me. I cannot manage to believe that it is *there*, in *that* calculation, that the meaning really operates. Just as I cannot manage to believe, let us say, in the enumeration and alleged mastery of the parameters set into play by the "vertical" breakdown of the fragment.[27]

The stumbling block would therefore seem to be in the disparity, the real "gap" between the formal work itself and the level of formalizing rigidity which characterizes Eisenstein's analyses. On the one hand, we have formal analyses which do not manage to account for the ideological determinations at work in the film text and which, despite their subtlety of accommodation (think again of the analysis of the sequence from *Nevsky*), remain little more than a sort of "grid" for perception. On the other hand, there is all the *force* of the work of giving form, which is not empirical, far from it, but which plays, nonetheless, on what must certainly be called the author's inventiveness, his intuition, even his inspiration.[28]

I am exaggerating, of course, but only in order to give a better idea of where the theory is situated, i.e., between these two activities. The theory is first of all the cement of principle which fills in the gap. It is the sole reference (in the sense in which that word implies a taking out of guarantees, of security) of the "creative work," of the actual productions and finished works, as well as of the analysis, of the after-the-fact justification. And this appears to me to be most particularly true of the little form/ideology dialectic set up and constantly used again by Eisenstein—from the "materialist approach" of 1925 (guaranteed by reflexology and Marxism) to organicism (in which the system of references is extended almost endlessly, always under the cover of the "dialectic").

But theory does not intervene beyond this level of principle. In a way, Eisenstein never stops developing "laws of form," always with the central idea of adequating the formal work to the ideological work (and of a simultaneous, double reading of the film, at both these levels). But these "laws," with all their scientificity, with all their conformity to the "natural" laws of the dialectic, have nothing about them of universal formulae; they do not permit one to define *a priori*, outside of each specific case, the form necessary to such and such a film. It is not that Eisenstein did not dream of proposing, if not *the* method, at least some methods of producing "correct" forms. Indeed, this served as the very basis for justifying his own research activity. Here, for example, is what he said at the 1935 Congress in response to the violent criticism from Sergei Vasiliev, who reproached him with walling himself up in his ivory tower:

> I do not look at statuettes, I do not contemplate them abstractly when I am seated at my desk. I work on problems which will be raised by the coming generation of filmmakers. And, if I remain seated working at my desk, it is so that you will not lose time at work tables and so that you can continue to make films as remarkable as your *Chapayev*! (RW 2, p. 128)

But whatever desire he may have had (consoled by his masterly practice of directing students and of "collective improvising"), he constantly warned students and readers against the hasty and abusive use of his research work—he doesn't give out recipes, such is the oft repeated warning. He is not seeking to make disciples: he even goes so far as to advise a certain distance in the application of his principles (and recommends "stepping back a little before reaching the outer limits"—RW 3, p. 421), the danger of their blind application being that of "obstructing the channels through which the work draws the spectator in" (Preface to *Nonindifferent Nature* , RW 3, p. 423). It is significant that right up to the end this concern with efficacy is given priority over everything else.

IV. Pathos/Ecstasy/Organicism

Let us return briefly to the point where we left the subject of efficacy, at the end of the second section of this chapter, stressing the dual (ideological/subjective) nature of its aim, and the progressive effacing of the first determination, or, rather, its reabsorption into a more and more stereotyped and invalid "political" discourse, in favor of a development, even a hypertrophy of the action exerted upon the spectator as a source of "energy." We shall now consider more closely this second determination, while examining the way in which it masks (or incorporates) the first determination.

As we have seen, in the early texts (from "Montage of Attractions" to "A Materialist Approach to Form"), Eisenstein constantly wants to subordinate lyricism and the spectator's pleasure to ideology, to the "moulding" of the spectator. The reversal of this perspective begins very early—in fact, with the first appearance of the term *pathos* in a text from 1926.

It should first be pointed out that in Russian the word does not have any pejorative connotations.[29] The *Great Soviet Encyclopedia* defines it as "passionate ardor, enthusiasm in the combat for a noble cause." And when Eisenstein introduces it, apropos of *Potemkin*, it is as a "positive effect," aiming at "leading [his] contemporaries to the necessary and correct, *left-wing*, active 'pumping up' " ("Constantza"). At this point, therefore, the concept of pathos seems to remain—with respect to its end-goal and its "functionality"—entirely in the realm of a problem of efficacy understood as transformation and (re)orientation of the spectator. Pathos "replaces" attraction. Cancelling the latter out as a concept, it comes to occupy the same place. Attraction shocked; pathos will aim at captivating, always in order to influence. And, if it uses precisely all the processes against which the idea of attraction, in all its violence, was conceived, this, Eisenstein tells us, is a simple tactical ruse, the processes in question being in fact submitted to a real "diversion." These "bourgeois" processes ("doubts, tears, sentimentalism, lyricism, psychology, maternal feelings, etc.")

> are ripped asunder from the harmony of their traditional association with the effects of "rapture," of flight from reality, and other effects of passification. . . . It is the bourgeois being forced to work on a "communist Saturday!" (Ibid.)

However, things are less limpid than we are being led to believe. Under the name of "psychologism," the same text of 1926 advertises a brand new preoccupation. Since the word sounds "regressive" (do not forget that Eisenstein is just coming out of Proletkult), it is surrounded with a whole apparatus intended to justify it, to acclimatize it, to "debourgeoisify" it. This will be a "new," "offensive" psychologism, very careful not to be "out of date," "figurative," even "narrative." It is nonetheless true that, above and beyond the rhetorical precautions, what is involved, and for the first time, is "that essential emotion of the masses," the "page of sentimentality" they need—in short, the spectator's subjectivity is being taken into consideration.

Naturally, I am not claiming that every card was played with the substitution of pathos (and its new "psychologism") for attraction. There will be many meanderings before the systematic reactivation of this theme occurs twenty years later in the second part of *Nonindifferent Nature*, entitled "Pathos." But, leaping directly into the theorizing of 1946–47, I shall begin by pointing out that the long text entitled "Pathos" starts out, paradoxically enough, by getting rid of the concept of pathos, for which, through a new displacement, the famous *ecstasy* is substituted (smoothly this time, almost surreptitiously). As early as the first few lines we read: "We have discovered that the principal index of the pathetic composition is a constant 'frenzy,' a constant 'movement lifting one out of oneself' " (RW 3, p. 72). (It will be remembered that this "movement lifting one out of oneself" is the way in which Eisenstein fairly constantly expresses the idea of ecstasy, through recourse to its "ek-stasis" etymology.[30] See in particular the chapter entitled "The Kangaroos," where those kangaroos never stop leaping out of one another's pockets.)

Ecstasy inasmuch as it suppresses/replaces (*Aufheben*) pathos, is first of all defined, or rather justified, very logically, in terms of efficacy. Even when he envisages certain forms of ecstasy which are related to introspection, or meditation, Eisenstein never presents ecstasy as a negative phenomenon. And, as in the case of pathos, what absolves ecstasy of all its idealist and bourgeois defects is that it is not an "effect of passification" either; on the contrary, it is an awakening which puts the spectator's emotional and intellectual activity into operation to the maximum degree.

Thus, in Eisenstein's vocabulary, the word "ecstasy" almost never has its most usual meaning, defined by the dictionary as a "state of exaltation which arises from an extreme joy or admiration," and which implies a sort of contemplative passivity, a "rapture," to use Eisenstein's word, to which he remains fundamentally opposed. Basically what ecstasy approaches most closely for him is its original meaning, its religious meaning, the "union with a transcendental object," provided that there is no contradiction between "transcendence" and, for example, "materialism" (an admission to which Eisenstein, for his part, seems quite ready to agree). At the cost of quite a considerable

change of object (substituting, for example, the tin-plated cream separator of *The General Line* for the Holy Grail), it is always a matter
of making the subject "leave himself behind," "transcend himself," or
"lose himself" *in* and *for* this feeling of union.

Ecstasy would therefore be presented above all as the means to
an end—and more precisely as the efficient (the most efficient?) means
to a *doctrinal* end. The achievement of unity, such a Stalinist ideological theme, and so appropriate to cap any conflictual (dialectical)
process. The doctrinal function then is obvious. As for efficacy, it is
no accident that ecstasy is presented so prominently as a kind of "me-
thodical" and methodological formalization of the idea of pathos.

Although the ideological function of ecstasy is certainly important,
I must say that Eisenstein seems to me to be eminently tactical (or
concessionary) here, and that ecstasy is not to be limited to being a
"new efficacy." It should not be forgotten that *Nonindifferent Nature*,
in which the concept is introduced and developed, was written between
1939 and 1946–47, indeed, between the release of *Nevsky* and the end
of the work on *Ivan*. Without wishing to reduce the matter to a simple
biographical coincidence, it could be shown that from *Ivan, Part 1* to
Ivan, Part 2, a movement takes place. It is a movement between, on
the one hand, the elimination of an ideological guarantee which leads
to glorifying Ivan as a "unifier of the Russian land," in the same way
that Nevsky was glorified, and thus in response to the same social
command, and, on the other hand, *excesses* of every kind: Ivan's madness, the doubts with which he is reproached so much, but also a
Scriptural excess, no doubt just as unbearable for official cinematography. Thus it is a movement that is not unlike the one which leads
from the presentation of ecstasy as an enlargement of the notion of
pathos to that other conception of ecstasy which aims to carry the
spectator to the highest peaks of pleasure. A movement from the "pathetic," which makes the spectator vibrate with the right feelings for
the just cause, to another type of ecstatic "vibration."[31]

Once again, I agree that there is much to be said about ecstasy.
It is undeniable that Eisenstein sets himself up as a master with respect
to the production of this ecstasy (Narboni). It is no less certain that
he aims at altering it, and that effectively it is altered, to the credit of
the Party and the State (Bonitzer). However, it still seems crucial (radically new in the Eisensteinian project and quite unthought of in reflection on the cinema) that it is *also* a manifestation of a consideration
of the "emotional experience" of the spectator, no longer envisaged
solely in terms of pleasure and reading. One has only, for example, to

reread the chapter of "Pathos" entitled "On the Problem of Supra-Historicity," which is very instructive in its "double-edged" aspect. Several pages into an analysis of religious ecstasy (in particular of *Manresa*), Eisenstein strives to demonstrate that ecstasy is a *technique* which has indeed been widely used for religious purposes, but whose essence is not inevitably religious. Thus he is led to insist, and at great length, on a certain "neutrality" of the state of ecstasy with respect to the "content" which will subsequently be proposed to the ecstatic subject:

> By a whole system of ingeniously developed technical processes, a state of exaltation, of nervous excitement, of ecstasy, is provoked in the "patient"—call it whatever you like. In itself, by its psychological nature, this state is formless. (RW 3, pp. 212–13; FW 2, p. 383)

But this insistence, if it does indeed empty ecstasy of any automatically religious content, very probably also empties it of the ideological contents whose privileged vector Eisenstein has used all his ingenuity to show that same state of ecstasy to be. If that state is so formless, one can always, of course, hope to orient it to suit one's own desires (and this is what Eisenstein does actually suggest). But it will nonetheless retain, as he himself says, a "pre-formal" aspect, which would lead one to believe that it is an end in and for itself.

> If there is a stage of thought in which notions do not yet exist. . . . there is yet another state, even more elementary and limited to sensation alone, which does not find any means of expressing itself outside of simple symptoms of that state itself. It is exactly thus that ecstasy presents itself at its outer limits—beyond notions, beyond representation, beyond imagery—beyond the spheres of any rudiments of consciousness to enter the "purely" passionate sphere of "pure" feeling, sensation, being. (RW 3, p. 213; FW 2, p. 383)

Let us make no mistake. Despite the safeguard of the quotation marks setting off this ecstatic "purity," the state of consciousness, or unconsciousness, at which Eisenstein is aiming, is in effect a borderline state of the mind.

The rule which Eisenstein suggested to his students should, of course, be invoked here—"stepping back a little before reaching the outer limits"! Not that I want to temper my evaluation of the excessive character of ecstasy, for it is there, and clearly there, at least in the text of *Nonindifferent Nature* (and also, let us not forget, in the color sequences of *Ivan the Terrible, Part 2*). But returning to the original, or rather to the filiation of the concept of ecstasy, it would be necessary to stress how it was produced as the last term of a chain which begins, as we have seen, with pathos, and whose constant characteristic is the absolute theoretical mastery exerted by Eisenstein. As in the case of the search for "laws" of form, this theoretical mastery and the theory itself play the role of an ideological cement of principle. At the same time as he transfers to ecstasy the qualities of pathos and of "psychologism," Eisenstein in effect develops the approach to the question of form that dominates all his thinking during the last ten years of his life, the famous "*organicism.*"

The idea of organicism intervenes first of all apropos of the construction, or overall form of film productions. A number of writers on cinema, starting with Eisenstein himself, have not hesitated to make retrospective applications of the concept of ecstasy, in particular regarding *The General Line.* In fact, in Eisenstein's silent films, there is "something" which simple "technical" analysis (even if it is as untechnical as his own) does not account for very well. No doubt it is that "something" which, as early as 1926, required that "the intuition necessary to its development" be spoken of, and which has recently been designated as "an authentic revolutionary desire. . . . a movement, a vibration, a laughing energy *that believes* in the transformation of the world" (Bonitzer).

More precisely, what is read (what Eisenstein reads) in *The General Line,* among other things, is a kind of representation, of miming, of the ecstatic process, *avant la lettre.* This formal miming affects the characters and the objects of the diegesis,[32] but above all, and most radically, the construction of the film is determined by it. On this point, Eisenstein is categorical. What distinguishes the ecstatic scenes (the one of the cream separator in particular) from other manifestations of ecstasy in the film is the quasi-exclusive recourse to "formal" means:

> The procession and the prayer for rain turn essentially on the means of production—one might call them "theatrical"—acting on the spectator through the behaviour of the characters. . . . As for the scene with the cream separator, it relies principally upon purely cinematic means and possibilities, impossible in that form and at such a volume for any other art. (FW 2, p. 123)

(Again I emphasize that these are late and ad hoc formulations. In the texts contemporary with the film and in particular in "The Filmic Fourth Dimension," no emphasis is placed on this process, for the text remains in the realm of "technical" descriptions.)

The explanation, or theorizing, of this mimetic resemblance is the object of one of the most persistent of Eisenstein's interrogations, and here, again, we find the problem of the laws of filmic form.

Eisenstein's own responses to that interrogation, as everyone knows, varied enormously. But I am compelled to observe that the *theme* of his response, at bottom, remained absolutely constant. *The laws of form could never be determined by anything other than the similarity to, and the closest relationship to, the laws of human thought.* Even the "brutal" and "primitive" theory of attractions conforms to this requirement. To a human psyche envisaged in the mode of a succession of reflexes (a series of action → reaction processes) corresponds a film form envisaged as the linking together of duly calculated elementary stimuli in a chain-like formation.

It is here, precisely at this point of the "laws of form"/"laws of thought" articulation, that organicism intervenes. As with ecstasy, the development of this concept begins with pathos, but the stages of its elaboration are perhaps more clearly marked. Before really getting to the idea of organicism (which carries yet another supplementary element, whose nature will be seen in a moment), Eisenstein had in fact put forth, in a sustained and detailed fashion, the hypothesis that artistic and, in any case, filmic discourse, can be compared to certain very specific forms of thought, notably the so-called "sensory" and "pre-logical thought" (concepts borrowed directly and without alteration from Lévy-Bruhl). This is the famous theory of "interior monologue," essentially developed in the no less famous intervention at the 1935 Congress. Interior monologue will turn up again later, apropos of montage, so I shall content myself here with giving an approximate outline of it, and, by way of example, this quotation, which brings out very clearly its *lawmaking* aspect:

> As for cinema, it seems to us that, by its specific nature, it reproduces phenomena according to all the signs of the method which produces the reflection of reality in the movement of the operation of the mind (there is not a single specific trait of cinematic phenomena or processes which does not correspond to the specific form of the unfolding of human mental activity). ("Pantagruel Is Born," 1933, RW 1, p. 249)

At the 1935 Congress, Eisenstein stated that the "sole condition for obtaining a valid work of art"(!) is to maintain sufficient balance between two "forms of thought," "logical" and "pre-logical." It is in particular in the latter category that he seeks at this period the explanation of "ecstatic-filmic" phenomena, whose importance he is beginning to suspect.

The theory of interior monologue was very short-lived. Perhaps the pretext for its disappearance was the *Bezhin Meadow* fiasco—since there is every reason to suppose that inspiration deriving from the model of interior monologue influenced the approach to the production of that film. But deeper reasons would have in any case imposed it. First of all, an external circumstance, the abandonment of the notion of "pre-logical thought," and the criticism of it by its own author, Lévy-Bruhl; and, above all, more immediately tangible, the accusations of subjectivism (he is compared, horror of horrors, to Proust)[33] and idealism which it brought down upon Eisenstein.

Thus, after 1937–38, Eisenstein's whole theoretical effort on this point will be aimed at picking up the same idea again while taking care to anchor it in firmer philosophical ground. Being very careful this time to refrain from relating the mechanisms of the psyche to remote and hypothetical "primitives," he turns to the guarantee of Engels and his *Dialectics of Nature*, which could not be more orthodox. From Engels's theses Eisenstein retains this potent idea: that nature is governed by laws whose essence is dialectical; and especially that in dialectical nature, transformations do not take place gradually, but by *leaps and bounds*. It is sufficient to thumb through *Nonindifferent Nature* to realize what a real theoretical find this idea represents for Eisenstein. Taking things to extremes, it might be said that the whole book is nothing more or less than a catalogue of leaps and bounds (a Piranesi engraving is transformed, by successive bounds, into another one; Frédérick Lemaître's diction or Steinberg's drawings are analyzed as a series of leaps, etc.). And against this background, ecstasy can at last find its perfect justification, as a particular instance of a general phenomenon (the dialectical leap): "the leap outside oneself (= ekstasis, ectasy) is necessarily the passage to something else, to something of a different quality, something contrary to what precedes" (RW 3, p. 61; FW 2, pp. 79–80).

But above all, perhaps the keystone of the entire edifice, this ecstasy which is common to the spectator (whom the work lifts "outside of himself") and to the film (for which it provides the formal logic) is also *what guarantees that both of them are in conformity with the laws of nature*,[34] with the great dialectical laws of incessant transformation by leaps and bounds:

> This sort of work has a very special effect on the person who contemplates it—not only because it raises itself to the level of natural phenomena, but also because the law of its structure is at the same time the law which governs those who contemplate the work, to the extent

that they themselves are part of organic nature. The contemplator feels himself organically bound to a work of this type, united, commingled with it, exactly as he feels himself united and commingled with his surrounding organic milieu and with nature. (RW 3, p. 46; FW 2, p. 50)

Eisenstein's theoretical (and almost rhetorical) *tour de force* can be clearly seen. Organicism is what gives the scientific laws of form (scientificity guaranteed by recourse to an "intellectual authority," Engels) by modeling that form on "nature" and on the structure of thought. That is in itself no mean feat. But beyond that, organicism appears to be something that miraculously sews up the rents in the fabric of the work created by fragmentation, suturing together the film fragments, those bits and pieces "ripped from the highly colored body of nature"— and it is therefore what protects against the breaking up of that "body," what insures its unity.

We have already encountered unity, as a typical ideologeme of Stalinist society (and very largely taken over by Eisenstein for his own purposes)—and, of course, this determination is not absent from the concept of organicism, which, ensuring the conformity of the work of art with nature, in the mode of the leap (of the dialectical conflict), also ensures its conformity to society, in the mode of unity (as "resolution of contradiction"). But I am struck in addition by the fact that through organicism, nature, a nature endowed with corporeality and with laws which are themselves organic, should be so strongly represented as Mother Nature—this Great Whole in which the spectator, the film, and Eisenstein all participate, and in which ectasy aims only at ensuring that one loses oneself, indefinitely.[35]

V. The Charms of the Dialectic

Eisenstein is the exact contemporary of the (re)discovery of a whole section of the Marxist Text, that section which deals essentially with philosphical questions, with the constitution of "dialectical materialism" in a body of doctrine. It was in 1935 that the first Russian translation of *Dialectics of Nature* appeared, and in 1929, Lenin's *Philosphical Notebooks*. A militant materialist, a convinced advocate of the socialist revolution, a committed artist, Eisenstein was immediately fired with enthusiasm, and his discovery of the Marxist (and Leninist and Engelsian) dialectic is expressed with all the ardor of the neophyte, in rather wide-eyed formulations: "The new factor of edification is cast in the crucible of the dialectical flame. The new social reflex is forged" ("Perspectives," 1929, RW 2, p. 42; FW 1, p. 196). Far from waning, with the passing years this enthusiasm will lead him to assign a central place to dialectical materialism in his theory of art (in his method as well as in his "epistemology"), and it is in his latest texts that we find formulations such as this: "This almighty, shining, miraculous method of cognition. . ." ("Intellectual Cinema," IM, p. 204; RW 1, p. 474). (In other passages, the dialectic will be called mysterious, bewitching . . .)

Now, while this enthusiasm remains equal to itself, the least that can be said is that in the meantime dialectical materialism goes on evolving. We are all familiar with the way Stalinist theory takes what was expounded, from Hegel to Lenin, under the name of dialectics (that "joyful, penetrating science, as it was understood and presented by Lenin") and hardens it into rigid *laws*, into "an indigestible skeleton of paragraphs and abstract propositions" (IM, p. 204; RW 1, p. 474). It was in September 1935, that Stalin's pamphlet "Dialectical Materialism and Historical Materialism" appeared, and it begins with these eminently apodictic statements:

> Dialectical materialism is the general theory of the Marxist-Leninist Party. Dialectical materialism is so named because the way it views the phenomena of nature, its method of investigation and knowledge is dialectic, and its interpretation, its conception of the phenomena of nature, its theory, is materialist.

In the text of 1943 which I have quoted, Eisenstein does not fail to note this withering of the Marxist dialect—attributing it, of course, not to Stalin, but to "bad teachers."Much more than that, he goes so far as to compare this ossification, this transformation into "paragraphs and abstract propositions," to what catechism was in the pre-revolutionary society.

Consequently, before dealing with any other detail, it seems necessary to insist on the essential ambivalence of the status of dialectical materialism in Eisenstein's thinking. Studies of Eisenstein, at least those few which are concerned with this issue, have in general a tendency to assume that a "young Eisenstein," who supposedly adhered to a particularly dynamic conception of the dialectic (the "struggle of opposites") must be contrasted with a second Eisenstein, the writer of the late texts, in whom this dynamic conception would have been flattened out, crushed by the preoccupation with "organicism," with "unity."[36] I am not saying that this scheme of things is entirely false.

It seems to me, however, that it overemphasizes a tendency that is in no way peculiar to Eisenstein, since it affects the whole dominant discourse on dialectics—and above all, it dismisses the fact that this contradiction, this struggle between a conception of the conflict and a demand for unity, for organicism, is *constant* in Eisenstein. There is not a revolutionary Eisenstein, the Eisenstein of the twenties, who supposedly thought in terms of struggle of opposites (and their dialectical unity), and then another, idealistic Eisenstein, the Eisenstein of the thirties and forties, in pursuit of the chimerical "total and synthetic art." There is, on the other hand, an Eisensteinian system (which is indeed constantly evolving), which constantly attempts to adjust itself to various theoretical and/or philosophical discourses, in particular, to "dialectical materialism," and clearly fails to do so, except in a way that is entirely unsatisfactory *from the point of view of those discourses*. But in this instance it seems to me that the important thing is not so much to gauge the degree of adequacy of Eisenstein's theories and their progress by one standard or another, as it is to define the internal movement characteristic of Eisenstein's research. It is therefore from this perspective, and without the slightest normative intention, that I propose to examine, not the evolution of Eisenstein's conceptions with regard to dialectics (a problem which is largely a biographical, even a psychological one),[37] but the transferring into his system of the terms of dialectical materialism, and, using the Stalinist idea again (solely for the purposes of expository convenience), of the "laws" of dialectics. Thus, first of all we have the theme of contradiction:

> objects and the phenomena of nature imply internal contradictions . . . ; the struggle of these opposites . . . is the internal content of the process of development.   (Stalin)

to which is linked, for example:

> For art is always conflict:
> 1. by virtue of its social mission;
> 2. by virtue of its essence;
> 3. by virtue of its method.
> ("Dramaturgie der Film-Form," 1929, *Schriften* 3)

We have already seen, and we shall see again in other contexts, how fundamental this idea of universal "conflict" is for Eisenstein. We shall see that it is at the root of his whole conception of montage (from the montage of attractions and harmonic montage, in which the "leap" from one fragment to the following one is always defined in terms of conflict, right down to "audio-visual counterpoint," in which the sound track and even the color are deliberately envisaged as "conflicting" with the image)—and it is also essential for the definition of notions like the fragment or the frame. But beyond this almost "technical" use of the theme of contradiction, there are abundant mentions (and in every period) of the "law" of the unity of opposites, of contradiction, in the most varied of subject matter areas and contexts.

This can be seen clearly in the texts of 1929 from which I have just quoted a fragment (a text subtitled "*Der Dialektische Zugang zur Film-Form*"). The essence of the text consists in a new exposition (often using the terms of several other contemporaneous texts) of the question of conflict as helping to account for the whole of film form—graphic conflicts, plastic conflicts, conflicts involving time, space, meaning, etc. Now, if the (numerous) examples given by Eisenstein are quite convincing when it is a matter of montage (conflict of a fragment with the one following it, conflicts within the frame), they are less convincing when he proposes to subsume slow motion ("*Konflikt zwischen dem Vorgang und seiner Zeitlichkeit*") or the use of distorting lenses ("*Konflikt zwischen dem Stoff und seiner Räumlichkeit*") under the same concept. Things become totally arbitrary when he extends his considerations to an "essence" of art as "conflict" between nature and industry, or to the "mission" of art, which would be conflictual in essence, since the task of art is "to manifest the contradictions of the existent."

For Eisenstein (in this text, but also more or less everywhere else), a conflict *must* be found apropos of everything—even if it means producing, as in "Dramaturgie der Film-Form," a classification which is more evocative of the famous Borgesian "catalogue" than it is of scientific explanation. He seems to believe, basically, that every conflict, every contradiction (taking those words in their most ordinary sense) participates in the dialectic, and he does not deny himself, when he sees fit, the right to define pairs of "antagonistic" terms.[38] Thus, in this area of "conflict," it is most important not to let Eisenstein fill us up with empty words. While his explorations of form appear innovative and productive, his efforts to account for them as consequences of the laws of the dialectic appear somewhat fantastical.

The theme of the conflict, moreover, can be isolated in Eisenstein only in a relatively artificial way, because it is so inextricably bound up with another "dialectic" theme, that of organicism. We encountered this term just a few pages back, and later on we shall return to a consideration of what it implies, more specifically, with respect to the conceptions of montage. Therefore, here I am simply stressing its conjuncture with a more directly political theme, one that is just as prevalent in the Eisensteinian text, that of *unity*.

Outside of any cinematic usage, the word "unity" evokes first of all, as has already been mentioned, an ideological theme that is particularly important in Stalinist society. It is no accident that in Stalin's tract, the first of the laws of the dialectic is stated in these terms:

> the dialectic regards nature not as the accidental accumulation of objects, of disconnected phenomena, but as a unified, coherent whole, in which objects, phenomena, are organically bound to each other, are interdependent, and condition each other reciprocally.

On several occasions, Eisenstein stresses the fact that if he had to define himself with one word, he would place his entire work under this aegis of unity. Behind all their apparent disparities, his films would be no more than "the alternate masks of the same face. The face is the embodiment of an ultimate idea—the obtaining of unity" (FW 3, p. 299; text dated 1943, not printed in RW; published in *Voprosy kinodramaturgii*, 4, Moscow, 1962). This *idea*, moreover, takes on a plainly Hegelian allure, and at times Eisenstein's texts turn into the saga of the adventures of the Idea: "The idea will wither and will be stifled, it will be attacked and distorted, it will be plotted against, it will be slandered."[39] But naturally, it is especially interesting to us to see that this theme is taken up at greater length in the theoretical work. Unity is first of all the "organic unity of the composition," a fixed and fetishized syntagm which is regularly trotted out, not only in the late texts, but as early as the late twenties.

Of all the laws of the dialectic, this is arguably the one Eisenstein cites and uses the most frequently. More and more it is the one which occupies the center stage of his reflections, coming almost to mask what it is nonetheless responsible for justifying, i.e., the principle of contradiction. Increasingly, Eisenstein plays both cards simultaneously—the card of contradiction (understood as conflict, the living nutriment of every phenomenon, and in particular the very principle of film montage) and the card of unity, understood as the reabsorption of contradiction.

> For, as a method, our montage is no longer the mere copy of the *struggle of opposites*, a simple reflection of the class struggle; it is the reflection of the *unity of those opposites*, an image of the culmination of this struggle in the dissolution of all classes, in the constitution of a classless

society, which radiates the *unity* of socialism throughout the multiform
multinational socialist unity, and which brings to an end the centuries
and epochs of antagonism. ("Dickens, Griffith, and the Film Today,"
1942, RW 5, p. 179)

I find this last quotation very significant in its complexity. In fact,
according to the tenets of strict "dialectical materialist" logic, there is
no incompatibility between the "struggle of opposites" and the "unity
of opposites." (The canonical dialectical thesis, for example, Mao's
"one divides into two," aims, on the contrary, at affirming that there
is always and everywhere a struggle of opposites, and that it is in that
struggle that their indissociable unity is revealed—no capitalism without a proletariat, no oppression without revolt, etc.) And it is the
characteristic feature of the Stalinist "dialectic" to read that "unity"
of opposites as "socialist unity," abolishing contradictions (that is the
famous theme of the "classless society").

It is therefore necessary to distinguish very clearly here between
a hasty and "conformist" adherence to the political theses of the period
(which will come as no surprise to us) on the one hand, and, on the
other, the development of the concept of organicism applied to work
on form. It seems to me that, in all the authors who, in these or other
terms, consider that the last Eisensteinian texts show a withering away
of the dialectic, there is either an ignorance of the history of "dialectical
materialism" (and especially of the importance of the theme of "organic unity" in Engels and Stalin for example), or, what is more serious
for an understanding of Eisensteinian theory, an overestimation of the
significance of the word "conflict" in the early texts (not of the phenomena of montage which it covers, and which are incontestable, but
of the generalization which it purports to give them).

What is moreover very generally striking in Eisenstein's use of
the reference to Dialectical Materialism is his tendency to "unify" its
different "laws." For example, the third of those laws:

the dialectic considers the process of development . . . as one that involves passing from insignificant, latent quantitative changes to qualitative changes; those qualitative changes are not gradual, but rapid,
sudden, and occur in bounds from one state to another.

We know that this theme of the "bound" obsessed Eisenstein, particularly in everything that has to do with the production of "ecstasy"
in the spectator (see above, section IV of this chapter). But what I
would like to bring out is the immediate distortion to which this concept is subjected:

1) First of all, by the overuse of this idea (albeit perfectly in line with a certain Marxist tradition). Eisenstein sees "qualitative leaps" everywhere—in the construction of the *Battleship Potemkin*, in Piranesi's drawings, who knows where else, and it is not surprising to see him describe the essence of the creative process in art as an application of this law (creation is simply the leap into something new, based on the accumulation of our experience).[40]

2) Next, because, very often, the only thing about this leap that is "qualitative" in his writings is its name. What is striking, on the contrary, is the predilection he manifests for heaping things up quantitatively, in his films, but also in the endless lists which fill his texts, the stubbornness with which he accumulates camera angles, points of view, reasons, the different "qualities"—for the sole benefit of a surplus of quantity (as Narboni has clearly shown).[41]

3) Last but not least, because he goes so far as to equate this qualitative leap purely and simply with the idea of contradiction, and to make of it a "dialectical reverse into its opposite":

> At such a moment an abrupt dialectical reversal of this stage into its opposite usually occurs. ("Our *October*," FW 1, p. 177)

> The leap. The passage from quantity to quality. The passage into its opposite. ("The Structure of the Film," 1939–45)

> However that may be . . . this curve [the logarithmic spiral] has been given precisely the meaning which, in our interpretation, is also found at the basis of the universal movement. It is precisely this curve which signifies, figuratively, the passage into the opposite. ("Organicism and Imaginicity," 1934)

This last quotation is particularly rich and enlightening, coming as it does, moreover, in a context in which not only the "leap" and the "contradiction" are combined, but also "natural" organicism (Eisenstein seems to attach great importance to the fact that the logarithmic spiral is found in the cross-section of the chambered nautilus shell), and, crowning the whole thing, of course, yin and yang. I believe there is no need to insist further.

Thus, the dialectic thesis to which, in the last analysis, Eisenstein most often refers is finally the most general one, the one which states simply that

> Nature is not a state of repose and immobility, of stagnations and immutability, but a state of perpetual movement and change, of endless renewal and development. (Stalin)

This uninterrupted, universal movement appears throughout all of Eisenstein's writings as literally fetishized, and his obsession is to find traces of it everywhere. Throughout all of the more or less fantastical and risky "applications" of the laws of the dialectic, what shows up most clearly is in the last analysis an unfailing attachment to this

> very principle of development and transformation, which is so bewitching in the phenomena of nature and which is so poorly understood in the creative process. ("Wie sag' ich's meinem Kind?!" 1946, RW 1, p. 244; FW 3, p. 137)

This attachment justifies the appeal to this "principle" in the strangest, most unusual, irregular, and sometimes most unexpected cases. *Movement* is what comes to unify all the specific cases, all the levels of the problem of montage (with Plekhanov, for example, as a guarantee);[42] elsewhere, it will account for the predilection for a "linear" drawing; and it is what finally comes to replace, or to enlarge, the *drive*, desire itself (this is very clear in the example, several times repeated, of the comparison between dance and drawing).[43]

Again, the point is not to repeat the dogmatic procedure of making Eisenstein accountable in the name of a "legal" dialectic whose model would be considered complete. That is absurd in the face of the reality of Marxist dialectics, and I hope that I have shown how aberrant, or at least how irrelevant such a procedure is in a consideration of the Eisensteinian project. Clearly, in Eisenstein's appropriation of dialectical materialism, there is both a very deep-seated desire to *found* his theory philosophically and a no less essential submission to dogma. Thus the catalogue of Eisenstein's breaches of Dialectical Materialism which has been compiled so often (especially by the Italian critics), seems to me to be a completely pointless undertaking, all the more so since it always comes *in place of* another, more difficult undertaking, namely, the evaluation of the internal consistency of Eisensteinian theory, and the definition of its real objects. Whatever may have been said on the subject, Eisenstein is not the Brecht of Soviet cinema.

Eisenstein Taken
at His Word

3

What follows is a "reading" or close analysis of "sequences" from two of Eisenstein's films. Such an approach poses several preliminary questions about methods and procedures:

1. Which films to choose? I had my choice of any of the films since copies of Eisenstein's six completed films were easily available at the time I was carrying out this study (from early 1976 to the middle of 1977). Thus the main criterion which determined my choice was the following: while it is banal and indeed patently wrong to claim that Eisenstein's work can be divided into two "periods," it is nonetheless undeniable that his films can be separated into two very distinct, large groups: on the one hand, the four silent films, and on the other, the two sound films (or three, if *Ivan* 1 and 2 are counted as two films). The methods of montage are very different in each group of films despite the common assumptions about it that they share. It thus appeared quite natural to choose one film from each of these "periods."

The General Line was my first choice among the silent films because, along with *October*, it seems to me to be the most coherent example of Eisenstein's approach to montage in the twenties. In addition, *The General Line* is accompanied by a whole body of writing which Eisenstein himself in 1928–29 considered to represent somewhat definitive positions.[1] I skipped over *October* (which is nonetheless one of his most obviously experimental or "theoretical" films) because it seemed absurd to work by myself on a film that has been for several years the object of an excellent group research project.[2] My choice of a sound film was simpler and very spontaneous since it was guided by my own personal tastes; as I did not feel capable of working on a film that I did not like very much, I thus chose *Ivan* (again, despite the fact that *Nevsky* is more experimental).

2. 16mm prints were freely available to me for a good period of time; the prints were from the United States and had been poorly dubbed, probably from commercial prints that were the worse for wear, hence the mediocre quality of the frame enlargements reproduced later in the chapter.

I was able to carry out my work under the most ideal conditions thanks to access to editing tables (belonging to the Universities of Paris-III and Lyon-II).

Finally, I did not notice in the prints that I used for *the sequences I studied* any differences from other available prints (notably those in the Cinémathèque Française).

3. My mode of presentation had to take into account both the particular nature of the objects and the specific goal of the study—namely, the demonstration in the most detailed way possible of a certain number of concepts relevant (or not) to the Eisensteinian system. This was more important than merely cranking out yet another "original" point of view on one or another of the films or their director. Although my own brand of reading is somewhat idiosyncratic (because of the emphasis on the "application" or not of Eisenstein's theories and the relatively little attention paid to other codes, mainly symbolic ones) my methodological debt to a certain number of theoretical texts is obvious.

At the risk of repeating myself I want to stress that my overall approach is one that schematizes the polysemy of the text along the lines of the now-classical model devised by Barthes in *S/Z*. My analysis of *The General Line* follows the thread of the filmic text, while the analysis of *Ivan* somewhat artificially groups the "levels" of the reading. That my analysis bears on pieces of film that make up only a small part of Eisenstein's work as a whole is of very little importance; in the first reading, respecting the order of the fragments makes it easier to show the metaphoro-metonymical work of the film, but this does not prevent one from taking into account the film as a whole in relation to one lexia or another; conversely, in the second (synchronic) analysis in which the filmic text is more obviously determined by scenic and figurative considerations, the organization of the analysis into subheadings does not neglect the diachronic aspect which can appear either in a latent or sometimes in a manifest way.

4. It is even more difficult to justify the choice of sequences. One could always claim of course that it had been made on the basis of a certain number of minimal criteria: the consistency of the chosen fragment, its representativeness with respect to the film as a whole (although this "representativeness" would be hard to determine), the "size" of the fragment, etc. At the very least, however, these criteria do not add up to a sufficient reason. In effect, I believe that I chose the sequences for the most part (and even at the price of some later setback) according to what I *hoped* could be gotten out of the analysis. I therefore carefully avoided the cream separator sequence in *The General Line*, not because it had already been widely written about, but because in its greater length it is doubtless more "monotonous" (in spite of its production of "ecstasy") than the dream sequence, which condenses in very little space a number of narrative principles and different representations. As for *Ivan*, the choice was even more arbitrary (I think in fact that any sequence would have done since the film is so "organic"); what basically determined my choice there was the wish to bring together into one "sequence" a fragment from each of the two parts of the film in order to play off *Ivan* 1 and 2, and their differences, against each other.[3]

I. A Soviet Dream

Hors-d'oeuvre (Fragment 0)[4]

The conclusion of the immediately preceding sequence: the agronomist in the dairy seated at the table on which we see the cashbox, the account book, the abacus; he raises his head, looks toward the camera, and gives a big grin.

No.	Duration (in seconds)	Description	
0			
1	36	The empty cashbox; then the falling coins	
2	21	The cashbox continues to be filled (with bills)	
3	30	Continues action from previous shot	
4	60	The hands move from right to left, putting the money in the cashbox	
5	74	Martha smiles while counting the money	

No.	Duration (in seconds)	Description	
6	40	Hands closing the lid of the cashbox	
7	115	Martha taps the cashbox, then rests her head on it	
8	98	INTERTITLE: "We've saved enough money—now we can buy a young bull!"	
9	80	Martha smiles and strokes the cashbox with her left hand	
10	94	Martha, very still, smiling in her sleep	
11	69	Clouds moving rapidly from right to left	

No.	Duration (in seconds)	Description	
12	57	Martha asleep on the cashbox	
13	138	A herd of cows enters the frame, moving from right to left; then they head toward the center of the horizon	
14	37	Martha asleep on the cashbox	
15	295	As the cows continue to move toward the left, the bull slowly appears	
16	45	Martha, asleep, a wide smile on her face	
17	70	The bull is still; cows continue their movement	

No.	Duration (in seconds)	Description	
18	70	At the end of the fragment, the pool of milk almost fills the entire frame	
19	50	Landscape with very cloudy sky	
20	42	A shower of milk	
21	42	Identical to no. 19	
22	39	Similar to no. 20	
23	18	Foamy milk being shaken back and forth	

No.	Duration (in seconds)	Description	
24	21	Similar to preceding shot. Shots 25–27 take up 77 seconds and are similar to no. 24	
25			
26			
27			
28	36	Foaming stream moving from right to left	
29	36	Oblique movement from right to left	

No.	Duration (in seconds)	Description	
30	37	Movement from left to right	
31	53	The milk arrives, and then begins to flow from right to left	
32	33	Like no. 28, but with movement from left to right	
33	61	The milk again, flowing from left to right	
34	37	Like no. 28 and no. 32; movement from left to right	
35	81	Cream runs down the sides of a ribbed cylinder, filling the frame	

No.	Duration (in seconds)	Description	
36	48	A waterfall in "profile"	
37	105	Follows no. 35: the cream continues to trickle down	
38	180	The milk rises simultaneously in two glass cylinders	
39	58	Disorderly movement of baby pigs suckling	

BEFORE/AFTER

Where to begin or end? This is a banal question which arises from any reading of a portion of a text since, even if one claims that the reading is going to simply follow the thread of the filmic text, one is immediately confronted with the arbitrariness of making any divisions in it. One can only do so by treating the thread of the text as if it consisted of discrete blocks of meaning, or the film as if it were *really* made up of sequences, which we know not to be the case. For example, I ought to count the shot of Lenin's double here as part of the sequence. Why not include it?

Of course it seems logical nonetheless: "Fragment O" is clearly the conclusion of a whole episode and a whole scenic organization (the burgled cashbox to which the agronomist causes the money miraculously to return); with respect to the fragments which immediately follow, admittedly from a *dramatic* point of view, the episode has changed, and from a *representational* point of view, the perspective has shifted. But even if one can make a neat cut between what might be called a "scenic" space and a "metaphorical" one, it is nevertheless true that the figure of the agronomist is engaged in multiple and systematic relations (textual, non-scenic) with many other fragments of the film.

This is only one example of a general problem with the segmentation of any Eisenstein film: even if the episodes are more often than not easily delimited, no fragment is reducible to its dramatic value alone, and thus ideally one would have to superimpose (at least) two segmentations of the text. As we shall see, however, this methodological problem has another side. Once the multiple levels of the text have been established, the reading of these 38 fragments will provide an account of the various patterns of meanings running through the film rather than an exhaustive, totalizing analysis. It is as if the body of the text were so "organic" (an idea that Eisenstein would have liked) that it could survive an occasional excision for the sake of the analysis.

Lexia 1. The Golden Rain: Fragments 1–3

Two things are to be noted here:[5]

—a fictional transition between two sequences through the repetition of a shared and abstract element (the cashbox/the money): the money being returned to the cashbox is the resolution of the preceding scene; the cashbox full of money represents the possibility of buying the bull, and thus the material for Martha's dream;

—an overdetermined metaphor: a metaphor of impregnation (see the myth of Danaë), but also of fertility (see the custom of inundating the new czar with pieces of gold at his coronation—at the beginning of *Ivan the Terrible*).

THE MATRIX

Let us examine these three very brief shots of the empty cashbox that gets filled with a shower of coins and bills. What is going on here? First of all, we are able to move from one scene to another by means of a tiny, intermediary element which ensures not a change of decor but a change of character: by focusing on the geometrically composed close-up of the cashbox (which turns it into an abstract object outside of any real space) and on the double miracle (the shower of gold and the triumph over individualism), the spectator pays little attention to the abrupt substitution of Martha for the agronomist. But these three brief shots also engender a series of symbolic and mythological references whose connotations, although elusive, are numerous.

What we see here in a very condensed form is the structural trait so characteristic of Eisensteinian beginnings: a double matrix which is presented to us at once, and is composed of two levels of simultaneous meanings and two modes of representation.[6] We can thus consider this tiny lexia (less than five seconds) a *debut*.

It appears that (even before considering the function of much more subtle codifications) the text progresses on two levels simultaneously, but according to different rhythms. The first level is that of a more or less classical diegesis (a fiction that progresses by means of its own logical connections); the second a system of fully developed connotations that extend over the entire film, but which are inscribed or inflected, perhaps, within each sequence or even each fragment.

Lexia 2. The Subject and Its Object: Fragments 4–9

In fragment 4, the object becomes concrete at the same time as (and because) it is seen being used: hands putting money in the cashbox. Next the subject is introduced, at first (spatially) separated from the object by the vertical division of the frame (4), then on a level with the cashbox (5). The space of fragment 5 is a scenic space even though it has not yet been established as such (mainly because of the sharp contrast between Martha and the cashbox in the foreground and the beams of light abruptly breaking against the wall in the background). And, as if to stress again the proximity of Martha and the cashbox, yet another axis of the composition places them in the lower right half of the frame. While varying slightly, fragments 6, 7, and 9 are repeated in an almost alternating montage. In fragment 8 the quotation marks in the intertitle ("We've saved enough money to buy a bull!") leave no doubt that it is Martha who speaks (to herself). Everything thus becomes focused on the emergence of a character with its classical attributes—its objects and its speech (interior monologue)—at the same time as the function of the sequence is introduced—the transformation of quantity (of money) into quality (the young bull).

MARTHA 1: "THE NEW MAN"

If in fragments 1-3 the cashbox becomes full, it is very much due to the agronomist and thus, metaphorically, Lenin himself,[7] because it is he who is ultimately responsible for putting the money there. Although the cashbox is isolated by itself in the frame and thus appears to be a magical object or one that is too real, nonetheless it avoids getting consigned to the imaginary because it is forthrightly seized or appropriated by the two hands. These hands are no longer those of "Lenin" because in fragment 5 they are clearly Martha's.

It should not be surprising that the film openly links Martha and Lenin. Martha, after all, as a poor, weak, but revolutionary, peasant women, stands as a perfect emblem of the Russian farmer of 1926. Moreover, if "Lenin," or his spiritual son, the komsomol with the wide, golden smile and hair like ripe corn—who anticipates the somewhat less colorful young hero of *Bezhin Meadow*[8]—can play an accountant or administrator, such is not the case with Martha. If she caresses the cashbox, and even falls lovingly asleep on top of it, this only literally indicates that she is so identified with the peasant collective ("*We*'ve saved enough money to buy a bull") that she dreams of nothing more than the prosperity of the collective farm (which is the object of the following sequence).

It has often been noted that in *The General Line* Martha was the only constructed *type* in a sea of stereotypes of all kinds (the kulak couple, the bureaucrats, the workers, the peasants, the Party man). It is almost as if she is the *vital man* called for by RAPP (which has something paradoxical about it). In any case it is certain that the character of Martha has—in this lexia but also throughout the film—a very special status. Martha has no "psychology," and her actions do not add up to a character. (It is for this reason that one cannot read *The General Line* as a story of consciousness raising, because it is instead a story of transformation—this is not Pudovkin.) But at the same time, Martha also cannot be reduced to a mere emblem or "hieroglyph," nor even to her *typage*. In order to designate her place in the double diegetic and symbolic economy of the film, the best word for it would be the Jakobsonian term *shifter* (*embrayeur*).

Sleep: Fragment 10

This highly composed frame includes, at the bottom and in the foreground, Martha and "her" cashbox (and also the accountant's abacus). At the top of the frame and in the far background, we see, on the left, three brightly lit milk cans, and on the right, the cream separator (I would almost call it the phantom of the cream separator). Each "object" in the frame is lit differently: the milk cans receive the most light, then Martha, then the cream separator. In this fragment of 94 frames (5 seconds) there is time to read the image[9] in such a way that Martha can be seen to be *between* the milk cans and the cream separator. In other words, her role is between the milk as an industrial product and the instrument which produces the cream (as well as ecstasy—see the "cream separator sequence"). Behind all of this, the windows mysteriously open, but to what?

SCENE AND METAPHOR

An extension of the scene begun in 4-9, fragment 10 reworks it by referring to a space that has already been used and given connotations; Martha dreams of "her" prosperity while asleep in front of the cream separator in the dairy. This space becomes the place and condition of what follows (her falling asleep). It is a pause which ends the lexia, as well as the "exposition" of her character, but also serves as the "guiding-shot" which directs us to read the fragments that immediately follow as a dream.[10]

In a parallel fashion, this fragment also marks a clean yet subtle break in the treatment of the space as scenic space. A double "progression" in relation to the immediately preceding fragments (the enlarging as well as deepening of the field) seems inevitably to include the sleeping Martha even more forcefully in both a decor and a scene. But, because the shot is so highly composed, because of the differentiated lighting, the obviousness and resonance of the symbolic system, and finally, the shot's absolute stillness, the representation is not at all naturalistic. Although this frame is the quantitative culmination of the construction of a scene, there is something even more powerful going on here which makes us forget about the scene.

In the stillness of this fragment which itself almost seems to *sleep*, we are presented with the dominant metaphors or metaphorical system of this text because four levels of signification are superimposed, knotted together or condensed there. To take the cream separator, for example, its first function is simply to remind us of the location (we are in the dairy); next, it serves as a plastic recall (the glaucous, milky light) of the image of anxiety and orgasm of an earlier scene; it is also an image of the theme of productivity as well as the sexual and social ecstasy that accompanies it; and finally, according to my reading of the image, in its shadowy mysteriousness in the corner of the room and the uneasiness evoked by this frozen tableau, the cream separator recalls Goya's monsters erupting from the sleep of reason.

FRAGMENT, CONFLICT

In no other part of this sequence is the nature of the Eisensteinian *fragment* so apparent as in this lexia, and this is particularly so because it represents a clearly fictionalized moment.

What, in fact, characterizes the classical system of narration/representation? (And what is it about that system which makes all of us who have been "classically" conditioned to almost automatically subsume every representation and fiction to it?) Roughly speaking, we could sum up its effects in the word "scene," because the scene is the result of the production of a temporal continuity and an imaginary spatial unity. And it is exactly this continuity and unity which is so characteristic of Eisensteinian representation. But I have already shown how this lexia, for example, cannot be a unified, isotropic, neutral, and simple imaginary repository of fictions. As we shall soon see, the systematic refusal to match the time and space between shots undermines any sense of continuity or unity. From one fragment to the other we have nothing but the effect of leaps or literal shifts (the camera changes point of view and discontinuous gestures are repeated).

We thus progress by leaps from the abstract object to the subject, to the scene, then to the *frame* in which the scene almost comes undone. Besides the contradictions from fragment to fragment, there are also the graphic, plastic (lighting), spatial, and representational conflicts inside the frame itself—the theoretical catalogue of "Dramaturgie der Film-Form" finally finds its application within a film. The fundamental conflict in this frame, however, is of course the one that entirely breaks up and scatters the imaginary reality of the fiction.

Thus the last fragment of the lexia (no. 10) would be archetypal in that it functions as a narrative nexus, a kind of "shifter," serves as a "guiding-shot" (directing the horizontal reading), is a condensation and overlapping of symbolic networks (the vertical dimension) and presents a stark indication of the fragment's lack of relation to "the real." In its stubborn fixity, with its celestial, aquarium-like lighting, and its sleeper drifting off into her dreams, it is a non-place, that of dreams, of anxiety and ecstasy.

Lexia 3

A "true" alternating montage begins. The montage will relate two autonomous series made up, respectively, of odd- and even-numbered fragments.

The Dreamer: Fragments 12, 14, 16

Three fragments show Martha isolated (abstracted) from the decor except for a view of a mysterious, out-of-focus window in the background. The camera is now on the opposite side of Martha from the preceding fragments and thus she is facing a different direction. A reading of the fragments reveals the following contradictory aspects:

—a basic continuity with the preceding fragments (diegetic continuity by means of Martha's continued presence, emphasized by the increasingly closer shots of her face);

—a double rupture within the scenic space resulting from the abstraction of the character (or rather, the figurant) from the decor, and the reversal of her position in the frame.

THE OLD AND THE NEW

The history of this renamed film is well known. Commissioned in 1926 by Sovkino and transparently titled *The General Line,*[11] work on the film was interrupted for a year (1927) in order for Eisenstein to direct *October*. He resumed work on the film in the spring of 1928, making no notable changes except for some slight modifications following a (famous) conversation with Stalin. After its completion the film was repudiated by Soviet officials (at least those in the film industry). It matters very little whether this was because, as has often been said, in three years the film had become "out of date,"[12] or what is much more likely, its form was no longer unacceptable to a film hierarchy striving to promote the dogma of socialist realism and which could only find irritating the film's *lack of humanism*. From then on Sovkino, which had produced and then refused to accept the film, distributed it under a new name judged less compromising for the Party and its line, *The Old and the New*.

It is interesting that, although the new title is doubtless less prestigious, it is certainly more emblematic of the film. For, in fact, a binary division of the old and the new structures not only the fiction of the film but also, as someone else has already claimed,[13] each episode and sequence of the film.

To look at this claim in more detail, let us return to the abrupt shift between the two images of Martha. At the point of stasis in fragment 10, Martha and the objects surrounding her are brightly lit and sharply separated from the back wall of the dairy.[14] The image, which is divided horizontally, isolates the new from the background of the old while bathing it in a halo of light. The same metaphorical code is present in the image of Martha dreaming, because the left-right reversal of her position, which disturbs the perception of scenic (as well as narrative) continuity, is accompanied by a radical change of decor. We no longer see the milk cans, the windows opening onto an imaginary peasant village, or the picture of the cow on the wall— nothing but the source of a quasi-celestial light which seems to suffuse Martha's face. It is as if Martha, who was at first displayed against the background of the somber and constraining Old village life (fragment 10), is now being seen "from the other side," set against the backdrop of her own dream, a dream of a prosperous New future (I am almost tempted to say that the dream enters through the window, just as in all the paintings where, for example, angels appear to saints).

Thus the split between the Old and the New can be found in the film's title, in the fiction, and thus in certain elementary narrative units. Here we are touching upon the Eisensteinian preoccupation with the "organic," or more precisely, what he will refer to from 1934 on as the "image" (*obraz*), this global image of a theme that the entire work of the film tries to anchor in the figurations (*izobrazhenie*) which convey the story.

EXPLOSION, ECSTASY, BRAKE

Taken together, the "trio" 12-14-16 has a clear function: to ease Martha into her dream (see *Martha, 2*). Two moments clearly stand out in this operation of focusing on the character:

—in fragment 12, a sudden close-up of the figure of Martha, reversed from her previous position, a "leap" that I have already tried to analyze.

—in 16, the smile which spreads across her previously almost expressionless face. This is the culmination of these three fragments and introduces a new "leap" which will result in Martha's temporary disappearance.

Eisenstein often spoke of these different phenomena in terms of ecstasy, or the "qualititative leap" (both, as we have seen, frequently and mistakenly understood to be the same thing). Or he would speak just as frequently, but more metaphorically, in terms of *explosion*, a metaphor developed to explain the importance of planting in the film "detonator" fragments[15] meant to increase tension. (There are many examples of this, particularly in *Potemkin*.)

Fragment 14 could doubtless be considered a "detonator" fragment since it is the perfect intermediary between 12 and 16, containing within it the resolute stillness of 12 and the emphatic closeness of 16. It is as if it were not possible to modify both parameters at once; the only workable or feasible strategy is to make the same point twice over.

Although this description is somewhat mechanical, it can still reveal the gist of Eisenstein's approach (not the process, which varied), one that involved ways of *braking* the progress of the narrative. Eisenstein envisioned a science of the means of delaying and suspending that progression and discussed its application with respect to the famous fragments used to postpone incessantly the execution of the mutineers in *Potemkin*. It would also be a science of the analytical breakdown of drama and fiction, and just how vertiginous and interminable this breakdown could be is best seen in Nizhny's course notes taken during the class discussion of the mise-en-scène of the Dessalines episode. Whatever the students over-hastily proposed had always to be postponed by further additions to the action. This was the approach he insisted upon throughout his courses at VGIK, particularly in the those entitled in the written version "Mise-en-jeu" and "Mise-en-geste" (1948).

This whole attitude is of course derived from the principle that no simple representation of an event is in itself significant. After analyzing the event, its meaning must be *constructed* through the organization of discrete units of signification (all the while maintaining, of course, a basic analogical figuration). The meaning of these Eisensteinian figurations cannot, however, be reduced to the reproduction of a "reality" which a spectator could "freely" observe, as in Bazin's democratic utopia of the image (it is not difficult to see why Bazin so disliked Eisenstein).

The Dream: Fragments 11, 13, 15, 17

The first division of the space into two areas occurs in a fragment empty of all animal movement; each is quite distinct and will be used in a specific way:

—at the top and occupying almost three quarters of the frame, are storm clouds rapidly moving (fast-motion filming) from right to left. Against this tumultuous background begins the slow and majestic rise of the figure of the bull;

—at the bottom of the frame is an indistinct, empty, motionless "wasteland"; gradually a herd of cows appears and swarms toward the middle of the horizon.

MALE/FEMALE

If these images can be read as a dream, it is not primarily because they are strange, unnatural, or have little to do with any "realistic" referent (because the gap between figure and referent is as marked in the whole of *The General Line* as it is in *October*). It is rather because of their position in the textual progression of the film (see *Martha, 2*) as well as their obvious "metaphorical" function.

The image is, first of all, and in every sense of the word, "trick" photography because it is the result of masking with the additional use of both fast-motion filming and, in the upper half, superimposition. In the top part of the frame two images are thus superimposed while the white line of the split-screen joins the top part to the lower one, and also serves as a horizon line dividing the image into two areas, each with its own look and content. It is this "material" structure of the image which elicits the following reading:

—first, the condensation of signifiers: the connotations of the stormy sky recall all (or almost all) of the myths of the bearded deities of sky and thunder (the male principle); the ascending figure of the bull is another quite transparent figurant of fecundity both in the figure of the bull itself and as a metaphor of "erection";

—second, the juxtaposition of signifiers: the earth, inert and passive, De-meter; below the large male sky is the space of the movement of the cows, almost magnetized, as it were, by the figure of the bull's erection. Male and female, literally conjoined in a metaphorical, overdetermined, but very precise image (this time in Eisenstein's broad sense of it: *obraz*) of copulation.

The couple male/female, which was the structuring theme of an earlier episode (the "marriage"), recurs throughout the text, but here its importance is at the level of the *image*, that term so insistently theorized by Eisenstein.

Old/new, male/female: along with these divisions the film proposes many more coupled opposites (human/animal, man/machine, etc.), as if Eisenstein had wanted to make it into a sort of silent or perhaps semi-ironic manifesto of his own obsession with "conflict."[16] The film comprises an interminably repeated binary structure manifested at every level (the persistent idea of "organicness"), in which the transgression of the paradigmatic bar points to the horizon: which is the most mechanical, the reapers or the reaping machine? who is the most beast-like, the peasants or their animals? and so on.

THE FRAME

For Eisenstein, Bazin's question about whether the screen is a frame or a mask would be meaningless. It is neither a screen-mask, a simple masking of a continuous and always recoverable reality, nor a screen-painting, the decorative filling of an empty frame. If for Eisenstein the frame has any relation to the profilmic, it functions, as we have seen, only in order to cut out or extract from it figuration, expression, or meaning.

The screen is thus neither an "open window on the world" nor does it merely give us the look of the camera. Above all, the camera does not "take its measure from man."[17] Neither scale nor point of view derives from man (as was the case, for example, with Griffith). Rather, in Serge Daney's words, the camera "takes its measure from anything"—the cashbox, Martha, the bull, the milk pouring from the spout, a hydro-electric plant.

Similarly, it is impossible in Eisenstein's system for there to be an off-screen which would serve to suture the intervals between fragments. There is only an *off-frame* space (see his definition of it in the article by that name) which is never the continuation of the space in the frame but the "place" from which it is possible to go from one shot to another. Also, and contrary to off-screen, off-frame cannot be conceived in terms of space but only in terms of writing (*écriture*). If the window in 14 and 16 which surrounds and bathes Martha with light opens on to something, it is certainly not something beyond the imaginary figuration which structures the scene, but rather the possibility of such relations (of light or movements, for example)—which moreover work by contrast—as well as meaning, as we shall now see.

ANXIETY/REPRESENTATION

What provokes the faint but irrepressible anxiety I feel every time I watch the scene of Martha's dream? Clearly it stems from the content of the figuration with all the elements of the fantastic, the ineffable, and the monstrous that Eisenstein could devise for these four fragments (it is not for nothing that the references to Goya's *Giant* are so explicit here), as well as the nocturnal and hallucinatory feel that it evokes. But there is also *something else*. When I see the simple yet unexpectedly slow ascension of the rigid figure of the bull, I cannot help but remember, perhaps irrationally, the kind of fascinated horror induced by another movement just as simple, silent, and autonomous: the opening of the window in the Wolf Man's dream.

If I see some relation between these two scenes (which perhaps has to do solely with my own personal history) it is less because of an improbable anecdotal similarity between the two (dream for dream) than the presence of certain traits in both Martha's and the Wolf Man's dreams that largely exceed the single figuration. No matter how much analytical passion is brought to the breakdown or interpretation of the scenes (and Freud and his patient certainly had more details to work with!), there is always something for which the analysis cannot account.

Hence what appears to be an extremely anti-Eisensteinian hypothesis: could it be that in this mania for meaning, this obsession with mastery, there is something unforeseen or not mastered? Or is it only an overly rigid conception of Eisenstein's method which finds itself contradicted here? Let us judge from the following:

> When it comes to the *object* or *composition*, I try never to organize shots merely according to what is *visible* on the screen. The object must be chosen, oriented and arranged in the shot in such a way as to invoke, in addition to figuration, a set of associations which increase the emotional-signifying charge of the fragment. This is how the dramaturgy of the shot comes about. This is how the *drama* takes root in the very *tissue* of the work. Lighting, foreshortened perspective, framing, everything must aim toward not merely *figuring* the object but also *revealing* its signifying and emotional aspect which becomes concrete at a certain moment in front of the lens. "Object" is to be taken here in the broadest sense. It refers not only to things—far from it—but as well to the objects of desire (people, models, artists), buildings, landscapes, cirrus or other kinds of clouds. ("Sergei Eisenstein," 1945)

This, however, is quite clear: not only does Eisenstein, through *obraznost'* (*imaginicity* is perhaps the best translation), make his figurations into signifying elements in direct relation to a theme, he is also concerned with the *emotional* associations produced by each fragment and each part of the filmic *tissue*.

What then could be more natural than that these associations would sometimes wander, slip away or escape their strict ideological function? In the dream of the bull it is exactly this "emotional" (or, to put it more directly, "erotic") overdetermination which is striking. Indeed, it is quite curious that these fragments which are more or less emblematic of the New should be so *dark*. It is as if the metaphorical machine which constantly functions in this film to convey the major signifieds suddenly begins to race (here, for example, in the celebrated fragments depicting the wait for the drop of milk to form on the spout of the cream separator—see Bonitzer's commentary). It is at this moment that the Eisensteinian strategy (and the sexual component of this strategy was certainly planned) becomes drowned in an excess of meaning, in a sea of erotic associations.

MARTHA, 2: WOMAN, MOTHER

The alternation of the two series of fragments doubtless indicates that a relation of logical causality structures the diegesis: the dream is "produced" by the subject, the character Martha, by means of an insistent contiguity. But Martha is also surrounded by "her" dream, immersed in it; it is the dream which opens and closes the lexia (and even if the delimitation of the fragment is arbitrary, the dreamer is nonetheless encompassed by it). The dream is so closely assimilated to the character that everything works, it seems to me, in reverse, because ultimately it is the dream which shapes and modifies the character: from the asexual Martha of fragment 12, artlessly asleep, to the increase of tension (14) brought on by the cows swarming into the frame, and finally to the widening of her smile (16) in the middle of the bull's ascension—the same smile she exhibits (in fragment 75, outside the limits of the fragment studied here) in front of the model sovkhoz.

The dream thus has a causal function. But it also suggests a symbolic equation in which Martha, as it were, "corresponds" to the herd of cows. Martha, in close-up, is included in the great female principle which is so forcefully and positively inscribed in the whole text, while this inclusion is echoed, at the level of the story, in the close relations uniting Martha and Thomka, the bull that she buys and raises, and who dies in (because of) her absence.[18]

Martha is therefore not only the emblem of the Russian peasant, but also the Russian soil, an earth-mother par excellence, for what is also evoked here is the overwhelming feminine sensuality of *The Earth*. This evocation is accomplished, however, through antiphrasis: there is no trait of sensuality in Martha's psychology, rather it is to be found in the film itself. This, I believe, is one of the reasons why the film was so coldly received. Its textual effects, read "in long shot," must have seemed a perversion[19] of the supposed innocence of representation, an innocence that socialist realism theorized ad nauseam.

Lexia 4

Again, a regulated alternation of two series, but shorter than lexia 3.

Sperm Becomes Milk: Fragments 18, 20, 22

As in the case of the dream, there appears to be a division of a single take into three fragments; the figuration of an unnameable white liquid which falls like rain and gathers in a pool.

RAIN

The major signifier of these three fragments is the white rain which rapidly enters the frame and remains there.

There is a system of rain in the film: the shower of gold (fragments 1-3), the rain of milk here, and the spring rain which fragments 19 and 21 will metonymically evoke, and which alternate with the shots of the rain of milk. But the rain in *The General Line*, the emblem of a fruitful and generous nature, does not just fall from the sky (see the sequences of the procession), but spews forth in eddies of drops from the spout of the cream separator.

It is a short leap from the "diegetic" rain (which the peasants hope will arrive to make the crops grow) to its symbolization, and thus the meaning produced solely in and by the fiction illuminates every corner of the text (as well as all the mythological connotations found there). This is a striking example of the importance of the global *images* at every level of the text, images that Eisenstein will later define as subsuming the partial configurations, and which here traverse and disperse the text.

ORGASM? (ORGANICISM)

It is not difficult to see that the sudden appearance of the white rain functions metaphorically as sperm, a logical consequence of the fact that fecundity (the mythical union of the sexes) is the theme of the whole sequence. More specifically, by following on from the stasis of fragment 17, this triple fragment ultimately appears as a figuration of ejaculation.[20]

If any further confirmation is needed, look at the similarly orgasmic moment which occurs at the end of the long cream separator sequence, and which is accompanied by an insistent ejaculatory (the stream of milk shooting up) and whirling (the machine) motion. Each sequence produces an image that is immediately readable as *jouissance* (this ecstatic culmination is analyzed as exactly that—with the elimination of the explicit sexual connotations—in *Nonindifferent Nature*, in the chapter "The Cream Separator and the Grail").

These two instances do not however offer us the same representation of orgasm (and there is yet another in the "marriage" sequence with its literal figuration of the "explosion" of fragments). With the cream separator the emphasis is on ecstasy (orgasm = discharge of tension) whereas here what is stressed is ejaculation, its physical and productive accompaniment. I would not even put forth such a crazy interpretation if I were not convinced that it is completely in line with Eisenstein's notion of organicness. And here we can see quite clearly one of the ideas that follows from this notion: the filmic as copy of the living reality of nature (although this copy does not depend on figurative analogy).

Natura Naturans: Fragments 19, 21

A less obvious repetition of the theme of heaven and earth seen in two fragments which are static and of identical duration. Also repeated, but more obviously, is the very similar fragment seen earlier in the film in the "peasant springtime" sequence (with its connotations of spring as young and fruitful).

FERTILIZATION/FERTILITY

The film works with two signifiers, and what are they if not signifiers, on the one hand, of copulation, rutting, marriage, and on the other, of large herds, abundant harvests, and flourishing industries?

In the sequence of the dream, as in perhaps all the "strong" moments of the film, these two signifiers are constantly and simultaneously figured, always intertwining and crossing over each other. Thus in fragment 18, the longest and least "figurative" of this lexia (the figuration is obviously disturbed by the presence in the lower right frame of a white triangle that seems to have no interpretable referential meaning) the white liquid (as I have just pointed out) is readable as sperm. In fragments 20 and 22, the milk is seen (in part because of the interpolation of the two "nature" shots) as both an industrializable substance (= source of wealth) and a nurturing one (= one link in the chain of signifiers of procreation), in short, a symbol of fertility. (It should be noted that one could just as well read this double signified in the fragments of the dream, for example, as a metaphor of copulation, and the crowding of the cows into the lower half of the frame as signifying the theme of accumulation, wealth, or quantity.)

We can now see very distinctly the general direction of the sequence (which provides just one illustration of Eisenstein's fascination with synecdoche: the whole and the part as two forms of the same organic representation)—from the instinctual to the technical, from the organic to the rational. It is as if the drive existed only to be immediately channeled into Stakhanovism. What emerges here is an ideology of productivity (which is a better way to describe it than characterizing it as "economism") seen throughout the film (the pork being turned into sausages, the ballet of the tractors, etc.) as well as in many others of the same period, beginning with those of Vertov.

ALTERNATING MONTAGE

Alternating montage is used a great deal in this film and particularly in this sequence. Eisenstein obviously uses alternation in a way very different from that of "classical" cinema, for which it serves a more or less unifying function—to a degree that has made it one of the canonical figures of the constitution of the filmic scene.

Not surprisingly, in Eisenstein's films alternation is used to present "conflicts": the conflict of two points of view (on Martha and the cashbox, fragments 4-10); between two principal figures (Martha and her dream, fragments 11-17); and even the disjunction of previously connected elements (the mythological theme of heaven and earth/the metaphor of copulation).

Lexia 5. A "Gratuitous" Movement: Fragments 23-27

The movement in the frame abruptly shifts from the vertical to the horizontal: from right to left in 23, 25, and 27, from left to right in the two other fragments (the movements are almost equally long, 59 and 57 frames, respectively). As for the substance represented, it looks basically like a white liquid with surface foam.

DISCHARGE

In these five fragments taken together can be seen the same crossing of signifying chains: the milky white liquid originates in the liquid that falls from the sky (fragments 18-22), whereas the dark and geometrical forms which appear, still unreadable, at the edges of the frame, are already bits of the technical apparatus which will become prominent in the following fragments.

Two signifiers in this syntagmatic movement resist being absorbed into the rest: the foam (to be discussed later) and the horizontal shaking movement. This movement—if one disregards all purely formal considerations (ones certainly not considered negligible by Eisenstein)—can be seen as no more than a kind of supplementary delay, a reinforcement of the economy of suspense begun with Martha's disappearance, and which will end only with the revelation of the fact that we have left the realm of dreams or ancient mythology for reality and more current myths. An extreme instance of the principle of *braking:* the delay determines everything else (the coming and going as *discharge* [*dépense*]).

The Unrepresentable: Fragment 28

Very choppy foam on the surface of rapidly moving water. It is difficult to describe the violence of the first appearance of this fragment, a violence reinforced by a curious effect (clearly perceptible, but only as a sort of disturbance in two seconds of the projection), a sort of anomalous movement: whether the water is actually surging up, the film has been flipped, the shot has been taken from a strange angle, or any other rational explanation that could be given—the water seems to "flow backwards."

FROTH/FOAM

The five preceding fragments introduce a disturbance, or supplement, into the discourse which gently leads the sequence toward its end (and for its own ends: the model sovkhoz dairy). Fragment 28 introduces what first appears to be a rupture.

This rupture occurs in the hypothetical denotational level of the shot: why should we have the sea here, or its figurative stand-in? There is also a rupture in a level closer to that of the signifier: fragment 28 no longer plays a role in the double connotation (milk-sperm) on which the whole sequential logic up to this point has been based. These ruptures, however, only seem to be ruptures for they can be explained away; on the other hand there *is* a figurative inconsistency in this fragment which cannot be ignored: the foam on the backwards-moving water seems to be outside of the representational system, momentarily breaking the global image which is in the process of being constituted (that of the milk industry).

But: this trait which at first sight seems so aberrant or unexpected is nonetheless related through contiguity and even repetition to the fragments which precede it because of the matching horizontal movement (although it interrupts the alternation that has been established) and the similarity of the substance figured: foam here, froth there—in each case it is a substance that is both liquid and airborne, floating and heavy.

Like the fragments depicting the milk froth, these fragments also serve (among other functions) to delay as long as possible a nonetheless inevitable end. They help to maintain at any price and for the longest possible moment, a certain ambiguity. One cannot help but think that some other reason exists for these delays than simply the suspense that they bring. The reason very probably lies in the *lure* set up by the delays, a lure which is a very specific form of the pleasure of the text, one that involves a dream of endlessly writing or filming, never coming to a conclusion (a little like the digressions in his written texts).

THE "FILMIC"

The sea would represent here a new set of mythologies evoked by the text (the sea as the mythical origin of civilization, and according to Freud, the symbol of the mother, etc.); but even if, as seems to be the case when looking at the film again, it is not the sea which is being figured here, the frame enlargement of shot 28 is still rich in connotations of perpetual movement, pure force, and discharged energy.

Once again, however, it must be said that these connotations do not arise directly from the lexia or the sequence; perhaps they do not even exist in the "normal" viewing of the film (in projection rather than as frame enlargements) except in an almost subliminal or quasi-imperceptible way. These connotations are nevertheless there, somewhere in the text. What I have in mind here is very similar to Barthes's astonished insistence that he saw a "third meaning" in some frame enlargements from Eisenstein's films, an "obtuse" meaning which "resembles nothing," is almost a "counter-narrative," and which has nothing to do with the problematic of analogy, or the resemblance to "life"— but exists solely as a field of the signifier's "permutational" play.

Needless to say, it is not by chance that Barthes discovered his famous third meaning in frame enlargements from Eisenstein's films (and in almost no others). The Eisensteinian text (at least *The General Line*, but also some passages from *October* or *Potemkin*) although deliberately written to mobilize certain connotations, contains something which is not reducible to those connotations. What interests me here is how much the mythology of the sea as well as the idea of the "third meaning" match up to a whole Eisensteinian discourse around concepts like the "sonority" of the fragments, their "harmonics," etc. If the lack of focus or sharpness of the photograph, its luminosity, or even its graphic sonority can produce some kind of meaning ("obvious," signifying meaning)—there still remains a sort of supplement which, because Eisenstein calculated every parameter into a system, can be called a supplement of *écriture*.

I do not want of course to give any credence to the (absurd) idea of an Eisensteinian mastery so perfect that it could subject everything to its system. Nevertheless it seems to me that neither in *The General Line* nor any other films of Eisenstein is there a disjunction so radical as the one proposed by Barthes between the "third meaning" and the "anecdotal" level of the diegesis. On the contrary, the one *and* the other (at least insofar as Eisenstein could conceive this "other," in terms no doubt inadequate) are *part of the same system*. This is for example one of the lessons to be drawn from the stubbornness with which Eisenstein insisted in "Montage 1937" on the need not to neglect figuration (or analogy or the diegesis), without which no "image" can be constituted. At the very least the third meaning would not be as erratic as Barthes believed, and one could even ask, as Sylvie Pierre has done, if it is not after all "the very linchpin of the narrative."[21]

Lexia 6. Channels and Cascades: Fragments 29-32

This is actually three fragments plus one. There is a three-part division of the same denoted object, the milk, finally and clearly presented as such, and now seen channeled through the apparatus of industry. A simple division occurs: the alternation of the direction of movements, a closer shot with each cut, with the last of the three being notably longer. It is a canonical pattern whose closure comes by means of a repetition (except for the direction of the movement) of the punctuation of the lexia preceding the anomalous fragment denoting the "sea."

NATURE AND INDUSTRY

The milk, now in a useful form, is finally at the industrial stage. This is denoted by the fact that the flow of milk is now seen to be channeled; it no longer shares any connotations with the rain earlier on.

Let us note nevertheless how each of these three frames dwells on the presence of the miniature waterfall which results from channeling the milk, and which inscribes in a typically Eisensteinian way ("conflict" *in* the shot) a double connotation which contradicts any overly-strict channeling—namely:

—the naturalness of the milk's descent as opposed to the artificiality of the conduit (and also to the deliberately profiled waterfall which follows in fragment 36);

—the idea, even if it is an irrational one, of the potential energy of the falling milk as opposed to the inertia of the milk when simply transported or shaken (and from this point of view, the effect of the close-up is fully felt: abstracted from any context, the shots serve exactly as abstractions—there is, for example, no object in the frame to give a sense of scale, and thus, from the point of view of the figuration, the miniature cascades of milk are strictly equivalent to gigantic waterfalls).

Thus the contradiction nature/industry, which has been an insistent theme for some time now, is repeated, varied, and foregrounded. By means of a logic that is not yet discernible, the rational planning of human industry is first added to, and then substituted for, primitive, mythical, uncontrolled forces of nature.

The ideological resonance of this theme stems from Lysenko's "grand plan for the transformation of nature," a plan which did not yet exist in 1928 but which would come to leave its mark on the development of productive forces alluded to in the film. More specifically, we can see in the film an indication of the city/country relation as another version of the nature/industry relation. The film implicitly proposes the thesis that "the city is the future of the countryside" (thus it is the workers who come in from outside that bring class consciousness, along with tractors, to the peasants; and that moreover the country is bound to become urbanized, as is only too evident from the futurist silhouettes of the sovkhoz).

Idem: Fragments 33, 34

A repetition which brings together the elements of the preceding group while unexpectedly extending them: the apparent three-part pattern (29-30-31) gains an appendix (with 61 frames, it is the longest of the four fragments) which puts into question the very idea of the trio. Another trio, on the other hand, is constituted by grouping 34 with 28 and 32.

SEGMENTATION

While the beginning of the sequence was actually quite easy to segment because of the succession of marked, almost articulated, lexias clearly differentiated by their figurative content and arranged in simple patterns, the segmentation becomes increasingly problematic.

Although the structure of the fifth lexia seemed at first quite straightforward (a regular alternation of five fragments, with a sixth serving as a moment of pause), it becomes more complicated if one looks, for example, at the duration of the fragments: 26 and 28 are almost twice as long as any of the four others and are thus related, which is confirmed by their similarity at the level of figuration (close-up of froth, foam). It is as if fragment 26, while part of the series 23-27, serves to foreshadow fragment 28 (once again we see a slight variation on the braking principle).

By the time we get to the sixth lexia, where we are now, it becomes even more complicated: the division into two groups that I proposed (29-32; 33-34) is not the only possible one; the following division readily suggests itself: 29-30/31-32/33-34, which comprises two analogous blocks (31-32 and 33-34), including duration. Moreover, the first of these blocks repeats in its dominant direction that seen in fragment 29; the second, fragment 30; we thus have two series, symmetrical as to movement (29-31-32 and 30-33-34) and each composed of three fragments.

I have nothing of course to prove except that one can prove nothing; all I have shown is that the text is (probably) not segmentable in such an absolute fashion (at least not at this level). Eisenstein wilfully complicates the textual structure (the pleasure of the text again), and is able to do so with great ease since it is a montage based almost exclusively on the metaphorical (thus we can begin to see the beginnings of the idea of harmonic montage: the abolition, not of all structure—because it is highly structured—but of the "hierarchical" relations between successive shots presupposed by the very idea of segmentation).

THREE

I have just mentioned the statistically frequent occurrence of series of three fragments. To sum up: (1) the first is one of the series which opens the sequence (1-2-3): identical framings, similar durations—a simple dissection of a diegetic unity while indicating that each fragment represents a distinct portion of time; (2) a similar functioning for the series 5-7-9; (3) the series 12-14-16 (see above, *Explosion, Ecstasy, Brake*); (4) the series 18-20-22 (analogous to the first two); (5) the series 29-30-31, a simple grouping of three fragments all having the same content; (6) the two symmetrical series 29-31-32 and 30-33-34 (of which I have just spoken); (7) the final series 28-32-34, more original not because of its composition (three almost identical fragments), but because its elements have been used strategically to conclude and punctuate lexias.

This somewhat fastidious summary nonetheless serves to clarify the dual character of these groups of three fragments as seen in their frequency and relative monotony (always the same repetition and breakdown). This highly formal repetition recalls other instances in Eisenstein of his fetishization of threes—most notably in what has come to be recognized as his signature,[22] triangular arrangements in the frame (see, for example, in fragment 10, the three milk cans).

It would be enough to leave matters there were it not for all the "symbolic" readings of these "threes" proposed by Eisenstein's Freudianizing biographers. However tentative these interpretations may be, they clearly overlook the most important rule of any symbolic reading, which is that it must pay attention to the dynamics of the text. Whatever "universal" meaning one could finally attribute to the number 3 (even with Freud's approval),[23] its repeated occurrence either in *The General Line* or throughout Eisenstein's vast work cannot be reduced to any extra-textual meaning. As we have seen in *The General Line*, the film is made up of a whole complex and complete tissue in which no meaning is independent of others. No text, filmic or otherwise, can be read as a catalogue of symbols (any more than it can be seen as a collection of symptoms).

Lexia 7

An abrupt break with the three preceding lexias through (1) the reappearance of a vertical movement and, (2) most important, the appearance for the first time of machines including a ribbed black cylinder (part of an industrial cream separator?), a hydro-electric dam, and two containers which fill up with milk.

REFERENT/QUOTATION

We see here for the first time, then, some "concrete" objects of which until now neither the film nor the spectator has been aware. At the same time we notice a phenomenon that has been present all along but which only retrospectively becomes noticeable: the preceding fragments have had almost nothing to do with the codes of realism or figurative codes.[24] It is only at this point that the objects become recognizable as spatial/volumetric figurations, hence making it possible to establish their referent.

There is an emphatic stress on these indices of reality: the languid flowing of the cream, its consistency, its "thickness," heightened by the ribs of the black cylinder; the reflections in the water which rushes over the dam; the opaline whiteness of the milk as it flows into the glass cylinders. These objects nonetheless still remain largely unnameable—or even, in the case of the mysterious black cylinder, unidentifiable. (There is of course the problem of the obvious gap in *my* knowledge, or at least in the knowledge presumed by this film.) It is thus difficult to situate their referent "in reality." I would say that their status is that of quotation more than anything else.

This seems very clear in shot 36:

—it functions as a citation of a whole iconography that has already become almost stereotyped (to take only a very well-known example, see the similar fragments in Vertov's Odessa "trilogy");

—of the four shots, it is the one where the indices of reality are the most contradicted by the composition of the image: by the quasi-absence of depth of field (probably achieved with a long focus lens), as well as by the marked gap between two parts of the frame (the sinuous curve of the water flowing down the side of the dam/the horizontal movement and fuzziness of the little triangle in the lower left corner) which makes a little collage, a kind of montage in the frame.

WHAT IS THAT?

This is the kind of question raised by a conflict between the concreteness of the "objects" now appearing and the difficulty involved in identifying them, a question that has been latent for a good while but which the text has somehow eluded, never quite allowing it to be posed.

Let us recall the description that Barthes gives in *S/Z* of the hermeneutic chain as it is structured in the classical text. This code surely exists in Eisenstein's films (as we shall see with *Ivan*) but here it manifests itself in a minimal, or more precisely, sub-liminal way, because it is below the threshold, not of perception, but of *thematization*; after all the discursive delays ("to delay meaning is to manufacture it") we come to the revelation of the solution to an enigma that the text has neither stated nor thematized.

Yet again, such a strategy is very coherent. Classical film, which makes classical use of this hermeneutic code, does not just limit it to detective stories: the appearance of a new character, for example, brings with it an enigma to thematize, formulate, and pose. In *The General Line* the enigma posed by the figuration of a new element seems to be immediately reabsorbed or dissolved by the force of the metaphoro-metonymical work of the film and the emphatic linking of fragment to fragment ("horizontality"). Hence the disarray of the spectator when confronted with the sudden emergence of the real.

JUNCTION/LINK/ENGAGEMENT (AND MONTAGE)

There are a certain number of fetish-words in Eisenstein's vocabulary. We have already encountered some of them, and it would doubtless be instructive to do a more thorough (statistical or semantic) study. Take, for example, the word *styk* (junction, join, link). While this is not strictly an Eisensteinian concept and he uses it only in a very metaphorical way,[25] it is nonetheless difficult not to see there, once more, the young Eisenstein's obsession with "conflict." *Styk* seems to be able to include both the conflict from fragment to fragment and the unification of these partial conflicts in an "organic" (or "harmonic") montage, as well as the question of the *shifter* (which allows the passage from one fragment to the next, and which Eisenstein conceived of both in terms of correlations and "leaps").

Eisenstein's theoretical discourse during this period stressed the double nature of montage: the local conflicts, and the unifying junction—and their articulation through iconic groupings and parameters which serve *at once* to mark the conflict and its junction. Thus in fragments 18-38 (those which comprise the "dream"), we can begin to describe how montage is functioning here:

—first of all, there is a primary category of parameters, a good example of which would be movement in the frame;[26] it is easy to describe and is implicitly one of the criteria used to divide the film into lexias. All of this of course relates to what the Eisensteinian catalogue calls *rhythmic montage;*[27]

—another type would be, for example, the material or substance figured by the shot: milk as rain, frothy milk, cream—a regularly increasing density. Water, however, in its diverse forms remains secondary to the milk. This is a typical *tonal* montage, with its dominant comprised of purely sensorial parameters which are not yet linked to any connotations;

—and, finally, a third type which is the most abstract because it organizes the form (or rather, the representation) of the substance from the more symbolic level (the rain) to the most "denotative" (the industrial channeling of the milk). This is of course "intellectual" montage.

Two very general ideas about montage quickly emerge from this brief description. First, it is impossible to analyze this portion of a sequence using Eisenstein's own categories since almost all of them function simultaneously (and, as I have already said, this was probably the origin of the impetus to promote harmonic montage). Next, one must recognize the importance of the double principle conflict/junction. The leap from 38 to 39 provides us with a final example of it: here we have the first appearance of animated beings since fragment 17, which represents a move to a different kind of figuration and composition, and a return to a "realistic" referent. There is very much a leap here, and one which takes place at several levels. I will indicate only the most extreme:

in close-up (from fragment to fragment) the connection is made through "intellectual" connotations: the two glass cylinders filling up with milk metaphorically recall the idea of the maternal breasts and of nursing, which is immediately displaced onto the suckling pigs;

in long shot (from sequence to sequence), a transformation of the fertility principle (sperm, male potency) into wealth (lots of fat pigs and cows)—a transformation of quality into quantity, which, as I have already noted, contributes in Eisenstein to a perversion of the theses of dialectical materialism.

A final consequence of this fetishism of junction/conflict is the breaking up of the text. The frame fractures the real (especially with the close-up) while the body of the film is broken into fragments. Meaning too is shattered: the meaning of this sequence, for example, can only be constructed in the most atomized form, in the tiniest articulations of the text (exactly where we found them). This perhaps offers another explanation for the difficulty of segmenting the film (the uneven tone that exists between fragment and segment).

DREAM AND UTOPIA

We have seen how, toward fragment 11, the concatenation designated as a dream (and precisely, as *Martha's* dream) is constructed; it takes us to fragment 39, which, in turn, serves to introduce another new "sequence" (the farm animals, the sovkhoz). A little further on, this will be transformed into the sovkhoz itself, with its idyllic life set in peaceful nature, where the buildings are functional, and the peasants serenely occupied. The logic of these concatenations demands that all of this be seen as a dream, yet it is ambiguous (which is reinforced by the intertitle in fragment 74: "Is this a dream?"). It is thus a rude shock when a smiling Martha reappears in fragment 75 in "reality," and we are immediately forced to see the sovkhoz through her eyes.

What status are we then to give to these fragments of the sovkhoz, which were originally presented as a dream and then depicted in detail as real? Clearly, we are dealing with a utopia,[28] literally that which is located nowhere (and which belongs to no one). Similarly, the dream ends, having come to its conclusion (when? we do not know), no longer Martha's dream but the film's, Eisenstein's, or, indeed, that of an ideological imperative.

It is not unimportant that this ideal, radiant, perfectly idyllic future (the representation of the sovkhoz "resolves" in its own way many of the contradictions!) is depicted as a utopia. It has often been said that *The General Line* is a film about a miracle (all or nothing: it works—the cream separator—or it doesn't—the bridal procession). It would be safe to say that from this perspective there is an absolute coherence between the film and its aim: does the film itself, like Martha and the agronomist, not dream of bringing the spectator "fully" into the picture so that he too can participate in the collective miracle, or adhere to "the general line" ("Let the eyes of the spectators blaze up at the sight of the kolkhoz's tin-plated cream separator!"—"Days of Enthusiasm," 1929)?

In this respect, and many others (especially the role given to the peasant masses, seen as dark, amorphous, shifty, reactionary, superstitious, etc.), the film could ultimately be seen to promote the truth of the Stalinist ideological discourse. To borrow Jean Narboni's phrase, it would be its *analyst*.

II. Murder in the Bridal Chamber

1. Ivan, Part 1, Ivan, Part 2

We are dealing here with a sequence in two parts, which establishes a relationship between the murder of Anastasia "by" Efrosinia on one hand and, on the other hand, Ivan's "discovery" of the truth about that murder in the very same place, and with the help of the young Basmanov. (The reader will soon see why "by" and "discovery" are problematic notions here.) The first passage in this two-part sequence comes about three-quarters of the way into *Ivan, Part 1*; the second passage in the sequence is about one-third of the way into *Ivan, Part 2*. The film lends itself to this pairing in the following ways:

1. First of all, by means of the diegetic links between the two passages. A little detective mystery is introduced in the first part, and it is solved in the second part. In a broader sense, poisoning is one of the central mechanisms of the plot, thematically connected to Ivan's murderous madness and to his paranoid isolation, symbolically linked to his two false deaths—the one that fails to bring an end to his long agony, and the one involved in the unsuccessful attempt on his life in the cathedral.

2. Next, the scene of the death of Anastasia (and of the funeral) is the one in Part 1 in which Ivan "announces" most clearly his character in Part 2 (black costume, political and psychological solitude,

doubt—a "Russian Hamlet").[29] Conversely, the scene with Fyodor marks the beginning of Ivan's recovery of self-control after his entreaties to Kolychev (moreover it comes immediately after a sign of that recovery—the executions of the Boyars).

3. Lastly, the symbolic substitution of Basmanov for Anastasia is acted out in this diptych, as is the more general passage from the matrimonial order to another order (without which the appearance of the *Oprichniki* is absolutely inconceivable).[30]

All of these elements are involved in a generalized playing upon extremely insistent *rhymes* between the two passages. They are rhymes between the settings and the props, which are identical and identically arranged in both passages: the empty goblet (36/H); Anastasia's apartment, filmed in two almost identical framings (33/D); and the system of icons, which are never filmed for their own sake, but whose insistent presence in the background silently guarantees the idea of a perfect permanence—from one scene to the other, "nothing has changed."[31]

All these effects—permanence, insistence, immobility of objects and of places—are achieved by means of a deliberate and thoroughgoing attention to detail. Furthermore, it is more than probable that if these two passages were not filmed in continuity, only a short period of time, at the very least, separated the filming of each. Above all, this effect of permanency and immobility is achieved to the detriment of and with contempt for any sort of naturalistic verisimilitude. As proof, I shall offer only the example of the presence, in shot J, of the deadly goblet, in a framing very similar to the one in which it first appears placed there by the hand of Efrosinia (shot 41); in this passage the Eisensteinian system can be clearly seen as the antonym of any sort of naturalism. Having been used "in order" to poison the czarina, the goblet has nothing more to do there. Nevertheless, it is absolutely indispensable for it to be there: (1) so that it can be played off paradigmatically against the "innocent" goblet which has remained at the bedside; (2) so that it can take its place in the trajectory of the deadly goblet (we shall return to this point); (3) last, so that Ivan's movements in the first passage (in particular his series of looks back and forth from right to left, shots 37 to 42 and I to K) can be reiterated in the very greatest formal and figurative detail.

Even before any analytical work is undertaken, it can be seen how the relationship between our two passages is controlled by a logic of sameness, and reiteration, which, of course, will have to account for all the variations, all the substitutions (including for the central one

Shot numbers are in boldface, duration (in number of seconds) in roman.

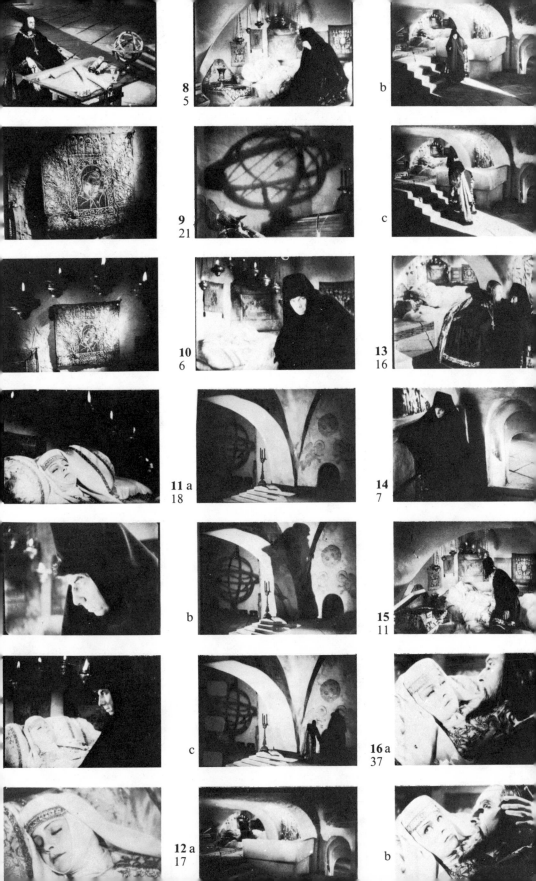

8
5

b

9
21

c

10
6

13
16

11 a
18

14
7

b

15
11

c

16 a
37

12 a
17

b

c

21 a
15

17 a
5

b

b

c

18
4

22 a
15

19
8

b

20 a
7

c

b

23 a
13

b

c

b

c

30
7

33 a
5

a

31 a
17

b

b

b

34
4

8

c

35
4

a

d

36 a
2

b

32 a
13

b

37
3

c

38a
5

41
8

8

b

42a
2

c

b

4

39
10

43a
10

4
5

40a
8

b

4
1

b

c

b

D a
3

I a
2

b

b

E
10

J
2

F
4

K a
2

G a
5

b

b

L
2

H
1

M
5

N
4

S a
7

O
12

b

P.
3

T a
16

Q
10

b

R
6

c

DIALOGUE

Shot 16a: You seem troubled, Czar Ivan.
(Ivan:) I am alone. There is no one I can trust.

16b: Kurbsky is far away, fighting in Livonia.
Kolychev is even further off, praying in a monastery.

16c: I have only you.

21a: (Messenger:) I come from Ryazan!
(Ivan:) It's from Basmanov!

22a, b: Again! The boyars again!

22c: Once again they are resisting our royal edicts!

23: Once again they are betraying the Russian Land. They are pre-
venting Basmanov and the people from defending Kazan, and
they want . . .

24: . . . to surrender it to the Khan.
(Anastasia:) Be strong!

25: (Ivan:) I shall be. I shall crush them with my bare hands.

26a: I shall abolish their fiefdoms and their privileges.

27: I shall give their land to those who serve the state.

28: And from those who serve without honor, I shall take . . .

29a: . . . all their land!

30: (Efrosinia) You are going too far, Czar Ivan!

31a, b: (Sound of the drops of poison)

31c: (Malyuta:) Our armies . . .

32a: . . . under Nevel's command have been destroyed.
Kurbsky has been defeated.
(Ivan:) Kurbsky?
(Anastasia cries out)

39a, b: Could Kurbsky have betrayed me?

Aa: (Ivan:) By what right to do you pronounce judgment, Czar Ivan?
By what right do you wield the sword of judgment?

Ab: (Faint cry from off screen)

E: Take that goblet out of my sight!
(Basmanov:) Sometimes goblets . . .

F: . . . are filled with poison.

G1: (Ivan:) The goblet!

J: The goblet!

M: So she was poisoned!

N: Anastasia, my beloved lamb!

O: (Basmanov:) Who gave the czarina the last, the fatal goblet?

Q: (Ivan:) She took it!

R: She took it from *my* hands.

S: (Basmanov:) And who gave it to you?
(Ivan:) Efrosinia!

Ta: Efrosinia?

Tb: Can it be true? The czar's own aunt?

Ua: Silence! Say nothing of my suspicions to anyone . . .

Ub: . . . until I have found out the truth.

of Basmanov for Anastasia). One more point in this connection, while we have the character of Ivan "in long shot." On the one hand, there is a similarity in his gestures, in the mise-en-scène from one passage to the other; but, on the other hand, he is obviously not the same man. There can be no better way of reading the opposition between these two Ivans than by referring to the opening shots of each of the two passages. Shot 1 shows us Ivan "the Great Statesman" at the conclusion of his long conversation with Nepeya, Ivan the skillful diplomat, the enlightened ruler, the Renaissance man who wants to give his country access to the benefits of international trade and civilization, whose ambitions are on a global scale. Wearing a richly brocaded robe, he is seated in a comfortable armchair before a table laden with documents opposite an insistently present globe (more cosmic than terrestrial).[32]

In shot A we have before our eyes a brutal dictator who has just unleased a wave of savage executions (it is true that he feels some guilt over them). The robe has disappeared (very significantly, it has "stayed behind," at the entrance to Anastasia's bedchamber, see shots 13 and V). The table and the atmosphere of work are also gone—we are now in the lair of a wild beast. And the armchair upon which he leaves a bearskin coat as he exits, through its "gothic," "barbaric" appearance, participates in this atmosphere of savagery and madness.

Behind Ivan's same features then, one character has been substituted for another. But are they really the same features? Not exactly—there are numerous variations in the appearance of Cherkasov's makeup, even if they are only those which account for Ivan's aging (and hardening). But here again, these variations (created, we know, laboriously and at the cost of hours of suffering for the actor!) hardly respect verisimilitude in the progression, or the regression, of the character. Ivan the diplomat seated at his desk (shot 1) still very much resembles the young husband, the conqueror of Kazan. When we see him again (in the diegesis, a few minutes later) at Anastasia's bedside, he already shows signs of his aging (37, 42). But the most striking thing to me is the similarity of Ivan's face when he comes back into the bedchamber (our second passage) and his face at the burial of Anastasia, whereas in shot A he looks much older. Once again, at the expense of "realism," this similarity is clearly determined by the necessity of reproducing a situation, and thus a meaning (things must be repeated as faithfully as possible in order for Basmanov really to be able to take the czarina's place).

In spite of the (narrative, diegetic) space separating them, it can be seen that our two passages very quickly reveal themselves to be closely linked—and further analysis only confirms this relationship. Therefore, we shall henceforth refer to them as one and the same "sequence."

2. The Scene: Positioning Things

Perhaps the most visible characteristic of this sequence is its treatment of space. Representative in this respect of the whole film, it depicts for us a closed and strongly unified space, using a single architectural structure as a referential support. The reader will recall how much importance Eisenstein attached to these structures, notably in his courses on directing. Thus it is essential to emphasize from the outset that they are always determined on the basis of two competing criteria, historical accuracy and function.[33] (That is, they are determined, in anticipation, by the mise-en-scène which will be inscribed in them.) That is exactly what we will find in the passage under consideration.

The preparatory work for *Ivan the Terrible* is probably the most extensive that has ever been done for a single film. For two years Eisenstein accumulated readings, notes, drawings. Almost all the drawings (some of them quite well known) date from the same period, from March to June 1942 (almost a year before the shooting began). The most striking thing about these drawings is the fact that they almost never correspond to the frames of the future film; but, at the same time, they are stupendous condensations of the whole of a future scene into a single representation.[34] Hence, the curious impression produced when they are compared with the film—they resemble without resembling. They offer the "idea" of the space and the event that will be presented by the film, but without the point of view which will be that of the camera.

Take, for example, what has been called "Anastasia's bedchamber." The scenario, extremely precise in its succinctness, tells us that Ivan rushed *v svetlitsou terema Anastasii*, into the "svetlitsa" of the "terem" of Anastasia. Those two words, both of them rather obsolete, designate ancient architectural conceptions. The word *svetlitsa* (related to the root *svet*, light) designates an especially well-lighted ceremonial room. As for *terem*, it is "an apartment located in the upper part of the house" (definition from the *Ojegov Dictionary*, which specifies that the word is no longer used), and clearly seems to imply the idea of a

kind of gyneceum, even a kind of harem, as is plainly suggested by
Eisenstein in a completely different context (in "Mise-en- jeu" and
"Mise-en-geste," 1948).

I am not qualified to evaluate the historical accuracy of the "reconstruction" offered by the film. But it seems obvious that the few
lines of these definitions can be seen, absolutely literally, in the setting
in which our sequence takes place. The shots which allow us to see
the whole set (12, 15, 21, etc.) stress at least four ideas: (1) It is an
apartment, connected, of course, to the rest of the palace by two doors
and a low window, but at the same time separate, and appearing clearly
closed (almost a place of seclusion). (2) The room in which Anastasia
lies has a *ceremonial* character—there is no intimacy in this space,
which neither Malyuta, for example, nor the messengers from the front
fear to enter. (3) The area is strongly *illuminated* (if not very brightly);
there is an emphasis on the many lamps and a contrast with the darkness of the first shot. (4) Finally, it is *elevated*. It is entered by climbing
a few steps. The window, although at floor level, overlooks a courtyard
(see shot W). Above all, a small parapet at right angles clearly marks
this elevation.

But, as "realistic" as these characteristics may be, how can one
overlook the fact that their principal determination is of a functional
(fictional) nature? We will see this in greater detail shortly. The elevation was indispensable for Ivan's comings and goings, and for his
threatening looks. The lighting with its violent contrasts participates
in a generalized playing upon the blacks and whites. Finally, the effect
of the whole is to define a closed space, focused on the sources of light,
on Anastasia's bed.

This last detail is perhaps the most essential one. That will be
seen in the discussion of the depth of field, but it can already be pointed
out that the clearest feature of the spatial arrangement is the way it
contributes to the production of a rather simple topology, determined
by a great cleavage between Anastasia on one side, and Ivan and Efrosinia on the other.

Anastasia is presented from the very beginning as both immobile
(she "cannot" leave her couch) and expressive. Throughout the first
passage, with her gestures (including the slightest movements of her
eyes) and her cries, she provides a commentary on Ivan's speech, giving
it an unexpected, extra-political dimension. (This system culminates
in shot 32, with the cry and the fainting, marking Kurbsky's betrayal
and at the same time the double—erotic—meaning of that betrayal.)

Ivan is presented as plainly disturbed, i.e., agitated, fluttering about like a moth blinded by a flame, from one corner of the space and the frame to another (see shots 22, 26, 32, 38), making a "political" speech completely out of place with respect to the reality of the scene being enacted before our eyes—in a word, Ivan is in the grip of a symptom whose truth is pronounced by Anastasia.

Last, *Efrosinia's* position also contrasts with Anastasia's, but according to a principle of excess that is the opposite of Ivan's. She slides over the space, slinks along the walls, melts into the darkness in which she participates morally, a maleficent nocturnal beast (see shot 12, in which she is glued to the spot, like a bat blinded by the violent light which penetrates the room as Ivan enters) investing the off-screen space and the match in the same way that Ivan occupies the frame, excessively.

What I am attempting to describe here is dual in nature. First of all, there is a polarization of the space around Anastasia's bed, and the production of meaning in the sequence will radiate outward from that polarization. Next, and even if only in a more or less mythical sense, there is the first phase of Eisenstein's work, the positioning of the actors in space, which Eisenstein calls mise-en-scène. It is as if the film (as a text, as a tress of meanings) referred directly, not to history or any reality of the characters and the events, but to *theater*. Naturally, I am not taking much of a risk in suggesting this idea, since I know that was the way Eisenstein worked, empirically, at least in the context of the didactic and analytical relationship he maintained with his students at the VGIK. We have only to recall how the filmic representation of the episode with Dessalines is set up "first of all" as a mise-en-scène for the theater, and "then" as *mise-en-cadre* (the breaking down, reinterpretation, rewriting) of the so-called mise-en-scène (see Nizhny, Chapter 2). Whatever the case may be, this phase of the work is always emphasized by Eisenstein (the preparatory drawings referred to would be one of its traces), and it is during this phase that the architecture of the scene is defined, in accordance with the dual exigency that I have stressed.

Whether or not the articulation in two distinct stages thus posited really accounts for the actual work done, or whether it is an imaginary formulation of that work, is in any case impossible to determine and of secondary importance. On the other hand, there is no denying the presence of this first stage of the fiction, in the form of traces which can be located in the literal structure of the filmic text, and which act as an a priori and internal guarantee of all the work of fragmenting (*mise-en-cadre*, montage). In addition to performing the general task (common to the whole film) of articulating the text according to a discursive logic, in this passage, the process of fragmenting performs a specific task—the production of the fatal error. And with respect to this whole work of writing, of fragmenting, of radiating meaning outward, the "prior" level of the mise-en-scène thus functions as a binding agent, assuring and assuming all the effects of coherence and continuity. Thus the space, fragmented by the cutting/editing, deformed by the framing, nonetheless remains unified and continuous. And this is quite obviously due to this scrupulously thorough positioning of the figures in the space. More generally, each one of the occurrences of the *film scene* (that imaginary space-time of which the filmic representation aims to give the impression) will in a way be split by this contradiction between a unifying principle and a principle of dissemination (this will be seen in connection with the matches as well as in other respects).

If it were necessary to lay additional emphasis on the imperious necessity which characterizes all this "preliminary" work, I would remind the reader here of everything that contributes to an extension and explicitation of the action (a kind of flattening out of the events). We have already had occasion to mention how insistent Eisenstein was, in his work with his students, about demonstrating that there was always "something to be done" *beforehand*. That the meaning could not be crystallized in any single given moment of the action, but had to be brought out constantly, made necessary, irrefutable. Now the work of *prolonging* the action is far from being limited to what Barthes has called the "catalyst" function in narrative. It is always motivated, determined by an assertive, "faultless" logic. (Example: In which direction will the *aide-de-camp* who has just taken Dessalines's saber away from him make his exit? "He will take the shortest way out," answer the students, anxious to get this bit player off stage. But, no! On the contrary, he will take the longest way out, in order to make very clear the fact that Dessalines is disarmed. All of Eisenstein is contained in this transformation of the *insignificant* into the *significant*.)

There is no need to emphasize how vital this process is for the functioning of the passage we are examining. Thus the poisoning, which is the principal element represented (denoted), is perpetrated as a consequence of a complex strategy in which nothing is enunciated without its cause being explicitly marked, and which simultaneously accumulates retardations, delaying actions (all of them equally significant—see, for example, the empty goblet in shot 36, reiterated in H and L). I emphasize—this strategy and this accumulation are not solely linked to a supposed "suspense" function of this episode. They are, on the contrary, typical of the use of the filmic system conceived as text, which plays with time as well as with space, by dismantling both of them.[35]

3. The Scene: Figuration and Representation

Assuming, then, the existence, at least ideally, of such preparatory work on the scene, in its theatrical dimension, we now turn to the analysis of its "screenification" (representation in filmic terms).

To begin with what is perhaps the most striking feature, the treatment of the space, one is first of all struck by the obsessive insistence on perspective and depth of field. The latter would at first seem to provide the distinctive criterion of a major dichotomy which would divide all the shots of the sequence (according to whether or not they emphasize depth of field). At the two extremes one would find:

1. On one hand, general shots showing the whole "chamber" from a variety of angles (the shot that is the "richest" in topological information is certainly 12, from which the bed, the two stairways, and the low doorway can all be seen at the same time; shots 14, 21, 32, C, and V might also be mentioned), and above all playing on the forward or backward movements of a given character in relation to the camera (among the most typical of such shots are 20, repeated in B; 15, echoed in D; 21, 29, 38, etc.);

2. On the other hand, close-ups, which can be categorized chiefly as either close-ups of faces (Anastasia, 47; Basmanov, F; Ivan and Basmanov, O; Efrosinia, 17 and 30) or as close-ups of objects (the goblets, especially 40 and H, the icon, 2).

And it appears to follow that the rest of the shots could be distributed "between" these two poles according to size (and depth of field).

Now, this distribution does not exist. A much more accurate description of the sequence would be given by saying that it contains *some* depth and *some* close-up—as though these qualities settled on, better yet, circulated throughout all of the shots, so that it is impossible to say absolutely that such and such a shot is exclusively marked by either one of these predicates.

This calls for some explanation. For the objection will not fail to be made that, while depth of field can indeed, at the limit, be considered a quantifiable "quality" of a shot (i.e., there can be "more" or "less" of it), a close-up is relegated to the scaling system of shots which is an unwritten law in the practice of filming. Now, as Bonitzer has shown, reflections on the question of the scene and of representation can only gain from displacing the problematic in order to take into consideration the ideological history (the ideology and the history) in which that problematic is inscribed—which he describes as a contradiction between classical ideology (homogeneity/continuity, and their imaginary preservation at any cost) and a "dialectical" (or "heterological") ideology.

Thus, if the close-up is absorbed into the classical system as a term interchangeable with every other term in the scale of sizes (marked symbolically, at least in English and French, by its reference, explicit or implicit, to the image of the human body), as a "principle of the close-up" (as one might speak of a "principle of montage" independently of any given form of montage), in relation to the classical economy of representation, it is inscribed as a permanent danger, that of the elimination of depth, of the loss of recognition:

> Thus, if we are interested in the close-up, the reader will have understood, it is not as such, "in itself," according to a "photogenic" (photological) sense. But rather, we are interested in it because it marks and remarks the discontinuity of the filmic space and absorbs the vision, the image, into the substitutive movement of writing. (Pascal Bonitzer)[36]

I could not put it better myself. At the risk of being perhaps excessively metaphorical, in dealing with that depth of field (it, too, imaginary, fictive, feigned), I shall emphasize what it implies of *presence* in the decor, in the place, in the scene; and conversely, in the close-up I shall emphasize what escapes (at least insofar as figuration and representation are concerned) the scenic analogy and tends to become *writing* (*écriture*). (The close-up consequently standing metonymically for everything which functions as a "supplement" with respect to the scene.)

Besides, this metaphor is not so daring. At any rate, it is wholly Eisensteinian. One need think only of the three (at least) texts whose titles mention the close-up.[37] All three of them are devoted to a call for a thorough study of the figurative means (of montage, and particularly of montage in the shot) going well beyond the simple question of "scale of the shot."

(Once again, the courses given at the VGIK are extremely enlightening here. The fixed position of the camera, the depth of *mise-en-cadre*—all this cannot fail to call to mind the work on *Crime and*

Punishment. Now it will be remembered that, in that work, in which the camera remained immobile and the same lens was used throughout, all the effects were obtained by means of the actors' movements towards or away from the camera, in the form of a violent contradiction precisely between effects of depth of field and close-up effects.)[38]

Returning to our sequence, what now appears there is not so much a term-to-term opposition between close-up and depth of field, but rather their co-existence, their complementary nature, and naturally, their conflict. This is particularly clear in shot 38, for example. It is quite obvious that the violent movement of Ivan's bursting in upon the scene from the background of the shot, and his crossing of the space of the frame in the same agitated mode, are supported by the presence of Malyuta, motionless, save for his eyes, in a close shot. Within the frame there is a violent contrast (conflict) between these two principles. The admirable thing here is that this conflict, far from being fixed, formal, is dynamic, integrated into the representation, and finally subservient to the meaning. That is true for Malyuta's obstinately immobile face, projected forward "in close-up" by his position in the foreground of the frame, by his very immobility, and above all by the stark lighting which strikes him from below, just as much as it is true for the fluttering figure of Ivan, who fills and emphasizes the depth of field as well as its width. These two figures, then, contradictory as they may be, find their resolution and their necessity in the production of one and the same "global image"—that of blindness, of "not seeing."

Thus, the following can be said concerning the "close-up" as a writing principle, i.e., as a principle in the system of the film as text: (1) First of all, it is inseparable from its "opposite," depth of field (a "unity of opposites" whose profound reality we have just seen, for the truth of the matter is that it is in *Ivan* that all the developments on the dialectic in *Nonindifferent Nature* find their principal justification); (2) It is even more essentially inseparable from the editing, since this potential unity of opposites is realized in the form of the co-presence (or sometimes in the successive presence, see shots 29 and 30) of both terms within the frame. This is the first indication (there will be others) of the fact that in *Ivan the Terrible* montage is less than ever to be found exclusively in the leap from shot to shot, but instead it is disseminated in the most subtle ways.

The reader may wonder why I have stressed this point of the field (or rather, its depth or lack of depth) at such great length. If I insist so much, it is because it is of fundamental importance to emphasize clearly the way the principle of montage takes specific form by playing on *both terms* of the conflict. First of all, of course, this is a fundamental point in demonstrating that Eisenstein is the antonym of a "cinema of depth," (one in which depth is produced so that the viewer can lose her/himself in it). But it is also especially important in order to combat an image of Eisenstein which would tend to freeze him in that antonymy, to consider his cinema as an absolute refusal of depth, of any scenic value, of any representational process, and, in an almost dogmatic gesture, to relieve it of the burden of "reality,"—a reality to which Eisenstein attached enormous importance.

The danger of such a position is not entirely avoided by Bonitzer, although he rightly contrasts Eisensteinian editing with classical editing, "a function of the dramatic quality, of scenography." Consider this statement:

> Eisenstein was never really interested in depth of field. Scenically he is interested in the frame, not in depth.[39]

And from there he moves into an analysis of the famous shot in which Ivan, who has withdrawn to the Alexandrov Palace, watches (head in profile, in close-up on the right-hand side of the frame) the supplicating procession of the Russian people (a long serpentine line stretching off into the distance on the left-hand side of the screen) coming to seek him out. It is easy for Bonitzer to point out that this is "the juxtaposing . . . of two opposing motifs," and that "the effect of a receding perspective . . . is completely negated by the rigorous order of the composition." But if he is able to make his point so easily, that is due to (at least) two oversights on his part.

First of all, his analysis is based on a still photograph, and it therefore neglects everything in the duration of the shot and in the movements (even minimal ones) inscribed in it that has the effect of tempering the rigor of the composition, in particular by insisting on the flatness of the right-hand side of the frame (Ivan's head) and the depth of the left-hand side (the procession).[40]

Next, and in order to support his argument, he has selected a shot which was composed by Eisenstein precisely *in order* to obtain the effect described by Bonitzer[41] (a montage effect between two half-frames, strongly "disjointed" in plastic terms). On the other hand, this argument falls completely flat for dozens and dozens of other occurrences in *Ivan*. (We have seen this with shot 38, and it could be shown with other examples.)

Let us repeat—Eisenstein plays every card, and he plays the card of depth of field as much as any other (a little more than quite a few others). He is content to redefine the rules of the game. Another example, perhaps the most spectacular shot in the sequence, no. 43, will confirm this for us. Divided diagonally by the little parapet on which Efrosinia has just placed the deadly goblet, it joins *and* separates (a new unity of opposites of which other examples have been seen in our analysis of *The General Line,* and which here is indispensable to the discourse) two half-frames. On the lower left, a figuration of Efrosinia who is "in close-up" (in particular, here again, as with Malyuta, thanks to the violently arbitrary lighting); on the upper right, an almost empty space, where Ivan appears, seizes the goblet, looks without seeing, and goes out again. Of course, in Bonitzer's description, the first thing that strikes us is the written aspect of the event. The freeze frame shows flagrant traces of writing. For example, Ivan's gaze meets Efrosinia's in a way that inscribes the fact that, without seeing each other (in the scene) they "look" at each other (this detail will be returned to shortly). Or, on the contrary, at other moments, there is the parallelism of their gazes (to be read in relation to the off-screen presence of Anastasia— but there again, without any eyeline *match*).

Yet, here again, invaluable as it may be for analysis, the text of the frame enlargement is deceptive, or at least insufficient. It causes the loss not only of time, of the duration, the tempo of Ivan's gestures, opposed to Efrosinia's immobility (or the exacerbated, cautious slowness of her gestures), but even the loss of perception of the space. As limited as the space afforded him by the framing may be, Ivan's movement is in large part executed in the depth of the image (a depth which the point of view, the "shortcut" marked by the camera, leads one to imagine as unfolding along the diagonal), and that space itself, independently of the figure of Ivan (before his entrance, after his exit) is anything but flat (it can be imagined, even in the still photo, from what we see of the beginnings of the ribs of the vault, arranged from right to left).

Now all of that, which is more or less eliminated in the still, is obviously essential. One might repeat here Sylvie Pierre's statement:

> The cinema does not have two bodies, one atemporal, the discontinuous chain of still frames, the other temporal, the unrolling of the images; cinema has only one body, in which time is inscribed.[42]

Of course, I am not denying that Eisenstein treats space in a very *written* mode. Whether he "flattens it out" (as with the case of the shot of Ivan at Alexandrov) or whether, much more frequently, he hollows it out by distorting it (his fondness for the 28mm lens is well known),[43] the space always participates in the "dynamic" of the *distance* which is to be maintained between the means of expression and the objects filmed. *But*, he does not, for all that, deprive himself of producing, simultaneously, an imaginary space in which, through the fragmentation and distortion, the spectator can situate her/himself, *in order to understand the meaning better.* This relationship between analogy and signification (not to mention *signifiance*),[44] which is perhaps more hierarchical than dialectical, is of capital importance throughout the entire textual system of *Ivan*. It is in any event what controls the representational economy of our whole sequence, as will now be shown quickly, by touching on a few other points.

A few remarks have already been made concerning the frame. Here, as in the silent films, the frame functions as a relatively autonomous unit, and all the more openly because it is based on a more immediate referent, the one posited by the existence of the prior mise-en-scène. This autonomy of the frame is constantly asserted by every possible means. Thus, in this sequence, one has the impression of a maximum variety of framing angles (of the points of view of the camera and their perspective orgnization). Take Anastasia's bed, for example. As far as can be determined on the basis of stills, there are no two identical frames; there is always at least one parameter that varies between any two of them.

More fundamentally, each frame determines its own off-screen space and its relationship to that space. In a general way, the frame is very "centripetal" (to use Bazin's expression). Without absolutely excluding the idea of an off-screen space from which something can emerge (although the temptation of such an enclosure can be sensed here and there—see shots 17, 23, O), this area outside the field never exists as an indefinite extension of the space of the field, homogeneous and isotropic with it, but exists only in a *discrete* way, in the form of individualized elements which are always *appealed to from within the frame.* Outside the direction from which it is deliberately evoked, from the frame (and notably by looks and gestures), and always with the aim of producing, of articulating a meaning, it can practically be said that the off-screen space, as such (i.e., once again, as a corollary of the field, i.e., the on-screen space) does not exist.

Here are some examples. In shot 19, when they hear the messenger coming, Anastasia and then Ivan designate the direction from which he will arrive, she with eye movement, Ivan with a head movement, towards the lower right-hand side of the frame. (Moreover, they are careful not to do this simultaneously—everything must be stated twice.) An even more obvious example is to be seen in the series of relationships established by the looks "exchanged" between Anastasia and Efrosinia, when the czarina is about to drink, and then drinks, clearly aware that she is being poisoned (47-48-49). The role of the off-screen space has nothing to do here with an imaginary opening of the frame (the "window open on to the world" dreamt of by Alberti and Bazin), there is nothing natural about the way the off-screen space comes to replace the field, but the signifier reaps a maximum profit from the operation.

Correlatively, then, the looks exchanged between the characters, the binding agent of any ideology of the "transparent" match, are directed strictly here. They are articulated in relationship to each other in accordance with a logic which, without ceasing to constitute the drama, must also and above all contribute to the emergence of the meaning, to the same degree as the other elements of the representation, in a completely unambiguous way. (And if there is any ambiguity in the glances exchanged by the actors, at least we can be sure that ambiguity was *calculated*; see for example the moment of Ivan's oversight, or Anastasia's last look, which has just been mentioned.) The looks exchanged articulate the discourse at the same time that they disarticulate the space.[45] In shots 26-27-28-29, for example, it is quite obvious that Ivan's looks (and his wrath) are directed at Efrosinia, whom, however, if the naturalistic dimension of the scene is taken as a point of reference, he does not look at—but whose look he crosses, from one frame to another, within the very surface of the frame. (To such an extent that the character at whom Ivan is supposed to be looking at that moment, i.e., the messenger from the front, is totally absent from these four frames!) The contradictory but perfectly clear result of this is that it is impossible to get one's bearings in the space represented, and impossible not to get one's bearings with respect to the meaning.

Here it would be necessary to look, one by one, at all the parameters of the figuration. For example, the gestures and movements of the actors, which are also marked by an essentially discrete, discontinuous quality, would have to be taken into account. There again, the meaning is articulated by shattering the "naturalistic effect" (and by causing suffering for the actors, from whom Eisenstein, who thought of them in essentially *visual* terms, demanded performances which have nothing in common with the "normal" behavior of the human body).[46] Or again one might look at the way the decor is handled, in particular the icons and the lamps. I will confine myself to calling attention briefly to two of these parameters, which, moreover, are related.

1. Mention has already been made of the systematic nature of the play of colors, in the insistent form here of the black/white contrast. Anastasia, dressed in and surrounded by white, contrasts not only with the "bad" Efrosinia, but also with Ivan and Malyuta (and Basmanov). This process of supersaturating black with meaning (variously predicated, in contrast with the single meaning assigned to white) ought to be examined throughout the film, as Jean-Pierre Oudart has shown. Black would be the attribute of the Assassin, the emblematic figure appearing throughout the film's network of meaning, placed now on one character, now on another (Efrosinia, Ivan, Pyotr Volynets). Thus the interesting thing is not so much to locate that contrast in the costumes of the characters in the sequence (which can be done quickly enough), but rather to read its calculated inscription *in the frame* (for example, we have a screen split up between black and white (16), black embedded in white (19), invasion of white by black (25), white embedded in black (32)), and especially *from one frame to another* (such as the collisions of Anastasia's whiteness and Efrosinia's blackness (39-40; 47-48)). This is a system of oppositions which should in turn be "opposed" to . . . its absence in the second passage of the sequence, since in it Basmanov too (as a metonymy for the *Oprichniki*) is clothed in black.

2. The lighting works first of all to reinforce and exploit this black/white opposition in the following ways. For example, the central position assigned to the bed and to its harsh lighting forms a hole of light in the midst of what, in the second passage, will appear more clearly than ever as a den, a lair, a recess (see C and V). Another equally important means by which this is accomplished is the penetration of the darkness surrounding the bed in various manners by a violent light, which is presented as coming "from the exterior" (the opening of the door through which Ivan arrives in shot 12, the light of which persists in shot 13; light coming from the other door, in shots 20, 29, B). But at the same time these lighting effects also accomplish their share of the work of signifying, among other things, by violently marking the faces (Malyuta's in 38, Ivan's in 42, Efrosinia's in 30, Basmanov's in F, for example). The remarkable thing here is once again the real duplicity required from the same element of figuration. The light coming "realistically" from sources whose position and nature

are suggested to the spectator, is also an "expressive" feature, one that is coded moreover (there is, for example, throughout the whole film, a systemic use of lighting that illuminates faces from below), and the two of them are *indissociable*. The ray of light which strikes and is etched on Malyuta's face (in order, as noted above, to project it into our vision "in close up"), is the light which entered with Ivan (12); and if, conversely, Anastasia's face is delicately sculpted (7, 39), that is because it is lighted in a diffuse way, by the little oil lamps arranged in a graceful curve above her.

One last feature should be mentioned, one which will bring out, rather emblematically, the salient feature of these lighting effects and of all the figuration. I am speaking of the very famous shadow which, in shot 9 and in shot 11, literally detaches itself from Ivan and accompanies, or rather, precedes and follows him, as though it had a life of its own, during the course of which, for example, it encounters the other shadow (that of the astrolabe). Like this shadow, all the figurative means are conceived, let us repeat, from the double perspective of analogy and signification. I find this shadow so "representative," because it manifests in the most obvious way imaginable the fact that Eisenstein thought of the question of figuration not so much in terms of painting, as has sometimes been said (that is not untrue, but it is somewhat restrictive), as in terms of line (lines of movement). Everything in the figuration is intended to contribute to materializing that ideal line, and all observers agree that he definitely seems to have had a perfectly clear vision of that line "in his mind."[47] (Whence for example, this statement: "Disney is lucky. If he needs a line, he makes it for himself, just the way he wants it" ["Lesson on Music and Color ... 1947," FW 1, p. 308].) Eisenstein's whole problem, in effect, is to "make" this "line" he needs—out of a material that is resistant to it.

4. The Montage

It is quite difficult to "segment" a film like *Ivan*. Or, perhaps it is too easy, since the film at first seems to be simply composed of very long sequences, linked to each other by simple fades to black. If, in an effort to confirm this first impression (the impression of a unity of narration), I refer to the triple criterion for the demarcation of autonomous segments in diegetical films, as established by Metz, and note that there is neither a major change in the course of the action nor a sign of punctuation in the first passage of what we are calling a "sequence," I am inclined to wonder whether there is or is not "a giving up of one syntagmatic type for another." And I am right back where I started from, with my difficulties of segmentation.

Let us look at the very beginning of our sequence. Could one not point out an alternation in it between the shots showing us Ivan at his desk and those which introduce Anastasia's "chamber"? (Shot 12, marking Ivan's arrival in the chamber, would then be a pivotal shot.) But that alternation is weak, indecisive. Ivan and Anastasia are in two different but contiguous places, as is clearly shown by the pseudo-match 1-2, and especially by Efrosinia's head movement in shot 10, emphasizing the fact that what is going on at Ivan's desk can be heard very clearly from the bedchamber[48] and already anticipating Ivan's entrance in shot 12). Furthermore, the alternation is very irregular. While the lengths of its successive terms are in no way too incommensurable, on the other hand, their structure makes it difficult to compare them. The three shots of Ivan are contrasted first with an extremely fragmented series of seven shots, in which the only movements are Anastasia's very slight head movements, then a single, brief (6-second) shot marked on the contrary by an abrupt and clearly visible head movement. Finally, in the second term of this alternation (shots 2 to 8), the nature (chronological or achronological? continuous or discontinuous?) of the succession of shots is not absolutely clear (this point will be examined again shortly).

Perhaps these "difficulties" are not really difficulties after all. (I mean, perhaps they are no more serious that those which are met with in any attempt to segment a film.) Yet, the very fact of the existence of quite a large number of doubtful points seemed to me to be a sign of the "distant" relationship which, speaking in very general terms, the narration maintains here with the classic narrative structure. We are dealing here with filmic units similar to traditional, classical forms. (It will likewise be noted that the passage from one shot to another is often effected in a mode which recalls "classicism.") At the same time, a whole series of disturbances are constantly modifying this classicism, playing on the points of articulation (from shot to shot and within the shots), and therefore on the editing.

Let us look again at the little sub-unit constituted by shots 2 to 8. It is a little narrative unit, introducing four principal diegetic elements: the two characters, the architecture of the room, and some props (icons, lamps, bed). The last shot in particular (shot 8) gathers these four elements together more or less (although it gives only a fragmentary notion of the architecture), marking a kind of provisional conclusion, of stasis. Nothing, so far, that is not strictly classical. Now, what *else* happens in the preceding shots? The first characteristic of the whole is obviously its fragmentation, the way it is broken up into pieces. One by one, two by two, the diegetic elements in question are presented to us in discrete fashion (shot 2: the icon alone; shot 7: Anastasia alone; shot 5: Efrosinia alone, etc.); the space, presented as a unified zone through the insistent plastic and referential reminders from shot to shot as well as by the way its characterization is accomplished in shot 8, is nevertheless, actually broken by this series of frames, a kind of "close-up effect" coming here again to underscore the fact that each term is to be taken not only as a constitutive element in the reproduction of an imaginary continuity (the scene's), but also a moment (not necessarily a "unit") in a more properly discursive rendering of the filmic chain, one that is, if you will, more written, more textual.

What I am describing here is well known. Let us take a very famous example, the opening sequence of *October*, particularly the first nine shots. Little by little, by means of a series of backward movements of the camera, by means of the accumulation of a more and more complete series of pieces of figurative information, the statue of Alexander III acquires a fictional existence (it becomes an object simultaneously identifiable in terms of volume thanks to the effects of reality, of referent); and at the same time, the insistence of the fragmentation, producing the crown, the scepter, the orb, the eagles, the czar's name before us in a hyperarticulated way, functions as a kind of written discourse (which in this particular case would come to represent something like a literal interpretation of the metaphor, "the czarist power was overturned in February 1917"). (This very typical example of Eisenstein's style has been analyzed in detail by Ropars and Sorlin.[49]) What strikes me is, of course, the similarity of the competition between the "diegetic" and the "emblematic" in the opening shots of *October* and in shots 2-8 of our sequence. Our shot 8, for example, which functions therefore as a summing up of the previous shots, and plays retroactively upon them by unifying them, is inversely affected by the breaking up or fragmentation which affects the previous shots, so that to a very large extent it can only be read as fragmented, "built up" out of all the elements it gathers together.

(This is all the more true in that this spatial "disturbance" is completed by a temporal disturbance. With the exception of a match on Anastasia's head movement between 6 and 7, there is nothing anywhere in that passage that clearly and unquestionably marks any kind of chronological order whatsoever. The brief and immobile shot 5 on

Efrosinia's face, for example, can very well be taken as a spatio-temporal "excerpt" from shot 6, or it could be "contemporaneous" with shot 5; there are even stronger grounds for treating shots 2 and 3 the same way, etc. In short, there is nothing to hinder us from thinking that we are dealing here with a passage of a hybrid nature, in which the *sequential* cannot be distinguished from the *descriptive*, to use again the Metzian terminology.)

No doubt this description could be improved upon. The important thing is the quasi-omnipresence in the film of this kind of operation in relation to the scene and working in part against it. For a long time it was felt that by comparison with his work in silent films, Eisenstein's sound films marked a regression, insofar as their use of editing was concerned. As a result of the acquisition of a better knowledge of Eisenstein's writings, this point of view has been revised. It is now felt that the sound films do not mark a decline of montage, but mark the appearance of new modalities. To go even further, editing does not fall into disgrace in Eisenstein's sound films; on the contrary, it is generalized and extended in those films. The dissemination of the "principle" of montage (at every level, at every articulation, every parameter) which defined "harmonic montage" in 1929 can also be found in *Ivan*, except that instead of simply denying the theatrical representation, it integrates it. From this point of view, the consideration of the dimension of sound (i.e., of a material that has to do with *time* more directly than the image does) is obviously fundamental to the "contrapuntal" montage of *Ivan*.

We shall return to this matter of the sound in a moment. But beforehand, it will be useful to describe once again the functioning and the effects of the editing, from shot to shot, and within the shots themselves. As is shown by a simple description of it, the sequence being analyzed contains a substantial number of matches (even if we limit our remarks to the "movement matches" alone, since, as we have seen, the status of the eye-line matches participates in general in this passage, in the treatment of the film as text and belongs to the order of the nonrealistic). Naturally, this notion of the "match" appears a priori rather incongruous. Is that not the very term that has been used and is still used to designate the (practical and theoretical) gesture whose purpose is to provide for the passage from one shot to another in the very act of denying that passage—the whole effect of "transparency" which the Eisenstein of the silent films so much abhorred? Indeed.

Let us take shots 21 to 26, for example. Each of them is linked to the following one by a "match." In every case, there is a movement match—and, what is more, half of them are axis matches (21-22/23-24/24-25). The narrative and representational continuity is therefore, at that moment, maximum. There is no temporal break, no ellipsis— a single flow, simply punctuated by cuts. Now, what actually happens in this passage?

First of all, it must be emphasized that the cuts are not the only elements in the articulation of the discourse. In shot 21, for example, we have the arrival of the messenger, Ivan's rapid movement towards the parapet, the gesture he makes to put the message down for a moment on that same parapet, and then, turning around, to read it by the light of the icon lamps. There are so many elementary events, almost separable, in any case clearly marked (and, let there be no doubt about it, each one of which could certainly be justified in terms of the meaning. It is very easy to imagine Eisenstein explaining to his students the why's and wherefore's of each gesture).

Next it should be noted that while they very obviously provide a link between two successive shots, the matches also underscore all the more emphatically the *calculated* nature of the changes of point of view, as the first example will demonstrate. At the beginning of shot 22, we "move closer" to Ivan just as he has turned toward the light in order to read. Now, this notable change of the point of view from which we see Ivan's face (it more than doubles in size from one shot to the next) is accompanied by practically no change with respect to Anastasia, due to the use of a very wide-angle lens (a "distorting" lens, which does not reproduce the movement of drawing closer on the same scale for the foreground and the backgound). Thus the cut, while dramatically pointless, is indispensable in a logic of the film-as-text, since it articulates a change in the relationships (figurative, representational relationships, and thus, in Eisenstein's work, hierarchical and semantic relationships) between the characters. Because of the match, the cut is of very little importance strictly at the level of the narration, and thus it becomes available for a function of an expressive order (or, rather, a writing order). Thanks to the match, the cut is not reabsorbed in a cumulative scene, on the contrary, it is articulated from it to a greater degree (used or conceived of as a signifier).

Again, I feel that in dealing with this subject of the "match," one must emphasize the competition of the two aspects of the dual, i.e., scenic and writing, principle in the filmic text, and to note that each element in the discourse has its origins in *both* of them. Concerning the matches, in particular, numerous Eisensteinian studies have demonstrated their very special nature in *Ivan*. But often they are viewed as being no more than a sort of trademark, the signature of an author who in the last analysis is very formalist. Now, while it is useful to note the *plastic* function of these matches (a preoccupation certainly not absent in Eisenstein, in the very precise form of the search for singular correlations from parameter to parameter), as Noel Burch does, for example, it is plainly wrong to consider them as reduced to that function, and, for example, as "mis-matches." (There could obviously be no "mis-matches" in *Ivan*, since there are no matches in the normal sense of that term.)

In this double movement which tends, on the one hand, to produce montage events within shots, and on the other hand, to use the match as a signifying trope, what interests me is therefore rather what can be perceived of the omnipresence of a principle of montage which is no longer practiced solely in the mode of conflict, but includes all sorts of contrasts, shocks, rhythms— what Eisenstein calls "accents"— by which he means:

> to capture the spectator's attention and perception in a new way, by interrupting the inertia of the unfolding of the sequence. . . . (*Nonindifferent Nature*, FW 4, 267)

It is the same principle which can be observed in other figures, in other parameters. To give another extremely simple example of this, let us look at shots E to M. They present themselves as a regulated alternation between close-up shots of Ivan's face and shots of the two goblets (+ Basmanov's face), according to the classic "seeing/seen" technique. As everyone knows, that is one of the devices most frequently used by the classic cinema in order to reinforce the imaginary existence of its characters and reciprocally to condition their credibility.[50] In addition, the last frame of every shot of Ivan connects up very exactly with the first frame of the following one (G with I/I with K . . .), with the exception of E/G, between which there is a little axis match. Once again, then, the number of seams in the textual fabric is maximized. And, once again, against the background of those seams, there is the incessant presence of a process of rupturing, of accentuation, here very simple and systematic: the use of the close-up for the goblets and for Basmanov, Ivan's 180-degree head movement in each of his shots.

If we turn back now to the short passage composed of shots 2 to 8 briefly described above, it can be seen that what was identified in it as fragmentation and summation would actually be none other than one of the possible modalities of this process of accentuation. There would be, in particular, at each passage from one shot to another, one or several elementary "correlations" which would produce a perpetual movement of the accent. In the movement from the icon shown in close-up (in the abstract, so to speak) in shot 2, to the same subject in shot 3, shown this time in a real decor by the gently swaying light of the lamps, the value of these icons as diegetic objects is accentuated. But from 3 to 4, with the appearance of Anastasia on her deathbed, the passage, effected among other ways by the repetition of the theme of the lamps, produces one of the possible metaphors of the character of Anastasia (in this sequence and in the entire film), that of the Virgin, or the Saint. From 4 to 5, moreover, the mode of passage remains analogous, in order to produce a more complete reversal of the accent—absolute contrast between Anastasia's face and Efrosinia's, etc. What becomes clear here is therefore the perpetual movement of the accent. Little by little, against the background of that movement, a stable configuration takes shape—Anastasia, the Holy Virgin, in her death agony, over whom a vigil is kept (funereal connotation of the oil lamps) by a bird of prey, Efrosinia.[51]

Naturally, other, similar sections could be selected from the sequence (in theory, every section of it) and the same relationship could be shown in them between the scenic reference and its framing (*mise-en-cadre*), the same interaction of the principle of montage and of accent—practically speaking everything that defines what Eisenstein at that time designated as "vertical" montage, and which I would rather term "organic" (for reasons which will become clear shortly). I therefore want to emphasize once again how this organic montage is defined among other things by the fact that the framing and editing effects are pregnant with metaphor. This film, which has so often been viewed either as a pure and simple return to naturalism, to dramaticity, to professional actors, to the anecdote, or as the debauch of an admittedly refined but gratuitous estheticism, or even as a "socialist realist" film(!), this film remains, in actual fact, the privileged locus of the application of the reflections on montage that took place during the years 1935–40 (in particular, the emphasis on the production of metaphors through the concept of the "global image").

This conception of montage will be examined again more specifically later. But it would be a grave omission not to evoke here, if only briefly, the music, and in a more general way, the sound track (the "audio-visual counterpoint"). I shall take only a single passage, the one in our sequence that has the greatest demonstrative value, i.e., shots 29 to 50. The music, almost constantly present, uses two themes in this passage:[52] the "betrayal" theme, written with rather staccato chords played on the strings, and the "death" theme, a kind of rapid chromatic descent executed by the solo violin. What strikes the attention first of all is the discontinuity of the sounds, the brutality of the entrances of the different sounds.[53] In shots 30-31, for example, the following elements intervene in succession, and each time at the cost of a direct cut in the sound track (facilitated by the distinct character of the betrayal theme):

> Efrosinia's phrase: "Ivan, you're going too far!";
> the musical theme (betrayal);
> the sound of the drops falling from the phial of poison into the goblet;
> once again the musical theme;
> finally, Malyuta's voice (off-screen).

This discontinuity is obviously to be read in relation to the editing. Efrosinia's phrase, synchronized with the image, and the beginning of Malyuta's phrase (off-screen, but connecting immediately with shot 42, where he is on-screen) contribute to a coincidence of image and sound which is in violent contradiction with the artificiality and the excessive asynchronicism of the sound of the drops (very amplified, "musicalized," this sound belongs more to the music track than to the sound-effects track). And, intertwined with these three elements, the musical theme scans the whole passage, or more precisely, it has the effect of putting the whole of the sound track, music, sound effects, and words, entirely in a relation of scansion with the image. When this effect reaches its most extreme development, nothing appears "real" any longer, not even Efrosinia's phrase (there is no longer anything that is only analogical). Each element, the sound as well as the visual, is here again presented as discrete—image and sound, one with the other, one on the other, one against the other, deliver a global signified (betrayal) of which each partial actualization (the musical theme, of course, but also the invasion of the surface of the frame by the black of Efrosinia's robe, and including the troubling strangeness of the sound of the drops) is already a micro-metaphor. (Very logically, the notion of the "global image" reappears here in the form of a single *theme*, which circulates from element to element, from actor to actor, each time bringing into play a different *material*, a different figurative principle, a new type of metaphor, etc.)

The end of the sequence, right up to and including the death of Anastasia, rearticulates these partial "figurations" while combining them differently, by introducing another theme (another "image"), that of death, or rather, of deadly love (Anastasia's love for Kurbsky, Ivan's love for Anastasia). The musical theme of betrayal, first of all applied to Efrosinia, will be applied to Kurbsky (31-33; although Kurbsky is not physically represented, he is nonetheless present in the scene, by virtue of the mention of his name and what that leads to); then it will be heard in the sound track as the fatal misunderstanding occurs (41-49). As for the musical theme of "death," it intervenes on two occasions: first in the shots 38-39, where it accompanies, logically, the already cadaverous face of Anastasia ("dead" as a result of having evoked Kurbsky—treason *and* love, both deadly) and also, more subtly, the immobile face of Malyuta (who thus perhaps does not fail to share at least in the symbolic guilt of all the participants in the action). The death theme next occurs towards the middle of shot 49, where it brutally replaces the theme of betrayal, logically with respect to the plot, and accompanies the fade to black which permits the passage to shot 50.

This is all still rather summary. (To complete things, at the very least it would be necessary to establish a record of the musical entrances in the second passage of our sequence.) Enough has been said, however, to allow us to posit the principle of this "counterpoint" and, above all, the effect it has of putting *all* the signifying elements, every one of them (image, sound, and every possible parameter in each of them), on absolutely the same level, so that they are equally and simultaneously used to produce both music (rhythm) and meaning.[55]

5. The Hermeneutic Code

At first glance, it would seem that nothing could be clearer than the event narrated here—the poisoning of Anastasia. This murder, committed by Efrosinia in the name of the Boyars is part of the desperate struggle between them and Ivan and his followers. (And, from this point of view, the decapitated heads of the Kolychevs will be one of Ivan's answers.) It is an attempt to punish Ivan for his presumptuousness and to weaken him by eliminating his sole moral and emotional support. These political determinations are amply exposed and commented upon, particularly in the funeral sequence (which, as we have already pointed out, Eisenstein viewed as the key sequence of the entire film, ideologically speaking).

Yet, if we look at it more closely, nothing could be less clear. In his text on *Ivan*, Jean-Pierre Oudart has described at length the unbelievable stage business by means of which, on one hand, Efrosinia sends her son to his death and, on the other, Ivan kills his wife. Let us recall the essential features of this description. The crime is committed by a proxy (Ivan), who does not know that he is killing. The murder weapon (the goblet) circulates throughout the film, from the marriage to the murder of Anastasia, and then at the orgy (in the song) and in Efrosinia's quarters, where it is not recognized by her. Finally, the murder takes place at the moment when "no one is looking at anyone else and when even Malyuta, the eye of the czar, is unawares.[54] I shall eventually have to make this description more specific (and even rectify it a bit), but it covers essentially what one experiences upon reading the still photo record of the sequence. We see how boldly and confidently Eisenstein on the one hand draws the path followed by the goblet (Efrosinia brings it out of nowhere between shots 30 and 31; it is then concealed beneath her robe, in 34 and 40; then it is placed on the parapet in 41, where Ivan picks it up to carry it to Anastasia), and on the other hand simultaneously inscribes that path in an interplay of literally absent looks (Ivan looking at the empty goblet, 35-36; Malyuta stubbornly motionless, and especially the series 41-42-43, where the goblet is seen in isolation, where Ivan turns his head to see it, then does not see Efrosinia, with whom he shares shot 43). The spectator is thus informed as to the *how* of the murder, since he or she sees Ivan and Malyuta not seeing and also sees the murder weapon in all its movements from place to place.

But this information is offered, constituted, only to be called immediately into question, contradicted, or at least complicated, by a whole filmic process. First of all, *who* is the murderer? Efrosinia, certainly, since after all she is the one who pours the poison into the goblet; but it is also Ivan, who causes that poison to be drunk (see, in shot 49, the heavy emphasis on his hand holding the goblet, very unrealistically, throughout the entire ingestion of the liquid, finally occupying the entire frame and very metaphorically occulting Anastasia's face). His complicity with Efrosinia is abundantly manifested— in shot 43, already mentioned, the moment when the death is decided, and in which the two of them share the shot; but it is also shown in shot 13, where Ivan has manifested his affection for (his complicity with) his aunt by an arm placed around her shoulder; and finally, retrospectively, in one of the most beautiful shots in the entire sequence, shot S, when, pressed by Basmanov (literally pressed—the frame squeezes them together), Ivan will admit that *he knew*: it was Efrosinia.

The next question is, *why* does Anastasia die? She dies first of all, of course, for the "political" reasons already touched upon. But also, as has already been mentioned, because of Kurbsky. In shot 39, it is the evocation of his betrayal (which has a double meaning, both military and erotic) which transforms her into a cadaver. As to her wide-eyed, fixed gaze in shot 49, it can, of course, be read "dramatically" (she was noticing Efrosinia, who in shot 48 had just stolen a glance over the parapet) and "psychologically" (she senses that she is going to die). But, it can be read symbolically as well (by connecting it to the horror with which her murderer, Ivan, fills her, or to her love for Kurbsky). And if Ivan kills her, it is precisely because she loves Kurbsky (and from this point of view, at the funeral Basmanov would replace not only Kurbsky, but also Anastasia, that is, *at the same time*, both the friend and the beloved). In any case, it is easy to see how much this murder, like the entire plot of the film, is overdetermined symbolically by the erotic setting (in which, as Oudart has shown, the murder of the Father and the Oedipal conflict are reenacted).[56]

It can also be seen (and here is what is most important to me) how the scenario (that is, loosely speaking, the scenic representation) is actually *contradicted* by the film (by the filmic representation). It would be interesting to confirm this by analyzing the way micro-enigmas, some of them quite elementary, are disseminated in the text alongside the major enigma of the plot. With no pretensions to being exhaustive here are a few examples:

1. Without warning, the icon in shot 2 suddenly appears placed in relationship with the shot of Ivan at his desk—in such a way that the viewer can imagine that Ivan is looking at it, until, shortly after (shot 8), it is seen to be a part of the decor in Anastasia's chamber.

2. Likewise, in shot 5, Efrosinia appears in close-up—it is a brief shot, there is no time to wonder about her presence before the answer is given (shot 6: she is watching Anastasia).

3. And the same process can be seen in Basmanov's presence on Ivan's heels, in shots C and D, and then his sudden appearance (also in close-up in shot F); this time the film explains nothing, or, in any case, makes nothing explicit (differing in this respect from the scenario[57]—but no doubt, in the last analysis, it is clearer this way—the diegetic explanation has disappeared and only the symbolic value of this presence remains).

Other examples could be given (where does Malyuta come from? we are not told, etc.) The important thing, it seems to me, is to show how systematic this is. It is as though, by contagion from the central enigma(s) of the plot, that of the murder, everything has become potentially enigmatic. And above all, it is important to note that here again the film avoids the classic narrative structure. The eponymous figure of the enigma in the classic narrative structure is indeed *suspense*, i.e., a narrative system in which the enigma is produced only as a narrative reserve which activates a "surplus of narration" by deferring as long as possible a *solution* (let us take that word literally, it is the moment when things are resolved or dissolved) towards which everything is imaginarily oriented. It would be appropriate to recall, along with Brecht, that in the *dramatic* system (the one to which Brecht opposed the epic system) the moment of solution is the one which takes priority in arousing the spectator's interest, and that consequently, for the spectator, suspense is only expectation (delightful or dreadful).

There can be no doubt that Eisenstein had not the slightest interest in making us wait for a solution. Not that he did not occasionally have recourse to a form of *suspension* of the narrative. We need only recall the way time is stopped in *Potemkin*, when the sailors are about to be shot. But never in his work does this suspension imply a fleeing forward; he never aims at displacing the spectator's fantasmatic investment towards a moment that is always to come. If he "suspends" time, it is, quite the contrary, in order to *fix* that psychic investment, to increase it *momentarily* and *instantly*. Expectation is not a factor in the Eisensteinian calculation. On the contrary, the spectator is meant to know everything as soon as possible, as quickly as possible, that is even the prerequisite for every possible efficacy in his system. (That, if you will, would be the "epic" side of Eisenstein, as Annette Michelson so aptly puts it.)

From its overall thematic level right down to its smallest detail, this sequence's "atmosphere" of enigma is therefore neither conceived of nor produced in the classic mode of frustration. It is readable—like every partial system in the film—only as a supplement of meaning and of writing.

The *thematic* function: *Ivan*, in its manifest text and in a good deal of what can be read there in the latent state, is a film about conspiracy; more broadly speaking, it is a *game* played for power (to be metaphorized into a game of chess, as Eisenstein did, or into a game of cards or a lottery, as Oudart does). Blows are dealt in response to blows, according to a sequence that is logical, but which is also at least partially mysterious and even random.

The *referential* function: The presence of Efrosinia, of Basmanov, the "absences" of Malyuta, because they are partially arbitrary, could be attributed to a certain effect of verisimilitude. It is shown to us this way, because that's the way it happened. ("It," i.e., the referent, and this time the story's referent, History—let us not forget, after all, that the project of the film is among other things to write, or rewrite, History.) I am perhaps making Eisenstein out to be more sly than he actually was, but it does not seem entirely improbable to me, given what various witnesses have reported about his conception of historical truth.[58]

Last but not least, there is the *writing* or *film-as-text* function. What is produced through this "hermeneutic" emphasis is a masterful discourse that is quite unique. Instead of adopting the procedure of the classic cinema and playing the card of the spectator's "supposed knowledge" (Daney),[59] here it is the filmmaker who grants the spectator *all the knowledge needed*: the spectator will learn everything *from within the film itself*: all the truth the filmmaker has set forth for him, but only that truth. Eisenstein is the one who knows—who knows how, why, who (who kills Anastasia, for example), but he also knows how, when, and at what pace to make it known to the spectator. He is *one step* ahead of the spectator, just far enough to ensure that he is calling the shots.

6. The Other Scene

We know how the principle of *character typing*, or *typage*, functions in Eisenstein's work. It is a translation, in terms of *physical appearance*, of moral qualities and/or of a social and political position. This principle, which is essential to the Eisensteinian system (and, moreover in its presuppositions very closely related to the concept of the "global image") is used here, it would seem, in a quite different way—not from the point of view of a principle of operation, but with respect to the effects it produces.

Let us look again at shots 2 to 8. As we have seen, a global image is constituted there of Anastasia as Virgin or Saint, while, by means of certain more or less discrete elements (the black/white paradigm which shapes the whole sequence, but also isolated gestures, such as Ivan's in shot 13), a global image of Efrosinia is produced, representing her as a surrogate and evil mother of the czar. She is moreover the mother of a pseudo-czar, half-witted and symbolically castrated. In a word, she is the *bad mother*. Opposite her is Anastasia, the *good mother*, the chaste mother of the legitimate heir.

Beyond its thematic value, the black/white paradigmatic system and everything accompanying it functions therefore as a kind of character typing. In a special actualization of the principle of character typing through clothing, facial features, gestures, an (obviously connotative) signified would be constituted, which would not be a social definition, nor even, properly speaking, a moral one, of the actors, but their *symbolic* definition. This process might be called *symbolic typage*.

It is important to emphasize that this is a mode of *typage* radically different from those previously used by Eisenstein. The Mensheviks of *October* are typed as Mensheviks, i.e., as occupants of a given place on the political chess board who have a given class allegiance. It is only subsequently and by means of a secondary process of connotation (character typing itself always being a kind of connotation) that this first signified can be applied to moral judgments (their sermonizing manners are *ignoble*, they are *spineless*, etc.). What is articulated in *Ivan* is of an entirely different nature. What can be read through images such as those as we have described is neither the social position of the characters, nor a simple moral judgment about them, nor even about their political position—but something much more archetypal, which is superimposed on all these other meanings.

Another example of this symbolic *typage* will show us how it manages to sidestep the issue of class determinations to a certain degree. I am speaking here of what could be designated as the mask of femininity. It is well known that that mask circulates in *Ivan*, as the sequence in color reminds us very literally.[60] In the sequence we are studying, the position of the Woman is occupied first of all by Anastasia, and then, as has already been pointed out, by the young Basmanov; it is no longer the diegetic and thematic substitution of the latter for the former that concerns me here; rather, I want to examine what it is about *the very appearance* of Basmanov that typifies him as feminine (as temporarily wearing the mask of the Woman, for like the explicit themes of the plot, the symbolic masks circulate from one character to another). There is the soft waviness of his hair, contrasted as much with Ivan's straight hair as with Malyuta's hirsute curls; his smooth, soft, clean-shaven or perhaps even beardless face; his frightened rabbit's eyes, when Ivan places his hand upon his mouth (shot U); that mouth itself, sensual, always open (without being over made-up like Vladimir Staritsky's, which is a caricature of femininity), etc. Basmanov's class origins, while not denied or expelled, are however, transformed by this symbolic *typage*. He is *plebeian*, and it is on the basis of this class allegiance, both vague (with respect to the Marxist analysis of social groupings) and specific (the plebe is defined as the lowest term in a certain topology)[61] that his representation as a feminine figure is brought into play.

This "symbolic *typage*" (never conceived of in such terms by Eisenstein, apparently, but which he would have without any doubt claimed as his own), is therefore a double perversion of "true" typing. This is so, first of all, because it produces its figures in a transhistorical field which is properly speaking that of the symbol, and, second, because instead of fully and durably characterizing such and such a figure (as is the case with the Mensheviks in *October* and of the *kulak* in *The General Line*), it is precarious. Basmanov is not reduced to his femininity, any more than Anastasia is reduced to her figure of the Good Mother (even though those features of her character which escape or go beyond that figure were not necessarily intended by Eisenstein, notably her love for Kurbsky).

Finally, on the scale of the film as a whole, it is one of the principal vectors of a process of overdetermination of the manifest scene (that of politics—maneuverings of strategies around power) by the other scene, the one in which the repressed erotic content is at work. This is particularly notable in the second passage of our sequence, where the treatment of the two characters insistently wraps a heavy veil of ambiguity around their relationship. This is true of all the convulsive, violent embraces which draw them together (N, M, T, U) and which the text contrasts with the gentle way Ivan placed his head upon Anastasia's conjugal breast (15, 18) or held her head up after her fainting spell (33, 35). It is the same with the two close-ups of the joined faces of Ivan and Basmanov (O, S), where everything, from the way they fully fill the frame to the amazed eye-rolling of the two figures, is excess of figuration and in which the representation, at times, becomes plainly that of a coupling (compare with the close-ups on Ivan and his wife, 16, 24, these, too, very chastely conjugal).

(Naturally, the symptoms of this erotic scene go well beyond the sole effects of symbolic *typage* alone. On this point, Oudart's analysis is again pertinent, when he notes the ambiguity between suffering and ecstasy, love and death throughout the entire poisoning scene.) Going further here would lead us into a detailed reading of the film, which is not my intention. It would doubtless also lead us to wonder again about the relationship between such a discourse ("the incredible familial cuddling")[62] and the Eisensteinian biography. In that direction, however, lie traps which we shall once again avoid.

On the other hand, I will lay emphasis one last time on the way this "second" (or rather, "third") discourse[63] reproduces (I mean, of course, produces once again) the disseminated, systematic, complete writing which Eisenstein intended, and which he developed so well, in theory and in practice, in the production of his manifest discourse.

Montage in Question

4

I. A Controversial Concept

We come finally to the concept of *montage*. First, it should be borne in mind how typically Eisensteinian it is. Critics and biographers are all agreed on this one point: Eisenstein equals montage. It is impossible to cite them all here, for the literature on Eisenstein is much too profuse. To take the two extremes, however, there are, on the one hand, those for whom Eisensteinian montage earns the highest praise: Amengual, for example, suggests that in *Potemkin* the use of montage "puts ideas into motion," that it "shapes the poetic form," "generates power" and "suspense," and "produces a sense of communion," etc., in short, that montage does everything. By contrast, we have Mitry, who is profoundly opposed to Eisenstein's definition of montage, although he accepts the principle as the source of all the signifying effects (and also most of the errors!) in his films. (This is not to mention the fixed adversaries, like Bazin, who prefer simply to identify Eisenstein with montage so that they can "proscribe" montage, without properly examining his theories.)

It should also be said that Eisenstein himself was unequivocal on this point (and here again there are countless references on record): montage is "the essence of cinema" ("Montage of Cine-Attractions,"

1925), and in case we missed the point: "The *essence* of cinema does not lie in the images, but in the relation between the images!" ("Béla Forgets the Scissors," 1926, FW 1, p. 162, my italics). Eisenstein, then, is the person for whom cinema *is* montage.

"The" concept of montage. Everything I have said until now implies and leads up to this sense of homogeneity: a history of the emergence of this concept in the films *and* at the core of the theoretical work. Such a history, of one single concept, traced out in successive theories, would probably be called "The Development of Eisenstein's Concept of Montage."

On this, however, we will have to have a more modest goal. If such theoretical accounts of montage, along with other general principles to which he constantly refers, can be "abstracted" incontestably from Eisenstein's work (and we have seen the difficulties involved in such abstraction), then the problems arise in recognizing that these theoretical accounts are neither rationalizations, however incomplete, of empirical givens and cumulative practices of filmmaking, nor are they simple, formal variations of any one, basic conceptual model—but that from one version of the theory to another, a project is being worked through, a theoretical space is being marked out. Or to put it another way, what is at stake in Eisenstein's work is not the elaboration of *methods* of montage, nor the formulation of one single concept of montage, but a kind of ongoing and even somewhat systematic study of the principle of montage (or the phenomenon of montage). This last statement will probably seem too vague: in any case, the whole of this last chapter is devoted to developing and clarifying it. Even in this discreet form, it nonetheless suggests ways of circumventing certain images of Eisenstein which are still quite current:

—although almost entirely obsolete, there is still the image that exalts the artist at the expense of the theorist (one can hardly believe that Umberto Barbaro's opinion of thirty years ago is still tenable today—"as an artist, Eisenstein is substantial; as a theorist, he is nonexistent *quia talis*");

—the equally controversial image of his work that retains only the rather unfortunate metaphor of "cine-language";

—and lastly, the most widely prevalent idea (even a "received" idea), that there is no *one* Eisenstein the theorist, but rather two (or three), and that the later Eisenstein contradicts and renounces the early Eisenstein.

These latter two together reproduce—and for this reason they will have to undergo closer scrutiny—the quantitative and the qualitative essence of the criticisms that have been made of Eisenstein's theoretical accounts of montage. To begin with, these accounts would be much too diverse for us to be able to really speak about a "concept" of montage, rationally worked out and scientifically defined; instead of this conceptual labor, there are only a series of more or less coherent attempts to present some thoughts about cinema in a certain kind of discourse, whether scientific or ideological. Are we not therefore dealing with something that is misconceived in every way, with a fundamental overestimation of the possibilities inherent in this notion of montage? Was Bazin, in his blindness, perhaps not correct to believe that Eisenstein was forgetting that cinema cannot escape so easily from *re*production?

1. An Overestimated Principle?

"Intellectual cinema," "intellectual montage," and "intellectual attraction" are all terms which Eisenstein introduces, at first in a rather interchangeable way, as a sort of terminal point for his theory and practice of silent cinema. Indeed, they very quickly become his theoretical sore point, attracting all the criticisms and misunderstandings (particularly over the word, "intellectual") that followed.

It seems to me that it all began with Balázs (at least among serious critics). We know that Eisenstein and Balázs—who otherwise enjoyed rather cordial relations—disagreed very early on over the montage question: in 1926, in "Béla Forgets the Scissors," Eisenstein scolds Balázs for overestimating the importance of the image at the expense of montage, in his eyes, a much more central function of film language (we can assume that the rebuke hit home, for in *Der Geist des Films*, four years later, the chapter on montage begins with a section entitled "The Inventive Scissors"). But in that same book, this is how Balázs presents the idea of "intellectual montage," although he does not refer to it by name:

> A group of young Russian directors have consciously taken up a particular "tendency" which eschews all wit and poetic quality in the interest of communicating ideas and information. These directors seek to achieve their ends by means of montage. . . . But not all ideas can be transposed into the stimuli of associations, and it is because of this that cinema will always remain an "art," and will never be reduced simply to the animated representation of ideograms and tables of statistics. More often than not, the Russians fall into the obvious trap of film-hieroglyphics. . . . Images ought not to *signify* ideas, but rather to *construct and motivate them*, the ideas then being generated as logical con-

The time-image

sequences and not as symbols or ideograms that have already been articulated in the image. Otherwise, montage no longer works, and becomes instead the reproduction of riddles and rebuses. It is not that the images of the filmic subject are rendered symbolic. On the contrary, what is involved are images that are already symbolic. We are invited to view ideograms and essays in hieroglyphics. The cinematographic forms of this genre would drag cinema back to the most primitive level of the written sign. Our system of writing, for all that, is more practical. (pp. 163–64)

The length of this extract is justified if only because it seems to me to anticipate, literally and exhaustively, much of what is at stake in this debate. We can, I think, distinguish two basic issues:

1. The celebrated concept of "cine-language," or more specifically, the so-called "filmic writing" which comes out of the encounter between cinema and *ideographic* writing (what Balázs, after Eisenstein, designated as *hieroglyphics*), or rather, as Metz puts it, "between the cinematic language system (*langage*) and the ideographic principle itself" (*Language and Cinema*, p. 275).

For many years, this was a burning issue. Scores of critics and theorists worked and reworked the idea of an incompatibility between the nature of cinema as a demonstrative art, aimed at the direct figuration of reality, and the expressive power of concepts, abstract ideas, linguistic events, and the "hieroglyphic theses" of Balázs, all of which are aimed at a "direct filmic expression of abstract ideas."[1] It was imperative, for example, to prove that "with the image, you can show a horse, a bull, a frog, a rhinoceros, but not the concept of animal" (Lebedev),[2] or, more generally, that it was impossible to take literally such concepts as "cine-language," "cine-sentence," "cine-grammar," etc. Even though this is no longer so hotly debated, since no one believes anymore that one could *show* the concept of animal, the majority still assume that one can *filmically evoke or produce* the sense of a universal (which is not, of course, the same as providing its general filmic correlative). A good example, to stay with "hieroglyphics," would be the chapter of *Language and Cinema* in which Metz describes not only the limits of the comparison between film and ideographic writing, but also the fundamentally natural and obvious side of such a comparison, or, at any rate, of the kind of "ideographic inspiration" claimed by filmmakers like Eisenstein.

Take for example (picked randomly from the list of instances of what Eisenstein called intellectual montage) the scene in which the *izba* (hut) is sawn in half in *The General Line*. Without criticizing it directly, Balázs includes it as an example of reproducing an ideogram, or, at least, a linguistic event (since he sees it as a clear-cut transfer of meaning, as a verbal metaphor: "breaking a heart"), a practice which for him is essentially alien to the cinematographic art. From completely the opposite standpoint, Amengual reaches the same conclusion:

> the *izba* is really a pictogram, shot through with the dynamism of the ideogram. . . . The subsequent discourse, attacking the idea of private property, is achieved through a series of equally ideographic variations. . . . What the shots reproduce is no longer an image of reality, but something that is already conceptual. This is the unmistakable mark of the ideographic. ("Eisenstein and Hieroglyphs")

Metz takes the same example and formulates it as a kind of equation ("saw" + "face" = "consternation") which, he says, "suggests an ideographic touch." (Of these three critics, moreover, he is the only one who acknowledges that the sequence in question not only has a symbolic or metaphorical value, but also refers to a fictional scene, a clearly marked level of dramatic action. Eisenstein himself always insists on this level, rejecting Balázs's simple allegorical reading.[3]

2. Eisenstein's equally celebrated use of "symbols." On this point, no one has gone further than Mitry in his critique of the montage of attractions (a critique, which, in the case of *October*, is directed instead at intellectual montage—under the circumstances, there is not much difference): "such an operation [the montage of "attractions"] is only valuable inasmuch as it uses lifelike elements (in the dramatic sense of the term) from which it draws its emotional power at the same time as its concrete symbolic meaning. Its value depreciates when it uses *arbitrarily chosen* symbols *applied* to, rather than *implied* by, the real" (*S. M. Eisenstein*, p. 46). In sum, what Mitry values most is "the linear development of the narrative" which one "treats" with "dramatic or psychological" meaning; other "abstract or symbolic" meanings are brought into play as a *supplement*,[4] and need not contradict the narrative element. Reality should not be "betrayed," nor are we justified in "interpreting" or "taking advantage" of it. Since Eisenstein pays precious little attention to the rules of the "lifelike," the "concrete," or the "implied," his crimes are almost complete, and Mitry scarcely has time, particularly with *October* and *Strike*, to deal with all the ways in which they deviate from his norms; there are whole pages in which he "invalidates" most of the metaphors in *October*, positing against their "bad" montage of attractions, a "good" *reflex montage*, by which he means a montage that "uses only those symbols determined by the

content. In other words, a montage of significant *facts maintained and understood* within the limits of the unfolding logic of the narrative action" (p. 59). Mitry's point of view (reaffirmed in *Esthétique et psychologie du cinéma*) presents the rough caricature of an image of "intellectual cinema" that is still widely accepted today: a kind of monstrous theoretical chimera (for a long time, the plan to film *Capital* was regarded as sheer folly), aimed at making cinema into a clumsy imitation of "archaic" forms of writing, and each film into a rebus, or a Chinese puzzle.

I have described these critiques (directed primarily, one suspects, at the Eisenstein of 1929) in a very summary way in order to be able to show how Eisenstein, indirectly, "replies" to them. To begin with, however, we must bear in mind that one of the most prevalent images of Eisenstein is that of a kind of erector-set freak, an inexhaustible *bricoleur* of meaning with a taste for manipulation. Which is not to say that he is a total stranger to this effect, because the theme of bricolage is an obsessive element of his discourse. Here are two short examples: the first is a technical term, a (period) trait that marks the appearance of the word "montage" in his theory:

> From the process of production, a technical term has passed into linguistic currency, designating a mechanical assembly, a set of water conduits, or machine tools. The beautiful word for such constructions is— "montage." ("How I Became a Director"—1945—FW 3, p. 243)

And even before anything had come of it, Eisenstein assesses it in terms of its capacity for artifice, anti-naturalism, and manipulation:

> What we need is science, not art. The word *creation* is useless. It should be replaced by *labor*. One does not create a work, one constructs it with finished parts, like a machine. *Montage* is a beautiful word: it describes the process of constructing with prepared fragments." (*Notebooks from 1919*, cited by Shklovsky)

Clearly, there is more to the distinction between these "prepared fragments" and the ready-made than what is merely lost in translation. As for the diatribe against creation, there is little evidence of it in, for example, the Eisenstein of *Immoral Memories* (who thinks of himself as an auteur, an artist, and secretly as a genius)—but montage always preserves something of its original anti-creationist birthright: if montage no longer involves a refusal of "art," it still claims to be an assembly of fragments constructed out of complete and autonomous parts.

The second example concerns his frequent claim that there are no relations, syntagmatic or otherwise, that can be thought outside of montage: everything must be montaged. We might consider what I said earlier about his writing (how difficult it is to distinguish, for example, in his written work, between what is rough and speculative, and what is thought out or "drafted": it is always the same, basically contradictory, blend of endless digressions and repeated interruptions), or even his distaste, in drawing, for all attempts to produce realistic effects, and his appreciation of pure "outline," or more explicitly, his analysis of drawings as montage. Everywhere we find the same "extremist" affirmation of montage: no discourse is tenable unless it is constructed, no intellectual operation is possible unless it is engineered.

Obviously, "cine-language" is not the only factor involved. Ultimately, it is only one of the most striking manifestations of the chief characteristic of Eisensteinian montage: it is employed, or at least invoked, at random, as an obsessional way of affirming the universality of manipulation, beyond any consideration of the specificity of the means of expression.

2. A Loose Concept

The other popular assumption is predicated upon evidence suggesting that there is no unitary concept of montage in Eisenstein, indeed, that there is actually more than *one* (two or three, perhaps more).

It is almost universally recognized, for example, that between the last two silent films and the two or three completed sound films, there are a number of differences, generally understood in terms of a disavowal, rejection, or regression, a "return to" less daring forms, to drama and to actors—and, of course, a repudiation of montage (or at least, of montage as a dynamic principle).

These obvious differences (which I hope my two earlier analyses of sequences have helped to qualify a little) carry over into our immediate theoretical concerns. Is there one Eisensteinian system so shot through with internal contradictions that it no longer has any meaning, or, at any rate, usefulness, as a system, or are there two or more distinct systems fashioned by the same person, but more or less incompatible?[5] The first of these propositions does, in fact, enter into almost all of the judgments about Eisenstein (among film historians for example) as well as a good number of the studies on Eisenstein, where it generally takes the form of a rejection of his identity as a theorist *quia talis*.

The second thesis is latent in most of the recent work, and has been clearly articulated by David Bordwell in a short article in which he argues quite openly for the notion of a radical mutation in Eisenstein's thinking: for him, there are, without a shadow of a doubt, two distinct periods, two Eisensteinian systems, each of which is "decisively shaped by the theory of mind he presumes"—a "dialectical" epistemology (based on a reflexology model) and a "behaviorist" or "associationist" epistemology (that leads to a concept of "organicity"). We have already come across these theses and discussed them—particularly in the light of their overestimation of the "dialectical" orthodoxy of the early Eisenstein. They appear again here because Bordwell, unlike others, provides a well-defined criterion for separating out the two periods he sees in Eisenstein's theoretical work. One can debate the choice of this criterion (and I shall) and argue that the epistemological standards to which Eisenstein appeals as support for his system are not *the* concrete determining factor, but it is clear that Bordwell's claim for an "epistemological break" is perfectly coherent, and not least because it explicitly questions the consistency of Eisenstein's corpus, where other critiques are more often less direct.

History, moreover, will attest that the montage question has been through many reincarnations, and before examining in more detail the "different" Eisensteinian conceptions of montage, I shall quickly review some of the determining causes of those changes, by way of a short biographical digression.

1. There is no doubt that the most outrightly normative determining cause was the effects of the widespread clamp-down on "formalism" during the thirties. The turning point in the official ideology of art was marked by the creation of organizations like RAPP and ARRK (for literature and cinema respectively) and events like the Writers Congress of 1934 and the filmmakers conference of 1935. Our interest in this history, which is not that well known at all, will be confined to noting its consequences for Eisenstein's position.

When he made *October*, Eisenstein was still, for everyone, the young and brilliant creator of the first revolutionary film of the Soviet cinema; even the many harsh criticisms of *October* were still couched in terms of axiomatic reservations like "Eisenstein's film is a failure, but he is still Eisenstein." It is not easy to determine exactly when things really began to go wrong; probably from the time of his American trip, as seen from the evidence, for example, of a comparison between two critiques, one of *October*, the other of *The General Line*, drafted by the same person, the officious Anisimov: the first (1928) is very guarded, and constantly refers to the "great artist," Eisenstein, while the second (1931) is infinitely more ruthless, and condemns the director as well as the film.

Whether this is accurate or not (and in spite of complex developments—on his return from America, Eisenstein, far from being harassed, was appointed as a teacher to the GIK in 1932, and as an official delegate to the Writers Congress in August 1934), the most concrete evidence of this critical pressure is the famous congress of January 1935, where he was attacked almost unanimously in unexpected and perfidious ways. Although his replies were apparently very successful, the next two years proved to be quite difficult ones, as we can see not only from the persecution over the shooting of *Bezhin Meadow*, but also from the widespread rumor, which had to be vigorously denied,[6] that he had been arrested and deported in January 1937. And although it is difficult to know if he was in any real danger, there is at least one indication that he was: the improbable number of occasional articles that he wrote and published in those years, and the stilted, stereotyped tone of these articles (see those mentioned in Chapter 2).

It is extremely difficult to weigh up the theoretical effects of this politico-ideological guerrilla warfare. Only two things are beyond question:

—during this period, and in spite of his copious self-criticism, he continued, almost without interruption, to pursue his theoretical work from the twenties; in 1933–34, he dictated *A Theory of Conflict*, now lost, to Pera Attasheva; in 1935, he transformed his intervention at the rostrum of the filmmakers congress into a plea *pro domo*; and lastly, in 1937 (scarcely recovered from the shock of *Bezhin Meadow*) we have the famous notes on montage;

—this continual activity, however, is also characterized, as we shall see, by displacements and transformations taken up in the cause of tactical considerations, with an eye for the "step forward" taken by the Soviet cinema, the step forward of socialist realism which obliged Eisenstein to work with the doctrine of the "vital man" that he had hitherto so ardently attacked. The extent of that compromise, often manifest in the most obviously concessionary statements, is difficult to estimate here.

2. The group of texts on montage in 1928–29 and those from the end of the Thirties form one coherent body of work, conceived as a whole: the book project entitled *Regissura*. We know that it was planned as a kind of theoretical and practical manual, incorporating in a pro-

gressive format the basics of Eisenstein's teaching at the VGIK. During that period, teaching was Eisenstein's primary activity, and so undoubtedly influenced his theoretical work. The published portion of *Regissura*, with more than 600 full pages, constitutes only one chapter out of the three originally planned, and anyway it has come down to us in the form of a stenographer's notes for the courses given in 1932–34. There is no way of determining the space that would have been given over to montage if the book had been completed; we can, however, say that it probably occupied a large part of the planned lectures, and in addition, for the first and last time in Eisenstein's known writings, montage is presented as a practical *method*.

In the course of addressing his students, for example, on the problems of moving from a theatrical to a filmic treatment of a theme, he proposes an analysis aimed at isolating increasingly smaller elements by breaking down each action into "cells of montage" (also termed "shot clusters") which "break down, in turn, into 'shots.' Since for each montage-unit the camera angle is the same, the various shots can, in principle, move towards or away from the filmed object" (see Nizhny's third chapter, "Break-up into Shots," pp. 63-93). This idea, the concrete application of which takes up a good part of the work on the Dessalines episode, is vague, and chronically disabled by its empiricism, especially when compared with the conceptual and theoretical subtlety of 1929. In the 1937 essay on montage, however, this idea will be taken up again and transformed as part of the much larger project of redefining the problematic of montage.

Forced to produce work that was no longer purely experimental (in the sense in which one could class Eisenstein's earlier films), it was more than likely that Eisenstein, in his didactic practice, was able to see the impracticability of concepts like harmonic montage, and that it was this confrontation that was responsible for much of the reshaping of perspective carried out in "Montage 1937." (As with the political determinations, however, this influence cannot be isolated as an autonomous cause: it is easy to make the inference, but hopeless to fully interpret its effects.)

3. What is most astonishing about this period of Eisenstein's life is the way in which he manages to continue his theoretical work *in spite* of the ideological pressure, and *along with* his didactic preoccupations. Even if there is little evidence in his texts published in the ten years before 1937, Eisenstein's work underwent a considerable development (which is to agree, in part, with Bordwell): in the period (a theoretical "resting place") of "inner monologue," for example, it

seems quite clear that his reflections about montage, and the principle of montage itself, took on an added dimension.

On the one hand, montage displaced and took over much of the foundational or conceptually unifying role that had hitherto been assigned to *conflict*. One result, for example, was to consider the idea that there is something "of the order" of montage even at the most elementary level, such as the movement from one frame to the next, since any two fixed images can, between them, provide an image of movement. At the other extreme, Eisenstein locates montage in the successive concatenation of different scenes (episodes). From micromontage to macromontage (Eisenstein's terms from "Montage 1937") by way of the "normal" montage of fragments, the concept or principle of montage can be seen as a guarantee of the ideal homogeneity which (in other terms but for the same purpose) conflict had once provided.

In other words, the concept of montage is almost bullied into service (as was the notion of conflict), and forced to assume responsibility, not only for signifying production but also for the much larger and more loosely defined area of production of "movement," whether purely physical (micromontage), completely intellectual (macromontage), or both at the same time.[7]

On the other hand, Eisenstein looks everywhere for evidence for the concept of montage, especially (since he is intent on proving that in cinema "it does not fall from the sky," as he puts it in "Montage 1937") in the forebears and "natural" (or cultural) predecessors of the cinema. The same extension of the concept to its limits occurs again a little further on, with respect to the idea of organicity: the production of movement (identified with montage—by way of conflict) is not only the very principle of cinema, but also of all processes of signification.[8]

In addition to the radical generalization of this principle, Eisenstein extends its field of application from a strict notion of editing (in his terms, everything that involves juxtapositions, shocks, and collisions) to the problem of shots and framing and also questions of sound and "audiovisual counterpoint," the details of which I will have more to say about later.

There are at least three contexts, then, which profoundly affect the way in which Eisenstein formally develops the concept of montage: the ideological, the pedagogical, and the epistemological, all acting in conjunction (to give only one example, Eisenstein's attitude towards the notion of "conflict" is clearly determined by the larger ideological transformations of his society).

However, even if these formal modifications (and the adjective is in no way intended to minimize their effects) strike us as perhaps the most visible element of Eisenstein's work in this period, I want to emphasize that they do not preempt any response to the basic question of the role of montage in Eisensteinian theory.

II. The Concepts of Montage

In this brief examination of some of the most common criticisms of Eisenstein's theories of montage, we will therefore respect the notion that, strictly speaking, there is no single theory of cinema (or theory of montage, since for Eisenstein the two are one and the same) to be constructed out of his work. This is not to say, as I have already suggested, that we can any more speak about several different theories, each succeeding the other, or else imbricated with each other. The sections which follow, then, are intended neither as a description of different categories within the same system, nor as an account of successive theoretical pronouncements—but as a rather simple analysis of some of the problematics that have come to be associated with montage.

I have chosen to discuss three of them (leaving aside for the present the "interior monologue," which I shall discuss later), or more specifically, I will look in turn at three sets of texts that are grouped around clearly defined periods, and examine the question or series of questions which they respectively address.

1. "Intellectual Montage"

The idea of "intellectual montage" appeared (under the rubric of "intellectual attraction") during the making of *October*. No sooner had Eisenstein formulated this conception of the cinema than it was immediately included in a "history" of the forms and types of montage. One recalls the famous typology at the end of "The Filmic Fourth Dimension," presented both as a descriptive catalogue of the different "methods of montage," and as a summary of the whole history of cinematographic montage (since the supposed origins of the Soviet cinema, which is to say, since Kuleshov). The dual nature of this classification, both artificial and celebratory, has been pointed out often enough: as a breakdown of the elements of montage, it is inapplicable; and as a history of the cinema, it is completely teleological—in short, it is put together to support and justify the need for a concept like intellectual montage.

Of course, this teleological aspect of the text (brought home to us by the fact that Eisenstein, in the future, only ever speaks about intellectual montage in the past tense) contains an ulterior, and quite contingent, motive, for it stems from the pressing need, at least from a tactical perspective, to justify two films that have already been accused of formalism.

This motive, however, plays second fiddle to Eisenstein's frequently voiced conviction that there is only ever one conception of montage being reaffirmed and developed from text to text, and from film to film, or rather that all of the categories of montage defined in the catalogue are based upon the same fundamental principles:

> The development from stage to stage proceeds from the fact that there is no difference in principle between the operational equilibrium of man under the effects of a crudely metrical montage ... and the inner, intellectual processes, for the latter operates at the same pitch, but solely at the level of higher nervous activity. ... From the point of view of "phenomena" (of effects), they may seem different, but from the point of view of their essence (as processes), they are undoubtedly the same. ("The Filmic Fourth Dimension," 1929)

Moreover, not only is intellectual montage the "logical" conclusion of the "theoretical" history of montage, it is also, in a practical sense, the direct and equally "logical" successor to Eisenstein's earlier work, and especially to the montage of attractions. This is implied in "The Filmic Fourth Dimension" (when Eisenstein claims that intellectual montage had been "propagated by [him] for several years already") but its most conspicuous appearance is in the "Dramaturgie der Film-Form," where it introduces another classification: "a series of formal possibilities, developing dialectically in accord with the following thesis: the concept of filmic movement (progression) is the result of the superimposition—or counterpoint— of two different fixed elements." We can summarize the successive features of this operation:

1. the simple "phenomenon" of the reproduction of movement, from one frame to another—a purely optical effect;

2. an artificially produced representation of movement (by a very rapidly alternating montage: the machine guns in *October*; by way of the "straight-cut": the destroyed eye in *Potemkin*; by "more illogical" means: the leaping lions, etc.) that always has a physical (physiological) effect on the spectator;

3. emotional combinations or syntheses which bring psychological *associations* into play (the slaughterhouse in *Strike*);

4. and last, a conceptual effect, the result of "an absolute liberation of the action from its determination by time and space" (in *October*, for example, the Russian soldier in a trench who is metaphorically "crushed" by a tank rolling off the assembly line in an armaments factory): the "movement" is generally "intellectual," for it is a metaphorical operation which governs the leap from image to image (in the example I have given, the meaning of the proposition emerges only if the spatial disjunction of the two shots is clearly and distinctly preserved, at the same time as we perceive the "fate" of the soldier).

This list of features is a valuable one. To begin with, it confirms what many Eisenstein critics (Pietro Montani, Marc Le Bot, etc.)[9] have argued: that in Eisensteinian theory and practice, intellectual montage has at least one direct precursor in the montage of attractions, based, as it is, upon "associations" and "emotional syntheses," and aimed at producing (in the cinema at any rate) a conceptual effect. Second, it gives us some idea of Eisenstein's direction: this section of "Dramaturgie der Film-Form" bears a rather disquieting subtitle: "Versuch einer Film-Syntax." A "filmic syntax" which seems doomed to fall back again upon the perilous idea of a "cine-*langue*." It is quite clear, however, that in "emulating the process of language," Eisenstein has no intention here of proposing a utopian "cine-grammar." Rather than posit an *equivalence* between language (*langue*) and film, he is concerned with a much looser analogy between certain semantic operations in film (related essentially to montage, in the limited, technical sense of the word) and certain "figures" of thought. We will return to this question, but I want to stress now that when Eisenstein discusses metaphor or synecdoche, it is never in the context of copying or *adapting* figures of rhetoric for the cinema, but more in the sense of models for the production of meaning. At another level, it is important to add that he does not identify the word with the "shot" (or the "fragment," or any other syntagmatic unit). For a while there is some uncertainty about this, but he finally comes to insist on the plurality of coded levels within the filmic image, and categorically rejects the dream of univocality, which does not of course conflict with the need for an analysis of each shot (an analysis in turn, which is not a reduction of the "shot" to discrete signifying elements).

This "filmic syntax," then, is only "syntactical" in its own indirect way. Hence the desire to make cinema a simulacrum of language is one which insists on the generalization involved in the operations of two notions, *conflict* and *stimulus*, whose ideological components I have already described.

It is also important to note that in its role as successor to the montage of attractions, intellectual montage is presented as an intensification of the range of possible stimuli, primarily because it takes the spectator and his reactions into account. Intellectual montage is clearly aimed at producing meanings stripped of all ambiguity (ideologically and semantically). But this pared-down meaning is never absolute, that is, without a referent; it is always addressed to a spectator (to the mechanisms, or at least assumed mechanisms, of his subjective activity); and it is a meaning whose necessary form is shaped by its intention:

> Only an intellectual cinema has the power to resolve the dispute between "the language of logic" and "the language of images"—on the basis of a language of cinedialectics. . . . A cinema with the utmost commitment to sensuality as well as investigation, and which draws upon its universal access to channels of action through visual, auditory, and bio-motor stimuli. ("Perspectives," FW 1, pp. 196–97)

> Intellectual cinema will resolve the antagonistic coexistence of physiological and intellectual harmonies. ("The Filmic Fourth Dimension," 1929)

> It is interesting that, outside of meaning and theme, these things cannot exist. . . . Abstract, formal experimentation is thus unthinkable (as in, for example, montage in general). There is no experimentation outside of the argument (take this into consideration). ("Notes on *Capital*"— 24 March 1928)

As for "dialectical" conflict, the other parent "principle" of intellectual montage, we have already discussed the kind of ambiguity which governs its implementation, and I shall not dwell any further on it.

Instead, I will try to describe as precisely as possible the character of intellectual montage. As has been pointed out, intellectual montage does not exist in the concrete sense of an achieved practice. For a long time, it was manifest only through these rather general declarations of intention that I have just quoted (and which are, of course, not without their importance, if only because of their attention to the question of spectatorship) or else in one or two segments from the films (basically the "gods," and "Kerensky climbing the stairs" in *October*).

From this point of view, the publication, in 1973, of Eisenstein's notes on the proposed *Capital* has proved invaluable. It is no surprise to find that these notes do not reveal a *method,* or define an "intellectual" *model* for the cinema, or even succeed in isolating fixed *rules*. They do, however, offer the most complete and precise development of the "intellectual" principle, and it is from this evidence that I shall attempt to *describe* the system of "intellectual montage."[10] It all begins with Eisenstein's assertion of a new historical "progression," one that repeats and corroborates the two we have already encountered. It is purely empirical and reproduces the order of the films—a drama (*Strike*), a poem (*Potemkin*), and an essay (*October*) "logically" justify the idea of a cinema-treatise (*Capital*). One immediately notices that what drops out of this "progression" is the drama, the history: in *Potemkin*, with the appearance of a "pathetic abstract" (lions which leap to attention), in *October*, with events which mark "the conclusion of a series of propositions": everything which "leads to a complete break with fact and anecdote."

This idea of "de-anecdotalization" is intrinsic to all intellectual montage,[11] and Eisenstein repeatedly returns to it, sometimes to emphasize how difficult it really is—"still very difficult to think 'like that' in images 'without any subject'. No matter—it will come!" (4 April 1928)—and sometimes categorically to assert that it *can* be done, not only from the point of view of making films, but also, and most important, on the part of the would-be spectator, whom, at the cost of a "reorientation" will transcend the cognitive difficulties posed by this new type of discourse.[12]

One direct result of this is to insist, initially at any rate, on the sheer insignificance of the anecdotal topic. The raw material is "banal and humdrum" (6 April 1928), "any old trivia taken up and animated" (8 April 1928), and it is in this spirit that Eisenstein's selection of material for *Capital* is restricted to "scenes of everyday life," especially domestic scenes (the soup cooking, the woman darning stockings, the chamber pot under the bed, etc.) which seem to him to represent the height of "trivia," in addition to meeting the categorical demand: "A film is cinematographic when its subject can be summed up in two words" (4 April 1928).

The anecdote only serves as an "ice-breaker"; it sets up a "chain" of stimuli[13] from which the film is constructed by working through controlled associations (we shall see how):

> The elements of this chain are starting points from which associations form, which in turn produce the play between concepts. . . . Every association depends upon a prior stimulus: without that chain of stimuli the work of association runs dry. The most abstract proposition loses

its rigidity when it is revealed as the effect of something extremely concrete, instinctual, and mundane. (4 April 1928)

The anecdotal must be purged, but it must also be devalued, or reduced to its humblest condition in order to emphasize that it is not the subject, and to foreground the subject itself in its best light.[14] With such a project—a series of potentially unconnected associations arising from an evanescent base—there is the danger of complete dissipation; since the anecdote no longer serves its cohesive function, the real subject must be defined (to bring the fragments together).

The essential characteristic of this subject, or content, is that it is political/ideological: "each element potentially points towards a content that is ideologically closed, though as far away from it, materially, as possible" (6 April 1928); and this "ideologically closed" content is of course (part of) the content of Marx's *Capital*, while its ideologico-political dimensions are affirmed in the didactic function of the film (the subject, if you like, has something to do with the theory: Marxist theory, in the scientific sense):

> There are endless themes to film in *Capital*: the one we want to film is Marx's method (8 April 1928). We know now that the basic proposition of *Capital* (its goal) is *to teach the worker how to think dialectically*. To show the method of the dialectic. (4 April 1928)

This general description of the political nature of the subject both in its substance and intention has a number of consequences:

1. Clearly film is not intended to represent things and events for their own sake, since things, facts, and places only acquire value (or meaning) as extensions of the associations they give way to, and in their montage with other associations:

> We are not looking ultimately for some perceptible reproduction, at least in the sense in which I have, until now, applied this in dealing with a battleship, a factory, or a luncheon. (4 April 1928)

The film must absolutely refuse to include any *scenes* that would be symbolic or, worse, allegorical.[15]

2. If none of the initial raw material has any semantic value of its own, it is, however, invested with *emotional* value. Besides, it is quite clear that Eisenstein selects the many anecdotes sprinkled throughout his work journal on the basis of a purely "emotional" criterion (that of his own personal reaction): anecdotes that are both extremely detailed and quite moving (scandalous, witty, and shocking).[16]

Eisenstein worries about this constantly, almost as much as he worries about didacticism, of which it is one aspect (all propaganda and educational work must have this emotional dimension—of the "lived," and of "pleasure"):

> This terrible desirability of the shot-in-itself (a palpable desire), a shot that could maintain itself without any semantic support (intellectual desire)—is absolutely necessary. Whether we like it or not, we should, and we will have to, come to terms with emotion. (4 April 1928)

This worry, it should be said, is probably the result, at least in part, of the close scrutiny to which his work since *October* had been subjected:

> How the "chaste young women" *of the moment* would react when I began to talk about *Capital* and intellectual attraction! . . . They prefer the emotionality of my work. (20 April 1928)

As we have seen, Eisenstein inveterately reaffirms that intellectual and emotional effects cannot be separated. In fact, it is part of the actual definition of intellectual montage to make some provision for the emotion of the spectator (in terms of its effect).[17] This moreover is not simply a point of principle, for Eisenstein will not rest until he has proved that this "emotionality" is not a pious pledge, or an abstract possibility, but a reality: in reality, "it works," he tells us, very powerfully, as, for example, during the screenings of *October:* the spectator not only understands the meaning, he is also moved—he laughs and applauds[18] ("the biggest reaction to 'Kerensky', thunderous laughter and applause" [4 April 1928]).

3. This raw material, as I have said, is useful in sealing the spectator's emotional attention, but is not essential to the film's content. To be more precise, everything in the filmic "past" which was phenomenal, becomes conceptual. Those *units* admitted to our rational faculty are no longer "phenomenal" units, but rather "intellectual units," secondarily elaborated by all the operations of montage and confrontation, from the primary material at the level of the anecdote. Each fragment expresses some of this materiality, but its value does not lie in the expression, its value lies in the partial (metaphorical) meaning attributed to the fragment by its place within a whole: the process of the production of meaning only retains one (or a few) of the whole range of connotations provided by these fragments and their representations: in filming China, for example,

it should be borne in mind that these fragments are not intended as a presentation of China, but as a presentation of a unified thought, through their confrontation with other fragments—New York, Egypt. (4 April 1928)

4. Finally, and contrary to what one might expect from what has gone before, the object privileged in Marx's work is not a theoretical one, like any of the key concepts from *Capital*. It is at another level entirely that Eisenstein selects his true object—the Marxist method itself.

In other words, it would still be a simplification of intellectual montage to see it as the mere substitution of one content for another (a cinema which would "tell the story" of surplus-value rather than any other story): it is a much more radical operation, the transformation of the status of this content, and, above all, of the relation of the spectator to this content. Hence, what Eisenstein means when he speaks of the "didactic" relation is not so much the revelation of a truth which the spectator will have to "learn" as a series of interactions between the various filmic elements: the initial stimulus (the "chain of trivial events"), the result (the associations that are formed), and the spectator:

Violently contrast the *stimulus* with the *final link* in the complex chain of conditioned reflexes. . . . Show the materiality of the stimulus in the crudest possible way . . . and then, the utmost spirituality of the final link. . . . Reproduce the mechanism of stimulation. Then, through a series of filmic stimuli, induce an emotional effect in the spectator, and present this text: "So, here you are at the point of . . . etc. . . . etc." (7 April 1928)

Here, the director is being stage-managed just as much as the spectator into a kind of initiatory set-up (a relation of mastery, if you like, which would not merely reproduce the "teacher-student situation").[19]

Thus, the famous project that Eisenstein takes on as the goal of his work on *Capital*—"to teach the worker to think dialectically" (4 April 1928)—is clearly not the only determining factor on this work, although it is, in some sense, the key factor. Even if a large part of the purely "formal" reflection, which we will now discuss, arises out of many different concerns (the question of montage, in particular, goes beyond any single preoccupation), one can at least assert that, in the course of all this formal effort, the thought of the *addressee* (what we earlier called efficacy) is always present.

It would of course be arbitrary to isolate (except for the sake of drawing attention to it) the "question of form" in the operations of intellectual montage. From the evidence of the *Notes*, however, we can say that Eisenstein devoted more time and thought, and developed more ideas and plans, around the question of form than anything else. Without claiming too much for the following breakdown (even in Eisenstein's mind, this is all very rough), we can distinguish:

1. principles of composition for defining the overall structure of an "intellectual" film—they are generally picked up from other works:

—first, the conscious decision to mix together genres and styles in patchwork fashion. Without harking back to the montage of attractions and its circus model, we can recall certain sequences in *Strike* ("the thunder sequence, an explosion of pure American comedy in a long and serious work"—31 March 1928) or even better, everything in *October* and *The General Line* for which Eisenstein was attacked on the grounds of digression and irrelevance—but also the great source of inspiration for the *Notes*, Joyce's *Ulysses*: "The formal side will be dedicated to Joyce" (8 April 1928), and this is certainly not ironic, as some have suggested;

—second, the idea of "circularity," or interlocking of narratives. The models for this are generally from the literature of the fantastic or fables (*Arabian Nights*, *Tales of a Parrot*, etc.), and, more so than all the others, they are totally abstract ideas, which Eisenstein is deeply apprehensive about using ("For the present, this is all probably distasteful enough"—7 April 1928). The most interesting aspect of this is probably the sense in which the last chapter would act as an ideal or intellectual resolution of this endless imbrication as opposed to a fictional one): "As for the last chapter, it must provide a *dialectical explanation* of this story without referring to its real (fictional) theme" (6 April 1928);

—and last, all of Eisenstein's reflections about his favorite idea of repetition. We have already looked at one or two examples (especially in the sequence from *Ivan the Terrible*), and we know that it is one of his most consistent methods, if not principles, so much so that it matches his own impulse for writing, efficiency, and mastery. We can see how Eisenstein explains and justifies this principle by looking at the way in which he describes the most elementary instance (two repetitive fragments): "The first fragment for the shock. The second for apperception" (4 April 1928). Moreover, it is not only the fragments that can be repeated: "[In *Battleship Potemkin*] you have this at the level of a double register, one, two—where, in addition to the montage fragments, completely emotional constructions ... are repeated with the same reinforcing purpose" (23 November 1927).

The common force behind all of these "principles" (or rather "methods") of composition seems to me to be an anti-naturalistic or anti-linear bias already inherent in the choice of subject—and one which always appeals to both the thought of the spectator (the spectator is captivated by this patchwork effect: the circularity turns back on itself, and reaffirms his sense of purpose as a spectator, while the repetition drives the point home) and the "dialectical" structure.

2. Similarly, the concrete *making* of the film (the shooting, the editing, the nature and function of the pro-filmic material) is thought out in terms of these two preoccupations—although in a much more integrated fashion. There are only fleeting suggestions about this, and they stem directly from discussions of the "content" of the film:

—the shooting of the film: at this stage, it is not a question of producing a "realistic" reproduction of the material, and in fact the only practical advice is about the possibility, if not the necessity, of shooting in a studio:

> For if we continue in this vein, we shall conclude that the whole of *Capital*—to save us "tracking down" the actual smells of Egypt—could be "constructed" in a studio. The Schuftan process. Glass. Models. You could shoot it in "Studio Three"!!! (4 April 1928)

In spite of its irony and its somewhat unrealistic shading, this comment is an important one:[20] in spite of his love of manipulation and his use of trick effects in some of the films (see especially *The General Line*), Eisenstein never actually did any shooting in the studio; for the silent films and for *Que Viva Mexico!* and *Bezhin Meadow*, he assiduously "tracked down" the smells of authentic sites (and in *Nevsky* and *Ivan*, the studio is used mainly, as we saw, for the purpose of realistic "reconstruction"). (On this point, the *Notes* are probably not to be taken literally: if he had pursued his work, it seems quite unlikely that Eisenstein would have given up producing the "smell" of authenticity in his films, if only because he would lose a whole world of possible connotations. As we saw in the analyses of the sequences, the strength of the "second" meaning follows on from the solidity of the "first");

—not surprisingly, the bulk of the work takes place after shooting, in the editing stage: the montage of "intellectual attractions" which is only described in terms of its formal resemblance to "emotional attractions." The same process, for example, is at work in the "gods" sequence, as in the following series (from *Potemkin*):[21]

> sad old man + lowered sail + out-of-focus tent + fingers kneading a beret + eyes full of tears. . . . (4 April 1928)

Here, paradoxically, in those *Notes* to a nonexistent film, is perhaps one of the clearest descriptions of the idea of harmonic montage: in the fragments of *Potemkin* cited here, the feeling, let us say, of sadness arises out of the confrontation between the fragments through which it resonates, while activating a different part (different parameters) of the fragment each time: an element of the figuration (fingers kneading a beret, tears in the eyes), the fact that the tent is *out of focus*, that the sail is *lowered*. . . . Similarly, when China, the Pyramids, and New York are invoked in *Capital*, it is certainly not as *themes* in themselves (4 April 1928), but rather in terms of what they have in common thematically;

—since things are not filmed "for their own sake," but only with respect to a specific network of mutual relations, the "impact" of the content will not correspond proportionally to the running length of the film:

> The question of volume is very interesting, and also very new; the mutual relations of quantity and the disparity between material and filmic length: "The impact of filmic length" (to answer the worries of Grisha [Alexandrov]: "What, you're going to include China as well as America ?" etc., etc.). (4 April 1928)

The *Notes* manifest a real fascination for the high *performance* achieved by this kind of montage: over the course of a normal-length screening, it not only generates a whole network of ideas, but also organizes a massive "impact" of raw material (which is proof again, in passing, that Eisenstein was not at all indifferent to the *presence* of this material, or rather, its "smell"). The fact of this efficiency in itself apparently almost justifies all intellectual cinema: "What we are looking for, finally, is an *economy of means*. And where better to find it than in the *immediate*"[22] (4 April 1928).

3. These "economical" means, then, are the essence of intellectual cinema, and thus they are described at length in the *Notes* which furnish an enormous variety of somewhat schematic and repetitive examples. At the core of this is the familiar principle of *associations*, which is to be linked up to the double movement of figuration in the proposed film:

The various elements of the material are recombined, not in terms of physical (or "sensory" as Eisenstein puts it) parameters, but according to semantic criteria: "the baroque Christ and the wooden idol are totally different, but they signify exactly the same thing. Balalaikas and Mensheviks 'resemble each other, in the abstract, and not in the physical sense' " (4 April 1928).

Similarly, one cannot "present" a theme by way of the image that would seem closest to it physically: on the contrary one should distance this image from its simple naturalistic representation: "Present the idea of exchange not by the Stock Exchange (*Mabuse, St. Petersburg*) but by a thousand 'little details' " (2 January 1928).

It would take too long to discuss in detail all of the sketchy ideas presented in the *Notes* (besides, they represent only an inconclusive portion of Eisenstein's thinking from this period). What is striking, however, is that they are consistently marked by two fixed tendencies:

—first, the metaphorical, or that which "stands for something else," the example (it is repeated at least three times) being the silk stocking, which could connote, all at the same time, art (the aesthetes who fight over every centimeter); morality (the stocking as a gauge of indecency according to how much it reveals); commerce, and implicitly, the market (the cult of fashion); and last, production, exploitation, and, the final phase, imperialism (the anecdote about the "Hindu" women forced to incubate the cocoons under their armpits (11 April 1928). The film would thus *condense* different meanings into a single element of representation, if not a single signifier, rather like the Freudian model. The result of this willful "economy of means" is that there is no need for the film to produce explicit meanings; much of the work is then done in the spectator's mind as he "processes" the associations.

It is plausible at least that this is what Eisenstein intended: to find a mode of representation which would encourage the spectator to take on the work of associating (backwards, this time) for himself;

—and second, of course, the mode of inscribing *within* the film the path of these associations, through the operations of a metonymic principle. Take for example the chain which

> starts from the pepper going into the soup. Pepper. Cayenne. Devil's Island. Dreyfus. French chauvinism. *Le Figaro* in Krupp's hands. War. Ships scuttled in port. . . . It wouldn't be a bad idea to cover up the sunken English ships . . . with the casserole lid. (7 April 1928)

Here, of course, we run right up against the most acute difficulties of the whole "intellectual" montage theory: it is always possible to claim that the film, starting with a representation like the silk stocking, can engage the spectator's imagination in the direction of one or the other association, but it is less easy to see how the chain of associations that begins with the pepper can really become a filmic chain. To go from "pepper" to "Cayenne," even from "Devil's Island" to "Dreyfus," is a simple process if it is limited to verbal operations (in the first example, it works through the fixed syntagm "Cayenne pepper"; in the second because the term "Devil's Island" represents nothing, it is only a denominator—contingently associated with Dreyfus by way of a well-known historical referent)—but in "filmic language," the most plausible process always involves an *expansive* development from a representation, and not the *limitation* of this representation to a single meaning (which limitation would oblige the spectator to work through the same process that produced the meaning).

Here we come back to the famous question of univocality (which includes the whole debate about ideography and cine-language). Again, there is no point in trying rigidly to categorize Eisenstein's position on this; it is a fact that he was tempted by the idea of the possibility of making univocal fragments. However, this is proposed only in the context of their montage (there is no such thing as a single fragment of montage, as we are frequently reminded), and it is clear that he views the temptation in the light of this problem: "The problem of framing for *Capital* will be a very unusual one. The ideology of the univocal shot has to be completely revised. At this point, I have no idea how. We shall have to experiment with different possibilities (8 May 1928)—and so he puts the problem aside for "later"; if we recall the last use of the phrase (24 March 1928), "there is no experimentation outside of the argument," this means that "experimental work" on the problem of univocality could only be undertaken within the process of making a concrete film.

If we had to sum up at this point Eisenstein's attitude, I would characterize it as the indefinite pursuit of a contradiction:

—on the one hand, all the abstract logic of association inspires his idea of producing "rebuses" like that of the pepper, a tendency which is encouraged, apparently by the success of the gods sequence, in which the transition from one representation to another is actually produced as a kind of movement rooted in the solidity of a signified (the "divinity" connoted by the images of gods);

—on the other hand, he knows from experience that a montage of several fragments, let alone one single fragment, is never univocal.[23] We shall do no more than note in passing all the work on the question of framing (alluded to, for example, in the quotation from 8, IV) and which afterwards finds its initial formulation in the definition of the fragment's parameters (what I have called its "vertical dimension").

Eisenstein's real answers to this question are not, in fact, to be found in the *Notes on Capital*. His practical response will be in the work done on representation in *The General Line* (where, as we have seen, the "sensory" parameters are quite central to the constitution of meaning), and his theoretical response will pass through a number of stages (the "interior monologue" among others) before it assumes rough draft form in the 1937 treatise on montage.

It seems unjust, however, to conclude with this image of intellectual cinema as inextricably caught up within its contradictions. Indeed, it seems to me that almost all of Eisenstein's commentators underestimate the role of the mental processes of the spectator (imperative not only with regard to the intellectual work necessary for producing "good" associations, but also with regard to the production of emotional "value").

Eisenstein, for example, maintains that the "sentence" represented by the gods in *October* is, of course, the "equivalent" of a verbal statement (of the type, "gods = zero"). To reach this conclusion, however, we must go through a series of procedures, which he roughly sketches out: first, the apperception of successive images as a formal chain; second, the identification of various representata as so many images of deities; third, the transposition of the formal chain to the level of content (thus positing a "metonymic" chain of deities); fourth, the correlation of this content with the anecdote (Kornilov's attack, from which the gods sequence draws some of its meaning, and which it qualifies, at the same time); and last, the emotional effect: the spectator laughs (or applauds, etc.). (This is a summary of the notes from 24 April, 4 May, and 8 May, 1928.)

In closing this discussion of intellectual cinema, I would like to emphasize, for the last time, the dissimilarity between this kind of breakdown of the function of the "gods" from Eisenstein's hasty comparisons between the juxtaposition of two filmic elements and the ideogrammatic principle (including, of course, some of Eisenstein's own over-hasty assimilations, contradicted, as we have just seen, by the essential practice of his work). Clearly, Eisenstein detested the idea that cinema was subject to analogy *tout court*; it would be wrong, however, to conclude that his intellectual cinema was intended to do away with all analogies, and make of film a machine that would be driven solely by "allegory," or "symbol." For there is no doubt that he has new plans for this machine, functions that are much more complex and mediated than that of simple, specular recognition.

It is to these designs, to this new conception of the *image*, that we shall now turn.

2. "Imaginicity"

In making a kind of surgical "cut," and leaping forward to the theoretical tangle of the 1937 reflections on montage, I am in no way oblivious to the problems raised by such a leap; first of all, I have suggested that there is no *gap* between intellectual montage and the montage of 1937, and we will therefore have to qualify this "intervening" period in more detail (I shall do this in a few pages); second, however, I would caution against attaching too much importance to any such periodization, since, as I have already suggested, it tends to reduce the textural density of a strain of thought to the consistency of a mere thread.

The years 1937–40, along with the last few years of his life, are undoubtedly the periods in which Eisenstein was most directly and explicitly engaged in a *theoretical project*. After the abandoned attempt (it will be taken up again in 1947–48) at the monumental treatise on mise-en-scène which was to become *Regissura*, this 1937–40 group of three "blocks" of texts—each different in aim and scope—which are devoted to the question of montage, mark one of the most powerful and concentrated stages of all his thinking.

One thing should be said about these three "blocks," as a kind of prologue: the first, which I have often referred to as "Montage 1937," is at once the most copious, the most complete, and the most structured. It is the only one which, properly speaking, presents a comprehensive perspective on the question of montage, and from this point of view we can say that it is the *base* of the other two (and a portion of *Nonindifferent Nature*). Of the three, however, it is the least finished, and was left in a state of rough draft, often on loose pages that are not always numbered, and which the almost faultless editors of the *Collected Works* have had great difficulty in sorting out. By contrast, "Montage 1938" and "Vertical Montage" are in much better condition, published during Eisenstein's lifetime (and even in two versions);[24] with many more examples, their tone is more concrete, and their aims are less exhaustive. They are, in a sense, a vulgarization of the original, since they recycle its major ideas, furnish them with a whole set of new examples—and temper them with the referential lesson of a practical application, that of *Alexander Nevsky*.

The major theoretical and ideological gesture of these texts (for the sake of convenience, they will be considered from now on as an ensemble) is their *return to montage*. That may not appear to be very significant, since Eisenstein himself had scarcely ever stopped thinking about montage. We have to recall, however, the situation of Soviet cinema at this point, and the extent to which it was dominated by the tyranny of dramatic naturalism, the insistence on a very crude interpretation of ideological content, and a conception of characters as "heroes" and "models"—all of which had established itself as if by chance at almost the same time as sound cinema, and thereby produced the "talking pictures" that Eisenstein had so dreaded.

In effect, this return to the theme of montage when it was theoretically and ideologically against the grain is undertaken with a certain degree of caution:

> There was a period of our cinema when it was proclaimed that montage was "everything." Now we are moving away from a period where it counts for "nothing." Regardless of whether montage is "all" or "nothing," we deem it necessary now to remember that montage is a constitutive part of filmic production, as obligatory as any of the other elements of cinematographic functioning. . . . This is all the more necessary because the period of "negation" of montage has wiped out even its strongest claims to validity, claims which should have been irremediably impervious to criticism. ("Montage 1938")

As he had already done in 1935, Eisenstein here renounces all claims for the primacy of montage[25] in an effort to purge from his discourse everything which would smack too much of aggressiveness or imperialism. It is difficult, however, not to see this attitude as double-faced (whether conscious or not): at the same time that he denies that montage is "everything," and effectively accords it a theoretical place along with problems that for him are almost brand-new (such as framing and acting), he arranges it so that montage, albeit in a strictly redefined way, will ultimately appear as the truly central principle of *all* of the effects of articulation and signification. In short, he proposes something like the following: "montage, the operation of juxtaposing two signifying elements, has been unjustly promoted by myself to the center of the theory of film: filmic signification is constructed through the participation of many other effects besides this montage-juxtaposition, and I propose to examine the general laws which govern *all* these effects." This, then, is the professed and actual aim of *Montage*—to show that these general laws can be reduced to a principle, a principle that Eisenstein will, however, discover is none other than . . . an extension of the concept of montage. And so it comes full circle.

He begins by shifting the historical perspective so that this "period" or "stage" of montage-sovereignty is sandwiched between the prior phase of "single point of view" cinema (the beginnings of cinema, before the "invention" of montage, and indeed all of the precursors of cinema) and the consecutive phase of sound cinema, the "audio-visual counterpoint" that Eisenstein had always dreamt of anyway.

We should also note, once more, Eisenstein's liking for historical periodizing,[26] for "dialectical" sequences on a grand scale (since he assumes that there is a qualitative "leap" between each of these three phases), and also for his apologetic classifications, the whole aim being to better promote a certain "organic" conception of audio-visual counterpoint, presenting it in some sense as the end of history.

The same is true of his theoretical additions. Aware that it is not enough to deal with the question of framing as a particular element of montage, nor to proclaim, in a stirring manifesto, the future of sound cinema as contrapuntal, Eisenstein therefore decides to handle both of these problems, framing and sound, at once. He also throws in for good measure, and with an eye to ideological constraints, the question of the actor, though in a less clear-cut fashion.

Ultimately, these two operations, the historical and the theoretical, are presented as if they were intrinsically related; the problem of framing is the montage of the past, when it was the only compositional problem of a "single point of view" cinema; audio-visual counterpoint is (still) the cinema of the future, but also the sum total of all of the problematics of the past (as the theoretical extension of harmonic montage, audio-visual counterpoint takes up and elaborates the principles of composition raised with respect to the question of framing).

And of course what finally unifies, even subsumes, the double cunning of this classification is montage itself, in its newly defined capacity, both as the general principle of all filmic dynamism (every juxtaposition and every series of elements) and of all spatial or rhythmic composition.

From this perspective, *Montage* contains even further paradoxes; on the one hand, Eisenstein makes his first serious attempt to deal with specific problems which he had hitherto only mentioned in passing (under the category of "conflict"). Indeed, this is something which was clearly troubling him in this half-finished treatise. He would thus insist that he was discussing the problem of framing only because no one else had wanted to deal with it; and, as for his treatment of the sound-image relation, it was intended to demonstrate the radically new effects of his conception of counterpoint. On the other hand, and in spite of the sound evidence offered by numerous analyses, the most striking feature of the ensemble is the extent to which all of these specific problems (to which we should add the problem of the actor, mentioned earlier) can be reduced to particular instances just as much as to general principles—the difference being that the unifying principle is no longer conflict, but montage.

What *Montage 1937–40* achieves, in effect, is a stage of development (the contrapuntal sound cinema) which both preserves and goes beyond not only the preceding stage (harmonic montage), but also the one before (the frame); clearly, the structure of this kind of theoretical work is typically Eisensteinian, and probably stands as the most consistent *formal* definition of his own theoretical domain.

Apart from this epistemological operation of reorganizing, reassessing, and redefining the problematic of montage, the essence of the work carried out in *Montage* consists in a clarification and a systematization of the whole of Eisenstein's thinking about questions of form and signification, in the light of a concept which we have already discussed at length, that of *obraznost'*.

As Eisenstein makes a point of emphasizing in the introduction to "Montage 37," *obraznost'* involves questions of a much more general nature than the study of cinema, or montage—but within that context, cinema is considerably more advanced than its "sister" arts (which does not, however, alter the fact that more than half of the arguments are taken up through examples drawn from painting and literature). Similarly, in the universality and general influence it attributes to his conception of signification in *Montage*, it constitutes one of the most important, but not the most well known, aspects of all of this thinking. The double concept of "figuration" and "image" with which he describes the phenomenon of the production of "organic" meaning (these words are to be understood in a very specific and precise way),[27] does actually appear here and there in the texts from this period, published early on. "Montage 1938," for example, yields this definition:

> What does such a conception of montage actually involve? In this instance, each fragment of montage no longer exists as something autonomous, but as one of the *particular figurations* of a single general theme which permeates all of the fragments equally. The juxtaposition of such particular details in a given structure of montage inaugurates and foregrounds within perception this *general* quality that is the source of each detail and which *unifies* them, namely, the global *image* in which the author, and the spectator in turn, experience the theme of the film.

Compared, however, to the length devoted to the same issue in "Montage 1937," references like this one, in all of the well-known texts of Eisenstein, seem to be mere allusions (indeed, it is a consequence of the exhaustive and supposedly conclusive treatment in the earlier text that Eisenstein felt he could afford to be allusive elsewhere). The consensus of Eisenstein's commentators (or at least those who are not entirely unaware of it) on this double concept of figuration/imaginicity is quite revealing: even in the better examples, we find references which are always somewhat wide of the mark. It is surprising, for example, to see someone as precise and discriminating as Marie-Claire Ropars present this summary:

> [figuration], which is to say, the cinematographical material, is contrasted with the image produced by montage and which constitutes the tangible equivalent of the concept. [And] to [figuration] as a figurative imitation of reality, Eisenstein opposes the image as an abstract element produced by montage in complete independence of the elements of representation.[28]

—hence, the idea of an *opposition* that Eisenstein himself never formulates but attempts instead to transform in terms of a complementarity (a "dialectical" one, of course).

It seems important, then, to try to account, even if rather hastily, for the full complexity of Eisenstein's analysis; to do so, the simplest route is to follow (roughly) the expository order of the 1937 text, with its three parts determined by a chronologico-typological distribution: past/present/future—frame/montage/sound film.

I. "SINGLE POINT OF VIEW CINEMA"

It is under this rubric that Eisenstein places all the problems of signification in the "cinema of the past"—basically, problems of framing. What is initially striking about this strange phrase is of course the term "point of view," which is a throwback to an essentially pictorial problematic. Moreover, this question of "point of view," as I have pointed out, is discussed by Eisenstein—but from two different perspectives:

—first, from a "pictorial" perspective, in the course of his study of the specific laws of composition in the frame (whether pictorial, theatrical, or filmic): problems of framing but also of *mise-en-cadre* (and thus of mise-en-scène);

—and also from a more typically Eisensteinian perspective, in his study of the processes of signification at work in the fixed image (or in the *fixed shot* of cinema—which leads him to assert that the frame must also, and always, be seen as a link in a chain of montage).

This "single point of view cinema" is the source of the initial formulation of the golden rule that reproduces the double point of view of its author, a formulation which will help to develop and modify the double notion of figuration/image:

> To be expressive, a mise-en-scène must respond to two conditions: It must not contradict the everyday life of normal people.
> But that is not enough.
> In its construction, it must be the graphic design of what determines the psychological content of the scene and the interrelated actions of the characters in its "figurative" meaning.[29]

"Figuration," then, the first of these two concepts, is initially given a negative definition: the figuration of events or objects must not contradict the normal or everyday (*bytovoe*) perception of them. Generally speaking, this is the minimum condition of all "figurative" art, and it would merit no further comment if Eisenstein had not returned to it so often, and with such insistence (and not only in the *Montage* essay).[30] The result of his insistence is to emphasize quite explicitly that this "minimum" absolutely cannot be taken for granted.

Indeed, without embarking on a long historical digression, we should bear in mind that, even if he never belonged to a Futurist group, even if he never *was* a Futurist, his first Proletkult productions prove that he was attracted to a "nonfigurative" art, or more precisely, by the idea of constructing a nonfigurative theatrical art. Of course this idea had a certain currency at that time, and Eisenstein was well aware that painting, at least, was already far advanced in the art of abolishing figuration (besides, does he not specifically cite the cases of Futurism and Cubism?). And is this not similar to his own achievement, with intellectual cinema, in devaluing the anecdote?

A large part of Eisenstein's work in *Montage* consists in withdrawing from those ideas, and replacing them with an even more powerful emphasis on the primacy of figurality. Even for the Eisenstein of 1937, this, once more, is a heartbreaking step: it is easy to imagine how much this very heavy insistence on the necessity of figuration as a base tallied with the mood of the moment (the themes of "socialist realism" which we discussed), and did so even in spite of Eisenstein's holy terror of anything which came close to resembling cinematographic naturalism. Ultimately, however, and despite the tightrope that he sometimes had to walk, Eisenstein's manifest interest in figuration is not the simple result of strong social pressures, and the opposition he maintained between "figuration" and "abstraction" is not without its own dialectical force.

We are confronted with this same preoccupation that was his at the period of intellectual cinema: intellectual film, no matter how totally "de-anecdotalized" is still based upon a narrative, representational chain. The two dangers to avoid are still (1) pure conventionality, abstraction, or total separation from the real and (2) blind submission to nature or representation for representation's sake, as in the illusion of naturalism. The need to steer a middle course determines all the concretely worked out examples in *Montage*, thus the representation of an emblematic Barricade which takes up a number of its pages. The barricade figured will only be a Barricade as the result of a particular iconic activity of "schematization," or "generalization" (we shall deal with this presently), but this iconic work is secondary, because it only exists if preceded or accompanied by a work of figuration: "a model of incompleteness would be a picture which suppressed its figurative side, hoping to get by on its imagistic qualities alone. We would have a picture which could be . . . anything" (p. 349).

It is on these terms, then, that Eisenstein construes what he calls *obraz*, the *image*—by a succession of little touches, each one extending and modifying the one before:

1. the image is initially defined as "graphic design" with the word "design" understood, as Eisenstein notes, in the sense of "drawing" and not "planning" (see p. 342); regardless of its material form, figuration, in its composition and construction, must produce a design, in addition to reproducing the real.[31] A design of what? Of "what determines the psychological content of the scene and the interrelated actions of the characters": in other words, of an interpretation of this content;

2. in the subsequent stage, the process is described in more detail: the image of the theme is of a metaphorical order; thus, in the case of the Barricade, if one of the two representations (no. 2) is preferred

because "more expressive," it is because, in addition to the figuration of the object (the barricade and the street) it includes a metaphor of its essential content: the idea of *revolution*. Thus, in no. 2, the sign placed underneath the barricade (but an "underneath" only with respect to the space of the frame) will be read not as a "sign inverted or placed below" (which would have been the case if this "underneath" was referential), but as a literal rendering of the word *re-volution*, which exactly captures the meaning that this sign is supposed to have. Revolution—a reversal, with the bottom on top; herein lies the "imagistic" function of this sign, a compositional metaphor for this reversal, this "bottom on top." In "discovering" this metaphoricity (he provides several other examples: "a-version," "arrogance," "broken down" with sorrow, etc.), Eisenstein immediately claims it is one of his constants, whose presence he will trace all the way back as far as *Every Wise Man*: when Mamaieva "threw himself" at the portrait of his kinsman and rival, Kurchaiev, he really did "throw himself" at it, taking a dangerous leap through the circular frame which held the portrait;

3. and finally the image becomes *generalization*: responsible for expressing—always with the clause associated with its *interpretive* character, as we will see—the central *idea* that can be abstracted from the representation of a scene, and from this scene itself.

Here, in a succession of radically different, even contradictory, examples, Eisenstein examines the question of methods and aims. From Chinese "line" painting where "the generalization is so strong that figuration is in danger of being sacrificed" in the cause of "painting an outline of Real Form" (p. 350), and the Indian miniature representing through a kind of condensation (between the figure of the elephant and that of the intertwined maidens who form its interior) the idea of "royal bearing"(p. 354), to the barricade and the creation of a particular image from the general idea of struggle, an image adapted to the historical circumstances of this barricade. Clearly, then, there is no strict criterion at work. In addition, Eisenstein emphasizes that *generalization* (the idea) *is not everything*, and that there must be a final "social" determination, which will allow the *global image* to be a *particular* generalization (a particular interpretation, one which takes sides).

With a stroke of his brush, the Chinese artist expresses his own particular emotion before the essence of the thing he is revealing; the Indian miniaturist, whose subjectivity counts for nothing, expresses the divinity of Vishnu through the use of convenient stereotypes: Eisenstein himself envisages various images of barricades, "triumphant," "breached," "impregnable," and for each one—a different "elephant" (p. 355). There are *good* and *bad* generalizations, a constant theme, not only in *Montage* but also—and again it is impossible to say how much influence each had on the other—in the self-criticism of *Bezhin Meadow*.[32] And of course it is extra-filmic criteria—political criteria— that demarcate the good and the bad.

At this stage, we can see that the image is no longer simply a metaphor. Or to put it more precisely, in his analysis of iconic (and then filmic) metaphors, Eisenstein comes around to questioning the *nature of metaphor itself:* the process of transferring a specific "quality" or characteristic, from its proper context to a context with which it is not ordinarily associated—the important word here being "process," since, in contrast to this dynamic vision of metaphor, the global image, or generalization which incorporates all of the diverse metaphors produced in the course of the work of representation, is not a process but an end result (even if it retains "potentially dynamic characteristics") (p. 355).

In his discussion of metaphors, then, Eisenstein privileges productivity, or dynamics, as he calls it, without adhering rigorously to any customary definitions (metaphor as a rhetorical figure). This emphasis on the productivity of a signifying process, however, is nothing new—take for example this observation from 1929: "To me, montage is not an idea put together out of a series of fragments, but an idea that is BORN out of the encounter between two autonomous fragments" ("Dramaturgie der Film-Form").

Montage reaffirms this: a "worn" metaphor has no artistic interest; the image is constructed out of "fresh" metaphors (p. 355). And it is the very nature of montage to create in us (the spectator) the conditions for this cumulative process of constituting a global image. (Correspondingly, if cinema is dedicated to montage, it is because montage is the best way of maintaining this cumulative process.)

Montage also deals, at long last, with the criticisms so often directed against Eisenstein's neglect or contempt regarding the "content" of representation. The problem of content is posed quite clearly there, since the image is worthless, even nonexistent, if it does not express the "truth" of its content, a truth, we must add, that Eisenstein carefully divorces from all metaphysics.

In presenting, for example, the *danse macabre* conclusion to *Que Viva Mexico!* as an attempt to provide the *image* of the deceased bourgeoisie (as a class), he is apprehensive about the risks involved in such an idea: the risk of lapsing into "mysticism" crops up "every time the artist, in the heat of creation, strays from the paths of social generalization" (as had happened to Eisenstein himself in *Bezhin Meadow*) (pp. 366-67). This truth will only be an "authentic revelation" of reality if the artist has put himself "in the position of the proletarian class" (p. 369).

In the final analysis, then, the double concept of figuration/image represents for Eisenstein a unity of opposites (yet again). The revelation of the true content of the representation (the image, or the only correct image) can contradict the more simple "rendering"—as suggested by the famous tarpaulin used to cover the mutineers in *Potemkin*, a referential distortion to express a historical truth (see the text of *The Twelve Apostles*).

Moreover:

The true social meaning of the event arises out of the conflict between figuration and generalization in a global image. (p. 70)

And further:

When there is no tension between figuration and image, the danger is that of a simple, tonal symbolism (for example "good = white"). (p. 372)

These very typical comments restate two of Eisenstein's favorite themes: the necessity of foregrounding or calling attention to the means of expression,[33] and also the recourse to "conflict," whose methodologically unifying function, as Eisenstein triumphantly proclaims, now steps forward to subsume the problem of truth and/or its appearances.

Of course, we also find a corollary in the necessity of keeping "nature" at a maximum distance, a necessity all the more urgent as this nature lends itself, increasingly, to an unmediated interpretation—Mexico, for example:

I must note in passing that the compositional style of the frame was one of the fundamental problems of form in our Mexican film. Because of the intense generality of Mexican things and perspectives, it was extremely difficult formally to capture the style and spirit of Mexico in a way which would render it accurately. ("Torito," 1934)

In *Nevsky* and *Ivan*, there is also a mistrust of everything in "nature" which is "too" typical (Prokofiev, in agreement with Eisenstein, renouncing the true models of traditional musical forms in order better to reproduce them; or Eisenstein using numerous pictorial and photographic sources, but never portraits of historical figures, for the making of his "images"). In general, when nature itself is presented in terms of "images," any immediate representation of the referent is to be kept at a distance (but not suppressed). (Consider the metaphors suggested by Barthes, in noting how Eisenstein maintains a tension between on the one hand a will towards the "ideality of meaning"— as in Greuze—and a purely imitative anecdotal practice—as in Chardin) [in "Diderot, Brecht, Eisenstein"].)

II. "MULTIPLE POINT OF VIEW CINEMA"

The introduction of montage incorporates, *mutatis mutandi* (which is to say, in accord with the new temporal dimension of montage), everything that has just been said about the production of the image through the labor of composition. However, the initial logical proposition that follows from this move—if the frame is a spatial confrontation between objects (from the point of view of meaning, of course), montage is the organization of temporal confrontations between fragments—is dismissed by Eisenstein as being too reductive:

> For a spatial arrangement which is not designed with an eye to the successiveness of perceptions has nothing to do with composition. Conversely, a seriality set up through montage which would not simultaneously create the feeling of space would be just as far removed from our idea of composition. (p. 405)

If the study of montage is to have any relation to the study of framing, it will not be through a simple transposition of the latter into temporal terms, but rather an extension or generalization, or, as Eisenstein puts it, a qualitative shift. This is characterized by the wholesale extension of the concept of figuration/image, by way of a lengthy discussion of particular cases drawn from painting, literature, and theater. The essential element of this extension is the appearance of movement, in correlation to the introduction of the temporal factor:

—a purely physical movement, restored by the succession of the fixed frames (p. 400);

—an intellectual movement which constructs the "generalizing" image out of the succession of two figurations (two fragments, for example, but not necessarily)[34] (p. 404);

—and another intellectual movement, leading this time, by the confrontation of heterogeneous fragments, to the *concept*.

Once again, we find some old favorites: movement as the essence of all phenomenal effects;[35] the study of this movement, in effect, is central to all of the definitive properties of cinema, from the simple impression of reality (between two frames) to the recreation of the concept; and last, the relation between the global image and, on the one hand, the theme (the "physiological" aspect, to take up the 1929 term) and, on the other, the concept (the intellectual aspect).

The emphasis, then, is on the intellectualization of the whole process, by way of a critique of impressionism, for example, which he characterizes by "the dominance of the retina (the figurative imprint) over the regions of the brain (the imagistic reflection)." It is the latter, the image, which is highly valorized through its correspondence with what Eisenstein calls the very nature of our perception of the world:

> The principle of cinema lies in the reflection ... of an ultra-primary process—the eidetic. Reality exists for us as a series of perspectives and images ..., "extemporaneous photos" unified by the eidetic. (p. 402)

In other words, "to think is to generalize" (p. 401). The problem with impressionism is that "figurativity swallows up imaginicity"—the primacy of the visual and the negation of the expressive.

We can therefore assume that this notion of montage is quite close to the model of "intellectual" montage, with the exception of some of the specific details of the formal description of its working procedures. Roughly speaking, we could say that it is basically constructed around two principles:

1. *synecdoche*; the rules governing the production of meaning by montage are formulated in the following way (p. 408): (a) the fragment (primarily the close-up, which is the epitome of the fragment) represents a part; (b) according to the principle of the part for the whole, this part evokes the completed structure of a whole; (c) this is true for all fragments; (d) the chain of fragments of montage is then read off not as a succession of details, but rather as a succession of complete scenes (or of whole signifying complexes) and not explicitly figured, but rather evoked in the mind; (e) the successiveness of the fragments reproduces a movement: just as there is a "clash" of two concrete representations between consecutive shots, so too with two fragments, there is a "clash" of two figurations *implicitly* contained in the frame, since they are the whole of which the frame is the part.

This, then, is Eisenstein's notion of cinema as an art of synecdoche, and we can see it as a kind of modified version of the idea of intellectual montage. If cinema is inherently the art of montage, it is because, unlike theater, it lacks the means of showing the real "in the flesh," and must therefore pursue other channels in the production of its "images." As a result, each fragment is presented, not in terms of a slice of reality, nor even as the representation of a whole, but as a partial figuration which acts as a stimulus for generating associations (and then producing images from them) (p. 413).

2. *rhythm*; montage always involves the same two indissociable functions: producing narrative effects and simultaneously constructing an image of them "well beyond the limits of figuration" (p. 410). Eisenstein now posits these two functions in terms of a new unity of opposites, between a narrative principle and a "rhythmical" principle.

Naturally, the "rhythm" in question has very little in common with the ordinary sense of the word (a manipulation of the length of the fragments, accentuations, etc.): rhythm, in the ordinary sense, is only figurative (p. 451), whereas the rhythmical principle which governs the "imaginistic" capacity of montage operates at the highest level of generalizing the theme in its complete and concrete form (p. 410).

Here the 1929 position is quite clearly stated. Eisenstein himself claims (p. 451) that, ever since his lecture at the Sorbonne (1929), he had insisted on this *doubleness* (*dvuplannost'*) of montage, and that he is rewriting it now (1937) as the final form of the contradiction figuration/montage. The same reformulation is also evident in the *double* classification of types of montage put forward, first, in the "Course Outline" (under the title "the semantic ordering of types of montage"),[36] and second in "The Filmic Fourth Dimension" (which would be the "imagistic" typology); in the former, he lists various aspects of montage as a narrative principle, from "informative" montage to montage "which constructs a notion"; in the latter, from "metric" montage to "intellectual" montage, he discusses the principle of generalization through the image, hence the "rhythm" in the redefined sense of the word.

III. "SOUND CINEMA"

This is a new logical extension of the double base (narrative/rhythmic) which is fundamentally at odds with montage, an extension based on keeping this essential principle while making a few minor readjustments: the fact, for example, that the fragment, in the sound film, is no longer burdened with its role as a unit of *temporal rhythm* (even though it is still responsible for other rhythmical functions).

This expanded definition of the "rhythmical" principle falls between, on the one hand, what is left of it in the montage of fragments (and in the fragments themselves—in the "visual") and, on the other hand, what it acquires in the sound "outline," which partially replaces the purely graphic outline (in the instance of the frame) and the rhythmical movement (in silent montage). As a result, sound in the film avoids being a mere doubling of the visuals, or an adjunct element that is welded on—instead, its role is a totally integrated one, and thus the function of meaning is taken up concurrently by diverse "materials of expression" (*matières de l'expression*).

We end up, then, with a whole series of the synoptic lists which Eisenstein was so fond of, rigorously classifying the three "stages" of the cinema, the elements associated with figuration, and lastly, those responsible for the generalizing-imagistic function. This is how they are finally presented (p. 467):

	Figurative Principle	*Image-generalization*
First Stage.	Figuration of the object	Line of the contour
Line of the contour	Figurative outline of the object	Graphic rhythm (within the image)
Second Stage.	Frame	Montage
Montage	Narrative elements of montage	Rhythm of montage
Third Stage.	Montage-frame	Sound
Word-phrase	Object content	Melody of phrases
Melody	Melody of phrases	Rhythm
Music	Sonority	Intonation, melody, contrapuntal harmony

The governing principle of the "progress" of cinema is clear enough: whatever was responsible for producing the global image at any given stage is attributed to figuration in the consequent stage; and within each stage, the component of imaginicity is split into two (or more) parts: a "narrative" part, and a "rhythmical," or properly imagistic, part (this is the meaning of the second line of each stage, except for the third, which is somewhat more complex).

However—and this is what produces confusion at this point in the theory—each stage retains, in part at least, the features of the one before. In the cinema "of montage" (silent—stage 2), for example, the frame, in its composition, retains an imagistic quality, as does the visual montage of the third stage. Ultimately, Eisenstein goes as far as to imagine a completely new "mixture" of all the stages at the same time—instances, for example, where the function of figuration would be assumed by the music, and where the visual elements would construct the global image from this figuration (p. 463).

At this point in our commentary on "Montage 1937" (toward the last pages of the version that has come down to us), it would be appropriate to recall that this discussion of montage is probably the most purely theoretical text ever written by Eisenstein, particularly with regard to the last section, which is the least developed, and perhaps the least convincing (in part, this is probably because the practical experience it draws upon is nowhere near as substantial and significant as was the case with the first two sections). In any case, it is clear that these are absolutely not models or rules for practical applications ("those who look in my work for guidelines or recipes will be disappointed"— p. 427). On the contrary, the important thing here, besides the exhaustive insistence on the durability and preeminence of the principle of montage, is the discursive arrangement of a whole battery of figural and signifying elements. Although Eisensteinian theory in this period is far from stable, this base will remain unquestioned for the next (and last) ten years of his life. (Of all the treatises begun by Eisenstein, *Montage* is thus the most foundational; in spite of its incompleteness and hesitations, it is the one in which there is the most visible evidence of a theoretically systematic project.)

3. "New Problems of Form"

This base, among others, produces, in the making of *Ivan*, in the last courses at VGIK, and in his last essays, the "audio-visual counterpoint" that Eisenstein had prayed for and anticipated for more than a decade. In the analysis of the sequence from *Ivan*, we saw the way in which audio-visual counterpoint concretely appears, and I suggested the term *organic montage* for it. If we now compare this with all the work on figuration and global image, we can see how much is invested in its double structure: *abstraction* (in the active sense of the word), represented by the idea of synecdoche, which we have just discussed (and elsewhere, the idea of association); and *integration* of all the filmic fragments, together with what they stand for, into an organized and structured whole. This process of abstraction/integration, or of fragmentation/montage, is similar to the analysis/synthesis model except that the two moments of this process *always occur at the same time*, completely in line with the requirements of the Eisensteinian "dialectic." It is, in other words, modeled on the canonical dialectic form where each is determined by the other. Fragmentation (and the accompanying abstraction) can only be achieved if it is party to the idea of a totality. Conversely, the montage of fragments, or their contrapuntal positioning, presupposes fragmentation. In his last texts, Eisenstein absolutely insists on the overall totality and integration suggested by audio-visual counterpoint, or organic montage. This feature at once subsumes and is opposed to the intensification of conflicts, both local and global, which were more unilaterally foregrounded in silent cinema. This, then, is the situation in 1945:

> In our *Manifesto* of 1928, we proclaimed the stark separation and opposition of sound and image as a way of anticipating a future counterpoint. . . .
> In my opinion, what characterizes the new phase of audio-visual montage is its allegiance to the increasing homogeneity of the polyphonic harmony of montage. . . .
> Formally, the counterpoint of montage seems to recreate that delightful moment of becoming of consciousness, when the two preceding moments have been overcome, and the world, fragmented by analysis, falls back again into a whole, breathes life back into all the reciprocal relations between isolated particulars, and presents to a stunned consciousness the perceived fullness of a synthesized world. (*Nonindifferent Nature*, FW 4, pp. 165–66 and 171)

In the domain of film, where the color film on Pushkin he had dreamed about for several years failed to materialize, the major event in terms of the application of the theses on "organic" montage was, of course, *Ivan the Terrible*—where the use of this montage is particularly complex:

> When you really get down to the nuts and bolts of making a film in color, the difficulties are absolutely monstrous. You have to coordinate ten times the usual number of correlates. ("Lesson on Music and Color," FW 1, p. 280)

Starting from the laying out of all the elements, the specific "ratio" of the montage then determines the recomposition of these elements with regard to the constitution of the global image.[37] The crucial features of this process, as Eisenstein frequently emphasizes, are, first, the "equal rights" of the various audio-visual elements (figurations, montage, sound, color, etc.) and second, their common orientation with regard to the image, or dominant theme.

> Every element, from the role of the actor to details of the folds in his clothes, must be treated equally in the light of a single emotion, an emotion which determines everything and which forms the very base of the polyphony of a multi-layered composition." (*Nonindifferent Nature*, FW 4, p. 196)

(This pertains to the lengthy analysis carried out in *Nonindifferent Nature*, in which Eisenstein describes and demonstrates the double principle of dissemination/integration.)

One more thing should be said about this work on *Ivan*, and it concerns the appearance of the problem of color. In *Montage*, Eisenstein, as we know, had expressly dealt with the place of color in the audio-visual counterpoint. Thus, when color ceased to be a mere possibility, it assumed its natural place in the grand "polyphony" which had already been construed:

> Music has its necessary and specific place in film.
> Color has its necessary and specific place.
> Which means that both color and music have their necessary place at every instant and in every context, where they yield the fullest possible expression of what needs to be articulated, presented, and completed at any given moment of the filmic action. ("Color Film," 1948)

and:

> A navy blue shirt . . . is not only a manufactured object, but also a combination of very specific sonorities. ("Lessons about Music and Color," FW 1, p. 285)

—a polyphony which will also come to include 3-D, television, and many others. There is no need to emphasize this unduly: Eisenstein's statements about color have been quoted often enough (they often appear provocative when taken out of context, because they always stress the specific expressive value of color, independently, if you will, of its realist context), but generally speaking, they are only taken up as a way of affirming the "organic" nature of montage.

Eisenstein's final work does not deal with the essential features of this organic montage. It is not that this decade of intense and uninterrupted work did not raise "new problems of form," but rather, as we saw in the case of color, these new problems (perhaps in the long run they would have amounted to the beginnings of a much more substantial theoretical meditation) take their place naturally in the structure drawn up in *Montage*, a structure which they further enhance and elaborate:

1. the *accent*: in the concrete instance of the sequence from *Ivan, Part I*, I demonstrated the meaning of this notion, and above all, its fundamental association with organic montage; it conveys both the disseminated, protean nature of montage (the "sprinkling" of montage

into every nook and cranny of the chain of discourse) and its basically expressive nature:

> Just as the squeak must be dissociated from the squeaking boot before becoming an expressive element, so too the coloring of the tangerine must be dissociated from the idea of the color orange before the color can be included in the scrupulously arranged system of means of expression and influence. ("Color Film," 1948)

> While the image of a boot is associated with its squeaking, it does not as yet have any relation to the process of creation, but once the squeaking is dissociated from the boot, and registers on the face of a speaking character, you can say that you have started something going: you have something to express. ("Lesson on Music and Color," 1947, FW 1, p. 282)

> With the transition to audio-visual montage, the fundamental center of gravity, as a visual component of montage, is *internalized within* the fragment, within the elements included in the image itself. The center of gravity, then, is no longer what happens "between the shots," the shock, but rather what happens "within the shot," the distribution of emphasis within the fragment, which is to say, the very buttressing of the structure of representation. (*Nonindifferent Nature*, 1945, FW, p. 267)

This montage of citations could not be more clear: in its "visual component," montage is no longer simply a matter of the articulation between consecutive fragments, it has shifted on to ground internal to the shot (or fragment). This does not, however, mean the end of conflict, shock, or montage as articulation, for it is taken up, in a much more global fashion, and under a more general principle of organization, in the relations between the various components (sound, visual) of the "scrupulously arranged system of means of expression and influence": the autonomy of each element as an expressive element, the systematic and "egalitarian" combination of all the elements, and lastly, the production of a system aimed at maximum efficiency in its distribution of accent. Here we find again the problematic of *Montage*, and that of the "young Eisenstein"![38]

2. the *close-up*: the importance of this notion for Eisenstein is well known. It is presented, if you will, as a kind of particular instance of accent: the close-up, the "principle of close-up," as we saw it demonstrated in the interplay between depth and width in *Ivan*, is organically bound up with the expressive, imagistic, signifying function of audio-visual montage:

> ... the essential function of the close-up in our cinema is less a matter of *showing* and *figuring* as of *signifying, rendering significant, or providing a meaning.* This was one of the characteristics of our swift assimilation of the close-up and our very idiosyncratic conception of its nature—unlike in the practice of American cinema where it had scarcely been recognized as a means of figuration.
> From the very first, the methodology of the close-up had won us over with its astonishing capacity to create a new totality out of the juxtaposition of parts. ("Dickens, Griffith, and the Film Today," 1940–45)

As this last phrase indicates, the close-up is basically tied in with montage. A larger interpretation of the whole passage would conclude that the close shot has almost nothing to do with a cinema of scenic space: as Amengual puts it, "the close-up in Eisenstein is not a *closer* shot, it is a *magnified* shot," (in "Eisenstein and Hieroglyphs"). For Eisenstein, the transition to the close-up is not the adoption of a different point of view on the object from within the same scenic perspective: it is an actual "magnification," or affirmation of a meaning and its articulation (probably not without some figurative function besides). This is about as much as can be said, since we have already seen that Eisenstein did not write anything substantial on the subject; we can only point to the important place given over to the close-up as a sort of emblem in his texts.

3. although it does not give rise to any truly theoretical elaboration, one theme is increasingly and insistently foregrounded: that of organic unity (see Chapter 2). Before addressing it properly, I shall simply point to how this ideology of unity, present in the conception of montage in 1937-40, is pushed into the forefront of things (perhaps simply as a way of giving an ideological gloss to his theoretical work);

> One can only speak here of what is "comparable," so to speak, namely the movement which is as fundamental to the structural law of any given musical fragment as it is to the structural law of any given figuration.
> Here, the concepts of the law of the structure, of the process, and of the rhythm of the development of either of these two, actually constitutes the only solid ground for establishing a unity between them and others. ("Vertical Montage," Part 3, 1940).
> Once again: having explored each aspect of the means of expression to its limit, success is achieved through knowing also how to orchestrate, or balance, the whole, so that any single aspect considered on its own, will not detract from the whole, from this general compositional unity. ("Color Film," 1948)

III. From the Laws of Thought to the Laws of Nature

In trying to account for the panoramic array of Eisenstein's theoretical concepts, I outlined a distinction (in Chapter 2) between the two main areas of his research: other than his theoretical work on the filmic (montage), we can point to Eisenstein's study and theories of what has been called efficiency—a notion we have already encountered in many forms and many different topics.

Here we would be confronted with another chronology altogether: no longer a chronology of the so-called "periods" relating to montage, but a chronology of all the changing ways of thinking about how film communicates, transmits a message, or exerts influence. So widespread are these changes over the pages and the years, even in terms of vocabulary alone, that our first instinct is to ask, again, whether there are "several Eisensteins."

I think we could make our point very quickly (or at least *begin* to do so—the rest is beyond my scope and intentions) on the evidence of two observations:

—first, this is a constant, or at least recurrent, problematic in Eisenstein: from the manifestos on the "aggressiveness" of the attractions (theatrical or filmic) to the militant declarations of principle in his last years, there is no break—the "fundamental activity" of the Soviet cinema is "to reeducate and exercise an influence upon the people" ("Sergei Eisenstein," 1945).

—second, and more clearly than with the theories of montage, the question of efficacy is one in which Eisenstein seems preoccupied with grounding his reflections on rock and not sand: in discussing the hypothetical "laws of form," I have already noted this anxiety about the scientific *foundation* of his discourse. On this question of the relation to the spectator, more than anywhere else, Eisenstein wants to stick to a discourse which is as verifiable as possible.

We can only talk about a "development" or "periodization" here with respect to those philosophies or fundamental epistemes which have some lasting value in Eisenstein's work. This begins, as we know, with reflexology and the notion of stimulus: "The theory of stimuli and their montage within a specific orientation should provide all the materials for the problem of *form*" ("The Method of Making Workers' Films," 1925, FW 1, p. 27). What is at stake in Eisenstein's fascination for this mechanical theory of reflexes is, already, a *model*, or *laws*, not of thought itself, but of emotion, of the psyche, or the "superior nervous activity" which is Eisenstein's Pavlovian formulation.

Perhaps it was interior monologue that was the real breakthrough inasmuch as it really examines the laws of internal discourse, or thought. In effect, we could see a parallel between Eisenstein's own distinction between a harmonic montage producing effects which are "only" physiological, and intellectual montage—and the movement from reflexology to an investigation of the mechanism of thought.

The trajectory of this displacement could be traced back to a phrase from 1929 which anticipates the "direct filmic expression" [*écraniser*] of concepts "through a free accumulation of associative material" ("Dramaturgie der Film-Form"). It is followed by the first appearance of the "interior monologue" as such, in the form of a transposition (partly determined, at least, by the appearance of sound cinema) of this "free accumulation" of associations. In fact, the first concrete manifestation of the interior monologue, that of Clyde Griffiths in the adaptation of *An American Tragedy*,[39] is quite conventional, for it barely ventures beyond the descriptive, or the "rendering" of the mental state of a character, and therefore remains trapped within a dramatic, fictional, and scenic perspective. This never filmed script, however, was not without its consequences: on his return to Moscow, and to theory, Eisenstein applied himself to this problem from 1932 onward: "only a filmic element can capture the idea of a man's stream of consciousness in a state of emotion" ("Help Yourself!" 1932). This same formulation crops up again:

> The true material of sound film is obviously the monologue.
> And suddenly, in the course of the practical resolution of an unforeseen problem of expression, it all came together as the "last word" in the general area of montage forms. Theoretically, what I had been predicting for a long time, was now confirmed: in terms of structure, the form of montage is the restructuring of the laws of the grain of thought. ("Help Yourself!" 1932)

and again, a year later:

> As for the cinema, it seems to me that its specificity consists in reproducing phenomena in accord with all the features of the method for producing a reflection of reality within the movement of the psychic process. ("Pantagruel Is Born," FW 1, p. 249)

—going so far as to isolate, in the finest detail, correspondences between all the technical operations of the cinema and psychic, as opposed to physical, phenomena; the fade to black, for example, would not be echoed in the closing of an eye, but rather in the progressive fading of mental images, etc.[40]

A much more serious study of some of the sources of these ideas is needed (all the more so since, to my knowledge, this has been done only in a very sketchy way). Ben Brewster, for example, has suggested that the idea of "inner speech" can be attributed to Eichenbaum, who developed it at the same time as Eisenstein, and above all to the theoretical works of Vygotsky (which inspired the practical experiments of his disciple and Eisenstein's friend Luria, at the neurosurgical clinic in Moscow):[41] in effect, the connection between Vygotsky's 1934 publication of *Thought and Language*, and Eisenstein's comments at the 1935 filmmakers congress, on the theme of a "filmic language" modelled on the "language of thought," is more than coincidental.

On the other hand, we would need to ascertain to what degree the suggested analogy between the signifying structures of film and those of inner speech would have been able to serve as the basis for a new theory of montage. I am thinking especially of passages from the 1935 discourses which lean toward a *methodological* assimilation between cinematographic montage and the study of so-called "prelogical thought" (the models for which are chosen from a field that is radically heterogeneous to Vygotsky's concepts: Eisenstein caught red-handed in his pursuit of scientific legitimization): there is, for example the famous Bushman phrase, in which Eisenstein traces out for us the literal structure of a filmic type of editing. On this project, however— the story of which also remains untold—the clampdown came brutally and without any warning: even if Eisenstein did truly attempt to practically apply interior monologue in *Bezhin Meadow*, we will never be able to prove it. And in "Montage 1937" ("a period in which the excessiveness of certain positions from the twenties became apparent to him" as it is put, quite seriously, by the editors of the *Selected Works*), there is no trace at all of interior monologue; the emphasis there is no longer on a hypothetical conformity of filmic montage to mental structures (prelogical or not), but rather on the conformity of the image created by montage with the reality to which it is supposed to correspond (the theme of organicity).

Again, none of this, strictly speaking, is essential to any description of the systematic theories about montage. The way in which we had to link together "Montage 1937" with the texts from 1928–29 on intellectual montage, might even give the impression that interior monologue was only an episode, quickly concluded and forgotten. Such a conclusion would be much too hasty, however, and for at least three kinds of reasons:

—first, the question of inner speech (aside from the unfortunately recruited support of a concept so doubtful as Lévy-Bruhl's "prelogical thought")—or more precisely, the question of either the language(s) internal to thought, or of its (their) eventual function as a model for artistic discourses—is a very important question that has not had enough attention. As Emilio Garroni has noted in an important article, modern semiology has pursued the same question through different channels, picking up exactly at the point where it had been abandoned, in a rough and unfinished state, by Vygotsky's reflections and by Eisenstein's and Eichenbaum's attempts to turn it to account.

—second, and more specifically Eisensteinian: the problematic of efficacy, in general, or of the determination of "natural" laws of form in particular, has certain retroactive effects upon the conception of montage (inasmuch as the latter is instrumental in every concrete manifestation of these formal laws). Thus it would at the very least be necessary to determine if (and how) interior monologue is really, as Eisenstein himself puts it, a simple "resting-place" between his 1928 ideas of montage and those of 1937–40; in other words, an examination of its relations with intellectual cinema as much as with organic montage.

—and last, if interior monologue is itself absent from the treatise of 1937, its traces are certainly not. Given the very patchy state of our knowledge of Eisenstein's texts, it would be unwise to claim too much: suffice it to say that there does not appear to be an absolute hiatus between the theoretical place occupied by inner speech and that occupied by much more general (and vague) considerations concerning the question of "human expressivity," or the theme of organicity.

In order to specify its place and role as the philosophical "substructure" of the reflections on montage, we must say a little more about the concept of "organicity." The "organicity" of the montage effect does in fact assume the form of a philosophical determination: the social formation, mechanisms of thought, works of art, artistic techniques and processes, etc., are, at any given historical period, phenomena which develop organically at the heart of the totality which is the social formation—and, Eisenstein adds, upon a single base: man.

This, then, is the thesis (so reductively formulated that it is almost a caricature) which is hammered home throughout "Montage 1937," and it is almost redundant to point out once again how much it owes to the dominant Marxism of the period. A few telling examples should suffice:

The phenomenon of figuration/generalization is reflected in the process of the formation of general concepts (whether historically or at the level of individual consciousness). (pp. 352–53)

The principle of cinema did not fall from the sky. It came from the very heart of human culture. . . . And the completeness of cinema consists not just in figuration but also in the principle of overall composition, which is to say, in the form, or reflection of . . . Man. (pp. 399–400)

The basic principle of cinema . . . : a complete event is broken up into *nonautonomous* fragments which are put together in a new configuration. . . . It is almost like semen, which must die to be reborn. . . . A principle which embraces all of art, the cinema notwithstanding. (pp. 422–23)

The unitary image, corresponding to the unity of the mental image. . . . Finally, vital man, conscious and active, as the model, not only for representation, but also for structure itself. (p. 332)

Naturally, we stumble over the problems (especially in the last passage, with its astonishing "unity of the mental image") inherent to the whole notion of organicity: what does "vital man," and elsewhere, "human nature," mean? Without involving ourselves in the obvious critique of "Marxist humanism," we can outline the two tendencies affected most by the idea of the organic:

1. a whole series of approaches to the question of the actor, which are particularly notable because they seem to follow an evolutionary pattern.

Of course, this is a point which is often taken up to support the thesis of the "two Eisensteins": from the Eisenstein of the silents, who detested the very idea of the actor (for which he substituted the concept of *typage*) would emerge an Eisenstein who had gone back to theatricality, the actor, and acting, not only in his films, but also in his texts.

But in "Montage 1937," but also even in *Regissura*, the work of the actor is treated as montage (or more precisely, as *de-montage* and *re-montage*). For this is where we find a very detailed description of the "Stanislavsky system," which is surprising inasmuch as it actually marks the end of a long and hostile polemic by Eisenstein against the founder of Art Theater—but is otherwise perfectly in keeping with the Eisensteinian mode. Eisenstein's approach to Stanislavsky ignores the emphasis on psychological determination, and concentrates only on the rigorous analytical process by which Stanislavsky teaches students to break up a role into "fragments," and then reassemble them according to the technique for producing a montage of "global images"

(p. 423). Rather than make any further comment on Eisenstein's approach to acting, I will let him speak for himself: the "method of the actor . . . seems identical to that of montage in the cinema" (p. 417).

2. at the other extreme of the spectator, we find the same homogeneity, in this case, in the development of the concept of ecstasy. The place of the spectator in *Montage*, for example, is itself considered homogeneous in relation to montage, to all the work of signification, or the film-work: "each spectator makes his own choice of montage in selecting only certain aspects of the phenomena" (p. 412).

If montage, then, is presented as "an emotional technique common to both the actor and the spectator" (p. 409)—not to mention everything in between—the conclusion is hardly surprising: "not just a unity of method between frame and montage or between montage and the method of sound films, but also another important methodological unity: with the actor—with Man" (p. 422).

And so the ideologeme of *unity* surfaces again, in a new context: an organic unity of composition, a methodological unity of emotional and semantic phenomena (from the actor via the film to the spectator), a dialectical unity of nature—and finally, a political unity, the reabsorption within the "State of the whole people," of all possible divisions, and class struggle.

It would be wrong to end on such a reductive note. I want therefore to go back and emphasize for the last time the idea of *productive* montage. As we know, it is a notion which was often put forward (even in recent times) as a counter to both mechanical montage-bricolage and to simple (transparent) filmic continuity. It is also bandied about, often at random, and put through many changes: from the minimal definition, Balázs's for example, (a productive montage is "a montage through which we learn things that the images themselves cannot show") to the occasional tendency to celebrate the idea of the "production," or "work" "of the film"—which serves to fetishize words like "production" or "work."

For Eisenstein, the distinction is clear-cut: it is not the film which works or produces. The film is the trace or inscription of a specific labor of production (of meaning, for example) carried out by the director, or directors—and this inscription of a *process* must generate in the spectator, more or less mimetically (and that is the fly in the ointment), a new labor of meaning production. The job of the director is to "adjust" the film in such a way as to contain within strict limits the spectator's possible "responses."

In brief, the Eisensteinian system forges a link between the organization of the film (montage, in a general sense) and the psychic processes. This link is not just a transitory phenomenon of the theory of interior monologue: on the contrary, it permeates the whole system. We have already discussed it in passing, in the desire, expressed in "Montage 1937," not to make the global image a simple reproduction of "worn" metaphors, but to catch the metaphor in its emergent state. I have not, however, emphasized that in 1928, Eisenstein was already preoccupied with this same issue: in a response to questions from Bruno Frei, he claims:

> We have been wrong about the concept of the symbol. It is incorrect to say that symbolism has died out. The power of symbolization is still alive, for it is an essential part of human reaction to sensation.

At this point, Frei interrupts: "Ah ha, so you are a Freudian!":

> Of course, the cinema must face up to the fact that everyone symbolizes unconsciously. It is not the completed symbol that interests me, but rather the process of symbolization. ("Interview," printed in *Schriften* 3)

This emphasis on the process of symbolization is absent from the criticism of those who reproached Eisenstein for his abuse of metaphors: Eisenstein was only interested in metaphor and metonymy as figures of *thought*—as fundamental figures of the very processes of thought.

There is no shortage of examples. Amengual, in one of the most famous, argues that the stone lions in *Potemkin* function both as a metaphor for the anger of the people and as a metonymy for the town of Odessa (because they are made from the same stone). There are also a number of examples in *October* which have been discussed by Marie-Claire Ropars;[42] I will cite only one of these, the statue called "First Steps," which appears immediately after the scene in which one of the young defenders of the palace is reprimanded by one of his officers, who scolds him with "Think of your mother!" In the juxtaposition of shots, the statue can be interpreted, with some irony, as a maternal signifier, related to the strict regime exercised by the White officers over the young "junkers." The same statue, however, is soon found in another scene, where the female soldiers are exercising and where it serves to mark the relation between two kinds of female figures: the mother and the soldier (the latter characterized by a well-known misogyny). The image of the statue acquires a complex meaning from these appearances: it is a good example of *Symbol in Werden*, the symbol in the process of being formed, in the act of becoming.

To end here is a daring move. At the very most we can outline some of the questions which besiege the Eisensteinian problematic: can montage (the "principle of montage") be compared to any specific instance of the metaphoro-metonymical movement? Or, more generally: is the principle of montage a reflection of "thought" (the internal processes of symbolization which characterize human thought)? What would be the form of articulation between the reproduction of these processes by montage, and the production of meaning for a spectator? And would it be the notion of *ecstasy* that marks the "organic" fusion of the link between the "process of symbolization" and the efficacy inherent in montage?

 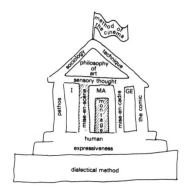

In the *Selected Works* appears this well-known drawing, representing the "building to be built." Eisenstein has this to say about it:

N.B.
If I were a lover of diagrams, this is how I would represent the task (*opus*) before me.
What is important here is:
1. the two levels of human expressiveness
2. montage as the door to a conception of image
3. the image erected on the base of human expressiveness
4. that all study is armed with the dialectical method—the *nec plus ultra* of philosophy and of the cinematic method, the *nec plus ultra* of the actual stage in the development of art.
5. *montage* is *already* written *vertically*, which means that it unifies everything right up to the latest ideas about sound, by dint of its own purpose.

This is probably the best emblem of the image which haunts Eisensteinian discourse, that of the "Building to be built," the system to be constructed. If this obsession is not actually spelled out until the last texts (notably in *Immoral Memories*, with the quotation from Blake: "I must Create a System, or be Enslaved by another Man's") it had been in evidence ever since *Regissura*, the first of the great unfinished treatises which mark the period from 1934 to 1948—if not, retrospectively, even earlier still, in the insistent desire for systematization which characterizes the texts of 1928–29.

Eisenstein, then, as the founder of a theoretical system—a statement which seems innocuous enough, but which clashes, as we have seen, with so many received ideas. The Eisensteinian system has a very specific make-up; in short, it is a system which is not properly conceptualized. This is not, of course, to say that there are no Eisensteinian concepts (in Chapter 2, I even tried to draw up a short list of them)—but they are concepts that hover freely above a fixed base which, if it existed, would be the only valid contender for the name of "system." Eisenstein's research, the projects which outline his system, would always be a displacement (and this would be its *experimental*, or empirical side) of this system. The filmic theory proposed by Eisenstein could never be formulated in fixed concepts, not even provisionally: it would always pine after a certain degree of theoretical license—the same license which determines that the notion of montage cannot be fixed, or defined, but only designated by the phenomena with which it is associated.

Hence, Eisenstein's ambiguous relation to theory, and even more so to philosophy and the sciences. On the one hand, he insists on perceiving his research as the construction of a systematic "edifice," but, on the other, he cannot be satisfied with a conceptualization of this system that is not as strict as its rationality demands. And this is why he looks to the philosophical, scientific, and ideological apparatuses, available there and then, for a *founding* base (the foundations of the "building to be built") or compositional substructure. This much is clear even from the above diagram of the building: the solidity of the plinth of "dialectical method," the roofing prudently furnished by "sociology" and "technique," the central and lofty position given over to the "philosophy of art" and the theory of language ("sensory thought")—and, by contrast, the wavering, almost unattached, quality of the small flag, "method of the cinema."

Let us not dwell, then, upon the details of those rather unsatisfactory approaches to Eisenstein which draw upon a philosophy (or a "science") for their founding impulse. Dialectical Materialism, in particular (or Marxism-Leninism in general), can only act as a closed framework in relation to Eisenstein's theories: a framework of thinking within which Eisenstein was never quite at home, whether he went out of his way to respect the doxa, or whether he parodied the canonical models (see ecstasy as a dialectical bond)—a framework, nonetheless, which commentators persist in applying to him, as if it were a prison or a tomb.[43]

I am not suggesting, however, that there is any more to be gained from stripping Eisenstein of this "framework"—especially if this means (as with Raymonde Hébraud's work)[44] seeing Eisenstein only in terms of a creative force, or protean adversion to form, etc., and ignoring the numerous statements in which Eisenstein himself insists on the importance of a theoretical framework (his own). I would be the last to deny that there are some bewildering moments in Eisenstein's films (the color sequence in *Ivan*) which one is tempted to read as a kind of vertiginous response to the frenzied willfulness of his writing; in other words, that there is in him an overriding energy, movement, or force, which is captivating, uncontrollable, and nevertheless delightful. Let us not forget, however, that these various manifestations of ecstasy are all acknowledged and accounted for in his system "to be built." This Eisensteinian ecstasy is interesting, not as some flipped-out state, nor as a dialectical leap—but as a calculated mastery of the former at the cost of a reduction to the latter, at least with respect to its place in a general system of filmic *form*. (This is to put things rather baldly, but I feel justified, nonetheless, in saying that Eisenstein had no truck at all with any kind of formlessness which he had not already anticipated and immediately transformed into a formal value.)

This study has been somewhat limited. If it had been longer, our first priority would have been to describe further the Eisensteinian system whereas here we have only been able to postulate its existence without really filling in any of the outlines. We have taken another look at Eisenstein, but a look which is far from undiscriminating, and without which it would be impossible to do anything with him except sing his praises.

With such a description (and only as a result of it), it would be possible to judge this system in all of its irreducible specificity—what it always was, so to speak—or else to put it to work by taking it for what it is: *one* partial, unfinished, and dated theory—but one of the very few we have—of filmic form.

NOTES

Wherever possible, the translators have referred to the titles of existing English translations of Eisenstein's essays. Two exceptions to this rule are the important texts "Vertical Montage" (actually three essays, translated as "Synchronization of Senses," "Color and Meaning," and "Form and Content: Practice" in *The Film Sense*) and "Off-Frame" (translated as "The Cinematographic Principle and the Ideogram" in *Film Form*). Where English translations were not available, the translators worked from Aumont's French. In his new bibliography, printed at the end of this volume, Aumont has translated the titles of Eisenstein's essays directly from Russian to English. When the title of an existing English translation differs significantly from Aumont's English, it too is cited in the bibliography.

1. Notes Towards a Biography

1. The beginning of a piece from 1944 (FW 3,227). For the sake of a clean reading, throughout this chapter, many of the sources for quotations from *Immoral Memories,* trans. Herbert Marshall (Boston: Houghton Mifflin, 1983) (most of them are from this book, referred to throughout as IM) have been purposely left out. References to RW are from Eisenstein's selected works in six volumes, *Izbrannie proizvedeniia v chesti tomakh* (Moscow: Izdatielstvo Iskusstvo, 1964–71), and references to FW are from *Oeuvres* in six volumes (Paris: 10/18, 1974–80).

2. Clearly, it is in keeping with the "rosy-hued" nature of *Immoral Memories* that it contains no references at all to his professional difficulties or failures: there is nothing about *Bezhin Meadow,* almost nothing about *Que Viva Mexico!,* or on the criticism of his work in the thirties, etc.

3. A repression corroborated by the little that we know about his emotional life. Although they do not recount the same stories (Shklovsky tells us that he was in love with someone called M.P. at Vojega in 1919, and that Judith Glizer was an intimate admirer; Seton describes her own affair with him, and confirms that Elena Telechova meant a lot to him, etc.), his biographers are all agreed that Eisenstein did not readily reveal his romantic interests. Marie Seton's biography is *Sergei M. Eisenstein: A Biography* (London: Bodley Head, 1952); Shklovsky's book is *Kniga pro Eisensteina* (Moscow: *Iskusstvo kino,* nos. 1, 2, 3, 4, 5, 10, 11, and 12).

4. This reluctance to reveal his emotional life extends into relations with friends. Even his friendship with Maxim Strauch, whom he knew from childhood days in Riga, stayed with for several years in Moscow, and continued to see right up until his death, does not warrant much mention (see the memoirs of Strauch, in the collection of biographical memoirs edited by Yurinev, *Eizenshtein v vospominaniiakh sovremennikov* [Moscow: Iskusstvo, 1973]).

5. For example: "Now it's nobody's business that my parents were divorced in 1909" (IM, p. 21).

6. "For I am unworthy to undo the straps of his sandals, even though he wore felt boots in the unheated theater workshop on Novinsky Boulevard" (IM, p. 75).

7. "How I Learned to Draw," (IM, pp.39–50).

8. This confusion about women is manifest in countless passages from Eisenstein's texts. Among them, we can cite the chapters "Souvenirs d'enfance," and "The Knot That Binds" from *Immoral Memories*. There are, of course, many examples from his films, the most obvious being the soldier-women in *October* (see the very relevant remarks of Pierre Sorlin in *Octobre, écriture, et idéologie* (Paris: Editions Albatros, 1976), pp. 149–52.

9. See the Foreword to *Immoral Memories*. The first three paragraphs contain a warning about the "immoral" nature of what is to follow—only to prove, however, that it is by dint of the book's highly cultured nature that it is "immoral" without being in the least bit "intimate." Indeed, there is no sex in it at all: "I read a book of pornographic memoirs [Frank Harris] and I can't remember a single one of the salacious scenes" (IM, p. 1).

10. We know that he had at least read *The Childhood Memories of Leonardo da Vinci* (see Jay Leyda, *Kino: A History of Russian and Soviet Film* [London: Allen & Unwin, 1960], p. 194: "Interview with Ilya Weissfeld," *Cahiers du cinéma*, no. 208), *The Interpretation of Dreams* (see "Interview with Bruno Frei" in *Eisenstein: Schriften*, 3, p. 259), *Moses and Monotheism* (see "Montage 1937," RW 1, pp. 416–17), and a book by Hanns Sachs and Otto Rank called *The Importance of Psychoanalysis to the Mental Sciences* (approximate title, cited in an unpublished text from *Method*, sent to me by the Eisenstein Archive in Moscow).

11. "I shall give you the basic slogan that has always guided my pedagogical work . . . my slogan has been, is, and presumably always will be: 'Tell all. Hide nothing. Make no secrets of anything.'

"A question immediately arises: Is not this very slogan, this position, this now long-established practice the sharpest of rebuffs to Papa? To Papa, who hid 'secrets' from me; to Papa, who didn't initiate me into them, allowing me to drift with the current and in one way or another come upon the discovery of the facts of life" (IM, p. 73).

12. "Program for teaching the theory and practice of film directing" (1936 version: RW 2, p. 131). The many stenographed notes from the course which have been published give us some idea of this teaching practice (see, among others, volume four of RW which is devoted almost exclusively to the courses).

13. Vladimir Nizhny, one of Eisenstein's students, wrote an account of the courses he attended at the VGIK, *Na ouvrokakh regissouri* (Moscow: Iskusstvo, 1958), translated into English and edited by I. Montagu and J. M. Leyda as *Lessons with Eisenstein* (London: Allen & Unwin, 1962; New York: Hill & Wang, 1963).

14. Jean-Louis Comolli, *Le réalisateur à vingt têtes*, preface to French edition of Nizhny, *Mettre en scène* (Paris: 10/18, 1973), p. 15.

15. The words "master" and "mastery" crop up in Eisenstein's writing with amazing regularity (taking into account that the words are more frequently used in Russian than in English) and are used much less to refer to a body of teaching than in the sense in which Eisenstein uses them to mean mastery as such. Of course, the terms apply most of all to Meyerhold, who is almost always described as "my master."

16. "Current opinion always holds sexuality to be aggressive. Hence the notion of a happy, gentle, sensual, jubilant sexuality is never to be found in any text. Where are we to read it, then? In painting, or better still: in color"

Roland Barthes by Roland Barthes, trans. Richard Howard (New York: Hill & Wang, 1977), p. 143.

17. Without preempting what I will say later, we can point to (1) his inability to finish (a book, a film), and thus the paradoxical fact that his only two completed books (*Film Form* and *The Film Sense*) were completed by editors; and also, on another level, his "relief" over a film like *Nevsky*, where he had been confronted with an absolute deadline to meet (Albéra discusses this in *Notes sur l'esthétique d'Eisenstein,* p. 12); and (2) the inability to work a theoretical concept through.

Ivor Montagu provides an interesting testimony to Eisenstein's "impatience" as it was manifest in the time he spent in Hollywood: "a person of fantastic energy, periods of fantastic laziness alternating with tremendous activity. Plans, schemes, ideas, would chase themselves around in his mind at times when he did nothing. But when the undertaking was launched, he would rest no hour of the day or night" (quoted by Ernest Lindgren in the introduction to the script of *Que Viva Mexico!* [London: Vision Press, 1971]).

18. "Wie sag' ich's meinem Kind?!" (IM, pp. 73–80). This is why it is quite absurd to try to reconstruct the conversation, as Shklovsky nonetheless tries to do in his biography of Eisenstein (even if he did have the advantage of personally knowing both the man and the period); indeed I would argue that Eisenstein's text, although obscure and bombastic, is more revealing than Shklovsky's quite mundane account.

19. A phrase attributed by Eisenstein to the Chinese philosopher Wang Pi (IM, p. 42). The essential characteristic of the Eisensteinian text seems to be a certain rapidity of impression (in the movement of the writing), and so from this point of view, it is difficult to believe Marie Seton's claim that "he would sit for hours over the wording of one sentence" (Seton, p. 260).

20. "Montage 1937," RW 2, p. 334.

21. Eisenstein says this outright when he quotes the French of Gaston Nandé: "Il n'appartient qu à ceux qui n'espèrent jamais être cités, de ne citer personne ("Only those who never expect to be cited, never cite anyone else), "Montage 1937," RW 2, p. 334.

22. See the two fragments appended to *Method,* respectively entitled "Twenty Years Ago" (FW 3, p. 291), and "Unity" (FW 3, p. 297).

This assumption of his authorial status is very often related to a fantasy: "If I were an external spectator, I would say of myself . . . " (a phrase which recurs throughout these two texts cited above). Indeed, Eisenstein frequently writes in the third person in these texts, or uses impersonal constructions as if to put some distance between the analysis of his own practice and the practice itself (I cannot agree with Pierre Sorlin's opinion that such impersonal turns of phrase are "rare").

23. See Rémy de Gourmont's famous maxim, which Eisenstein cites on a number of occasions: "Eriger en loi les fruits de ses observations personelles est une aspiration inévitable de l'homme, s'il est sincère."

24. The only one that has been attempted is Dominique Fernandez's *Eisenstein* (Paris: Grasset, 1975), and it is a rather shoddy affair (there is no other way of putting it): he does not read one-fourth of Eisenstein's published texts—especially *Immoral Memories*—he makes hasty conclusions about facts that are either unverifiable or have clearly been fabricated, and plagiarizes shamelessly from earlier work. In spite of the author's native intelligence, and his two or three pages of genuinely good analysis, the book is quite forgettable.

25. He also notes some other, more trivial failures: because he transforms obedience into rebellion, he cannot play the piano, or ride a horse, and lacks

any general knowledge of the finer social arts. Most important, however, as has been noted above, is his refusal to take the place of the father (see above, the discussion of mastery).

26. I have already mentioned his adoration of, or filial piety toward, Meyerhold. In his memoir of Eisenstein, Maxim Strauch gives an account of Eisenstein's visit on the day he had just recovered all of Meyerhold's artistic and literary papers: "You should have seen Eisenstein then! He was in his element. Glued to his chair from early morning until late evening, lovingly devouring page after page. He picked them up, read them, reread them, and could not put them down. . . ." As for his Oedipal "hate" for Meyerhold, Shklovsky tells us that Meyerhold's own advice to his students was—to hate him!

27. One of Eisenstein's lessons, which Nizhny describes in some detail, was about a possible mise-en-scène of the murder scene in *Crime and Punishment* (*Lessons with Eisenstein*, pp. 95–139, especially pp. 98–99).

28. References made here to *Nonindifferent Nature* and "Montage 1937."

29. "The moment I saw Tetlapayac, I knew that it was the place I had been looking for all my life" (Eisenstein's words, according to Seton, p. 195).

30. We should also note here that it was *Every Wise Man* which made Eisenstein a *master*. Following in the footsteps of Meyerhold (whose version of *A Doll's House*, according to Shklovsky, was equally radical), he courted his master's recognition of this, as witnessed by the dedication inscribed on a photograph which Meyerhold sent to him: "I am proud of the student who has become a master. My love to this master who has his own school already. To this student, to this master, to Sergei Eisenstein, my highest regards" (photo reproduced in RW 5, and in *Cahiers du cinéma*, no. 226–27, p. 55).

31. In my preface to *Au-delà des étoiles* (FW 1, p. 15).

32. The first of these statements dates from February 18, 1940, when he announced that "the pact of August 1939 provided a solid foundation for increasing cultural cooperation between two great peoples" (Seton, p. 398)—a cooperation that was to bear fruit, to name only one instance, in a production of *The Valkyrie* at the Bolshoi in the fall of 1940. The second statement dates from July 3, 1941, and is reprinted in the collection *Jewish Brothers of the World*, published in 1941 by the Gospolitizdat (State political press).

33. These pages were written before I had read the last part of Christian Metz's *The Imaginary Signifier*, which contains an analysis of the characteristics of Freud's style, an analysis which applies very well, I think, to Eisenstein himself:

"Freud was little inclined towards the type of statement which exhaustively enumerates the pertinent features of a concept in the form of an explicit, independent proposition. . . . He was more interested in the phenomena than in the naming process, and his doctrinal apparatus was often only gradually put together, via a series of slips and slides . . . rather than being assembled all at once and for once and for all, according to a directly conceptual procedure commonly seen as the only possible form which intellectual 'rigor' can take . . . Some of his concepts, appearing as they do several times in the same book or from one book to the next, are never exactly 'set out,' they progress, or rather they make their way . . . and he sometimes neglects to consider retrospectively the ways in which these semisuperimposable developments might be matched up." Can we not also find in Eisenstein's theoretical texts this same "remarkable way in which they manage to combine on the one hand a reiterative stubbornness and an *esprit de système*, on the other a frequent lack of concern for formalization, which is almost the exact opposite"? (*The Im-*

aginary Signifier, trans. C. Britton, A. Williams, B. Brewster, & A. Guzzetti [Bloomington: Indiana University Press, 1982], pp. 231–32).

2. Eisensteinian Concepts

1. The word "image" is used here in the ordinary sense of the term and not in the very particular meaning given to it by Eisenstein in a large part of his theoretical work, a meaning which is dealt with in detail in Chapter 4.

2. In a fragment very probably intended to be inserted into the major essay on "Montage" (1937) and quoted in footnote by the Soviet editors (RW 2, p. 548), Eisenstein begins a critique of harmonic montage which coincides with what is being suggested in the present work. He says that in the absence of the possibility of actually calculating all the parameters of a fragment, the danger of this form of montage would be that of falling, through laziness, into the practice of a montage based on a "meaning" attributed to each fragment. That, Eisenstein says, would lead back to the most primitive phases of the development of the art. (I am summarizing his argument very briefly.)

3. The respective references for these examples: Excerpt from a course on *Ivan the Terrible* given at the VGIK in March 1947 (RW 3, pp. 591 ff.; FW 1, p. 294); third part of "Vertical Montage," 1940 (RW 2, p. 235; translated as "Synchronization of Senses" in *The Film Sense*); "On the Subject of Directing" (subtitled, *Mise en jeu* and *Mise en geste,* in French in the Russian text, dated January 1948, RW 4, pp. 717 ff.); finally, "Montage 1937", in particular, RW 2, pp. 418 ff.

4. The reader interested in learning more about the development of the concept of the "profilmic" is referred to Etienne Souriau's article, "Les grands caractéres de l'univers filmique," *Revue internationale de filmologie,* No. 7-8 (no date).

5. Lest the reader wonder why Aumont finds it necessary to specify that the word "shooting" should be read as "active" in this context, it should be pointed out that the corresponding French term, *prise de vue,* uses not a present but a past participle, used in this case as a noun. Aumont is stressing the fact that in normal filming situations, and in the usual critical terminology, *prise de vue* is a frozen stereotype, in which the active notion of *prise* (from *prendre,* to seize, to take, to extract) is lost, and that Eisenstein's filmic practice and theory rejuvenated this expression, giving it a new and active sense. (Translator)

6. See in particular "Perspectives" (1929), RW 2, pp. 35 ff.; FW 2, pp. 189–190, and "Montage 1937," RW 2, p. 338.

7. "Off-Frame" (translated as "The Cinematographic Principle and the Ideogram" in *Film Form*) and "Dramaturgie der Film-Form," both from 1929. What is anticipated in this metaphor of the frame as a "cell of montage" (a proposition which Eisenstein opposes to Pudovkin's, the frame as "element of montage," referring to a conception of montage as a game of construction, erector-set-like) is obviously another metaphor, this one also biological, which will be condensed in the word "organicism." See below, Section IV of this chapter.

8. See P. Bonitzer, "Le Gros orteil," *Cahiers du cinéma,* No. 232, pp. 14 ff. In particular, Bonitzer brings out the way in which the question of the close-up is inseparable for Eisenstein from that of montage and from that of the fragment and bears witness in addition to the fact that these latter two concepts function simultaneously in Eisensteinian theory. For Bonitzer, the close-up is what "marks and remarks the discontinuity of film space and sweeps

the vision, the image up in the substitutive movement of writing." Curiously, the theme of the close-up which is ironically so "Eisensteinian," was not the subject of a special study by him. He only approaches this problem (frequently, it is true) from other angles, apropos of other theoretical questions and, above all, of course, in the texts on montage (see "Montage 1937," [RW 2, p. 456], for example, the analysis of the superimpositions in *Strike*, superimposing a close-up over a medium shot, and thus making clear the abstraction of the close-up; or again, see a later text, "Dickens, Griffith, and Us," dating from 1942 [RW 5, pp. 129 ff.; translated in *Film Form* as "Dickens, Griffith, and the Film Today"], the role of the close-up in montage; etc.)

9. Pascal Bonitzer, "Voici," *Cahiers du cinéma*, No. 273, Jan.-Feb. 1977, pp. 5–18.

10. Jean-Pierre Oudart, "La Suture," *Cahiers du cinéma*, No. 211, April 1969, pp. 36–39. (See *Screen*, 18, No. 4, for an English translation by Stephen Heath, entitled "Cinema and Suture." This issue of *Screen* contains other articles on Oudart's concept of the suture, grouped together under the general title "Dossier on the Suture.")

11. Eisenstein himself moreover specifically indicated that what he terms "conflict" is none other than a variation on the Marxist-Leninist concept of "contradiction." See in 1942, in "Dickens, Griffith, and the Film Today," this statement—"conflict (read, contradiction)," RW 5, p. 165.

12. "Im Gebiete der Kunst verköpert sich dieses dialektische Prinzip der Dynamik im KONFLIKT als dem wesentlichen Grundprinzip des Bestehens eines jeden Kuntswerks und jeder Kunstgattung." "Dramaturgie der Film-Form," 1929, *Schriften* 3, p. 201.

13. At the beginning of "Montage 1937," Eisenstein, in fact, recalls his positions in the article "Off-Frame," and in particular the "genetic" connection postulated by him between frame and montage, and regrets that his position of that period, according to which framing was only a specific instance of montage, would seem to have discouraged any study of the frame, composition, etc. He therefore announces his intention to do such a study in his essay, and begins, not insignificantly, by talking about a film which "poses the problem of the frame all the more pointedly since it has not been edited." —*Que Viva Mexico!*, see RW 2, pp. 336–37.

14. Indeed, as early as 1924, in "Montage of Cine-Attractions," Eisenstein develops this idea of heterogeneity by opposing the montage of attractions ("confrontation of subjects aiming at a thematic effect") to the process of "description," termed "theatrical" by him, and to parallel montage in the exposition of a subject, as well as to the simple process of "contrasted confrontations" (which, however, has the merit of "producing a precise and powerful emotional effect")—all of these processes have in common the defect of not producing enough heterogeneity from one shot to the next. See RW 2, p. 275; FW 1, pp. 131–32.

15. The first article (unpublished at present) in which Eisenstein sets forth the idea of an "intellectual" montage is, in fact, called "IA 28" ("Intellectual Attraction 1928"). See also "Intellectual Cinema," (IM, p. 207–8; RW 1, pp. 470, exact date unknown) in which Eisenstein tells the story of how this idea came into being.

16. Respective references to these slogans: "On the Problem of the Materialist Approach to Form" (1925), RW 1, p. 113; FW 1, p. 151; "Montage of Attractions," (1923) RW 2, p. 270.

17. It should be remembered that the *New Spectator* (*Novyi zritel'*) was the name of a magazine which appeared during the twenties.

18. I am borrowing this word, through Metz, from Gilbert Cohen-Séat, for whom it designates, "not the effectiveness of a particular procedure or a specific act, but the power possessed by a means of expression in its own right" (Metz, *Essais sur la signification au cinéma*, [Paris: Klincksieck, 1968] p. 40, note 1).

19. "The Method of Making Workers' Films" 1925, FW 1, p. 26. It is true that in later texts, other "failures" will be attributed to causes that are of a more formal nature, either completely contingent ones such as the slowing down of the speed of projection of *Potemkin*, required by the musician Meisel, which "demolished" the effect of the roaring lions ("Reverse Music," IM, p.98; RW 1, p. 321); or more essential ones, like the smile on Anastasia's corpse, that seems to approve Ivan's plans as he leans over her coffin, the effect of which was so ridiculous that Eisenstein cut it out (*Nonindifferent Nature*, RW 4, pp. 350 ff.; FW 4, p. 211); or like the shots from *Potemkin* which were originally inserted into the cream separator sequence in *The General Line* and which were removed on grounds of "inorganicism" ("Pathos," RW 4, p. 78; FW 2, p. 114)—not to mention the "intellectual" sequences of *October*, often criticized by Eisenstein, and which we shall return to later in this work.

20. See "The Little Horse of Viatka" (RW 3, pp. 500 ff.), in which attraction, in 1946–47, is once again valorized as one of the means of autonomizing expressive processes, of which it represents the essence. (This question of "autonomizing" is itself at the center of Eisensteinian reflections on color. This subject will be returned to in the second section of Chapter 4.)

21. Thus, for example, in *1935* we read: "The cinema is taking a new leap forward. Slogans expressing a stance with respect to matters of revolutionary theory and philosophy on the cinema front pose the problem of the passage from a revolutionary thematic in general, from the inflamed pathos of earlier stages to the taking of a position with respect to those themes. In the same way that the method of communism is the superior form of the scientific class struggle, likewise the problem of the living image of the Bolshevik is crystallized on the crest of the revolutionary thematic and the traditions of the revolutionary cinema. On the screen, we no longer see only the masses, only the revolutionary, only the event and the chain of facts, the initiator of which proves to be the wisdom of the party. On the screen the flesh-and-blood Bolshevik appears in concrete circumstances for a concrete task." ("The Most Important of the Arts," RW 5, pp. 239–240). In *1939*—"The mastery demonstrated by those whose collective efforts have made this production is admirable. The theme of the film is admirable. And equally admirable are the sentiments stirred in us by this magnificent film, *Lenin in October, Lenin in 1918* (films by Mikhail Romm), above all, it is Lenin in our hearts. It is Lenin, as he lives in the memory and the feelings of the many millions of our people. This Lenin whose great cause we are carrying out" ("Lenin in Our Hearts," RW 5, p. 256). In *1946*—"What are the films whose sounds and images have been spread so far and wide throughout the country and popularized the idea of the economic superiority of the kolkhoz system, which is the basis of the military successes we have seen? . . . What other film has sung with so much enthusiasm and *joie de vivre* of the unbreakable bonds of friendship uniting the peoples of our country? . . . What other film, in the very midst of war, has brought to the country's screens with so much colossal temperament, brilliance, and vehemence the thesis on the military combat of the party leader?" ("On Ivan Pyriev," RW 5, pp. 453–54). (Dozens of pages could be filled with passages in the same vein.)

22. "The experimentation with 'interior monologue' as a partial solution of the subject is a 'resting-place,' but in the same way that Gargantua, the

father, is a 'resting-place' between Grandgousier, the grandfather, and the grandson, Pantagruel" ("Pantagruel Is Born," 1933, RW 2, p. 303).

23. François Albéra, *Notes sur l'esthétique d'Eisenstein* (Lyon: Centre d'Etudes et de Recherches Théatrales, Cinématographiques et Télévisuelles, 1973).

24. At the famous Soviet Cinematography Congress of 1935, to which I refer frequently, he was one of only two people (Kuleshov was the other) to speak in support of Eisenstein and theoretical research in general.

25. On this point I differ with François Albéra, who sees things very clearly when he points up the confusion of the Eisensteinian vocabulary on the question of form, but whose analysis remains too ahistorical. Thus, for want of sufficiently perceiving the tactical movement which marks Eisenstein's attitude all throughout the thirties, he believes he traps him in contradictions which are only in the words. However, apart from this lack of historical perspective (which is not negligible!), Albéra clearly shows how the "Hegelian" formulations of 1935 are as opposed to the dialectical proclamations of 1925 as they are to the theme of organicism of the forties (*Notes sur l'esthétique d'Eisenstein*, pp. 52 ff.).

26. As Albéra points out very correctly, Eisenstein could have taken as his own this statement of Tretyakov's: "Ideology is not in the material which art uses, ideology is in the processes of the development of that material, ideology is in the form" (see Albéra, op. cit., p. 48). As for Eisenstein's dual struggle against formalism and contentism, countless quotations could be used to demonstrate it. I shall content myself with the following two, both taken from Eisenstein's last lesson, dated 25 December 1946:

> There are different ways of composing a work so as to bring forth and present an ideological orientation. It occurs that, when the interpretation of the work has been fixed in advance, it is mechanically divided into determined themes. Such a laboratory procedure leads to an abstract execution.

> Such a work, to the degree that it corresponds to certain rules, can act upon the spectator. But if these "laws" are fortuitous, they cannot penetrate the spectator deeply, nor can they act in the way they should, they do not conquer him, do not give birth in him to the feeling of reality, do not contribute to the realization of the subject. These works are thus inevitably formalist, because they are not founded on the desire to express in their totality real phenomena and the natural laws which derive from those phenomena. Thus is manifested the artist's arbitrariness, stripped of any foundation. ("Problems of Composition," RW 4, pp. 684 and 680, respectively)

27. In one case ("vertical" breakdown of the fragment) as in another (analytical description of the *Potemkin* sequence), an interesting symptom is moreover the use that is made of the word "theme," taken as something like the equivalent of a *musical* theme.

28. In another context (but already apropos of *Potemkin*) Eisenstein had lucidly recognized this necessary intervention of creative intuition: "The solution can only come from something new, that is, from suitably chosen material, from a correct theoretical point of view, and ... from the intuition necessary for its development. An intuition which, for the moment, it would not be possible to break down or analyze, but which for the moment could be accounted for as an unknown but powerful form of energy" ("Constantza," FW 1, p. 39).

29. Aumont is referring here to the fact that in French the word "pathos" has a negative sense covered in English by the term "bathos," i.e., "false or overdone pathos" (Webster). (Translator)

30. Naturally, here again it seems clear that Eisenstein is following his inclination to propose the most mechanical models and metaphors of psychic processes. Let us recall the answer given by Lacan, admittedly in a completely different context, to a questionnaire submitted to him (1966) ("Réponses à des étudiants en philosophie sur l'objet de la psychanalyse, *Cahiers pour l'analyse*, No. 3, May-June 1966, pp. 5–14) by a group of students: "Are you sufficiently enlightened not to require me to give an answer about the means of 'lifting someone out of his consciousness?' I am not Alphonse Allais, who would reply, 'Skin him alive.' " Here is a remark of Eisenstein's (still on the subject of ecstasy as "being lifted outside of oneself") exactly like an answer to Lacan's statement: "In its comical aspects, it is the famous bear which the Baron Münchhausen flogs, thus forcing him to step out of . . . his own skin and flee into the forest stark naked, leaving his 'overcoat' with the baron" ("Pathos," RW 3, p. 213; FW 2, p. 384).

31. On several occasions, the state of ecstasy is explicitly compared by Eisenstein with intoxication, dreaming, or drug-induced states. See for example "Pathos," RW 3, p. 211; FW 2, p. 379, or the "Afterword" to *Nonindifferent Nature*, RW 3, p. 424; FW 4, p. 339.

32. "There are good machines, the ones which contribute to productivity and which were imposed on the peasants traumatically as well as ecstatically" (P. Bonitzer, "Les Machines e(x)tatiques," p. 24). To which corresponds this passage in Eisenstein: "For . . . in that drop of milk . . . was reflected, as in . . . a drop of water, the fact of a handful of little landowners, peasants living in isolation, separately, but who, justly impressed by the separator . . . accomplish just as abruptly the gigantic qualitative leap towards the new forms of social development . . . 'mujhiks' become 'kolkhozians' " ("Pathos," RW 3, pp. 80 ff.; FW 2, pp. 118–19).

33. See "Pantagruel Is Born," RW 2, p. 301; FW 1, p. 247. Eisenstein must have been all the more affected by this reproach since he detested Proust (see the confession of this hatred in "Foreword," IM, pp. 1–7; RW 1, p. 212).

34. Eisenstein had already approached, although less systematically, this question of the similitude of formal laws and natural laws in a text of 1934, "Organicism and Imaginicity" (written in connection with the *Regissura* project). Among other things we find there the following remarks: "The very *law* of structure of a phenomenon is expressed in an analogous law for the structure of the work of art. The externally figurative side of the phenomenon represented may even disappear. Then, instead of a sculpture, we shall have an architecture, from which the figurative dimension is absent, but in which the dimension of representation of the phenomena of nature and in particular human nature continues to be present in the very laws of architectural proportions. . . . It is certainly not concrete representation, but the correlation between the proportions of the phenomenon represented and the characteristics of its structural laws which provides the bases for that" (RW 4, pp. 663–664).

35. Once again, organicism aims at anything but a naturalist imitation of nature. I have already mentioned, in Chapter One, the metal "virgins" with which Eisenstein's father had decorated the facade of one of his apartment buildings. They (also, more generally, the whole question of the servile imitation of nature) are no doubt what Eisenstein is thinking of when he writes, "At that period of degradation (the *art nouveau* period), nature was the object

of a corrupted imitation! Architecture did not seek to imitate the principle, the coherency of nature and its phenomena, but the appearance of the vegetable kingdom and the human body, especially the female body. And iron was bent into the shape of a vine. Stucco was fashioned into the shape of a lily. The form of the windows sought to reproduce the rippling circles spreading on the surface of the water" ("Montage 1937," RW 2, p. 478).

36. This is the thesis expressed by Bordwell: "With Eisenstein's casting off of his dialectical epistemology, tension drops out of the concept of montage—now he stresses organicism" (David Bordwell, "Eisenstein's Epistemological Shift," *Screen*, 15, No. 4, Winter 1974–75, pp. 32–46).

37. It may be asked in particular if the dialectic, which, as Eisenstein himself remarks ironically in "Intellectual Cinema," has in some ways replaced religion (catechism) in its repressive aspects, has not also replaced it *for him* in its positive aspects (coming to substitute new "articles of faith" for the old ones). In the absence of a sufficiently trustworthy biography of Eisenstein, I submit this as a simple hypothesis.

38. There are countless examples, of which I will give two that are typical. First of all, the accumulation of examples illustrating this statement: "Whatever may be the given conditions of a composition, the direct solution as well as its exact opposite prove equally correct and striking" ("More Thoughts on Structure," RW 3, p. 236; FW 4, p. 15); and this "application" of the dialectic to a contradiction between "the free flow of the line and the frame of the canons." "For this contradiction contains the fundamental conflict of the union of opposites, on which are based and transformed things as old as the world. And more ancient than the Chinese symbols of yin and yang which I am so fond of" ("How I Learned to Draw," IM, pp. 49–50; RW 1, p. 262).

39. "Peace and the Atomic Bomb," (September 1945, published in *Bronenosets Potemkin*, Naoum & Levina Kleiman, eds. [Moscow: Iskusstvo, 1968]). This theme was taken up again and expanded by Leonid Kozlov. Taking Eisenstein quite literally, he writes "Eisenstein's supreme quality as an ideologue-artist, as a theoretician-artist, is revealed precisely in the logic with which he puts order in the idea of his artistic universe. . . . In the persistence with which he leads his idea—the idea of unity—towards its content and its true meaning" (Leonid Kozlov, "L'Unité: à propos de l'histoire d'une idée," *Cahiers du cinéma*, No. 226-27, Jan.-Feb. 1971, pp. 228-38, first published in *Iskusstvo kino*, 1968, No. 1). These ideas looking for their adequate manifestation are enough to make you believe you are dreaming.

40. See "Torito," RW 4, pp. 634–35. It should be noted that here Eisenstein already uses the metaphor of the explosion: "Without a supply of power (cultural background and the actual experience of previous productions), no creative explosion can take place."

41. Narboni, "Le Hors-cadre décide de tout," *Cahiers du cinéma*, No. 271, November 1976, pp. 14–21.

42. "What is going to bind all of these phenomena together, the common language of the synchronism, will, of course, be movement. Plekhanov has already said that in the last analysis all phenomena could be reduced to movement. It is movement which will reveal to us all the deepest levels of internal synchronization, which can be determined subsequently. It is movement which is going to show us in a tangible way the meaning of this unification and its method" ("Vertical Montage," 1940, RW 2, p. 196). See also "Montage 37," passim.

43. See the quotation of a Chinese philosopher: "What is a line? A line speaks of movement" ("How I Learned to Draw"), and also the whole of this

latter text, which takes up other aspects of the same theme (IM, p. 42; RW 1, p. 262). The comparison between dance and drawing which appears there had already been used by Eisenstein in 1934 ("Organicism and Imaginicity," RW 4, pp. 658–659).

3. Eisenstein Taken at His Word

1. It should be pointed out that all of Eisenstein's films (with the possible exception of *Bezhin Meadow*) have been accompanied by essays on related theoretical issues. Even at that, the set of texts from 1928–29 form an especially interesting case; there are scarcely any important texts from the period of *Strike*, and all of the theoretically important texts on *Potemkin* were written several years after the film was made. It is not until the period 1937–45 that we find such a coherent set of writings, in effect, all of the "technical" texts on montage, sound, color, etc., which I am drawing upon here in relation to *Ivan the Terrible*.

2. I am thinking, of course, of the seminar at the University of Paris-8 (Vincennes) which brought together Philippe Desdouits, Michèle Lagny, Michel Marie, Guy Mikhaelian, Marie-Claire Ropars, and Pierre Sorlin. Working collectively from 1972 to 1979 with the help of "heterogeneous theoretical tools," their research has resulted in the publication of a whole series of studies about *October* under the general title, "Ecriture et idéologie."

3. An alternative would have been to choose Ivan's marriage and the color sequence (which is a parody of it); that, however, would have entailed an analysis of a much longer and more dramatically complex sequence in which the problems of composition and montage, which are of primary interest here, would have been swamped. Eisenstein himself explicitly designated the "key-scene" as the mourning sequence around Anastasia's coffin, "not only for the method of its composition, but above all for its dramatic effect. . . . In these key-scenes—compulsively and exultantly composed—everything which is formally characteristic and new about the film is revealed with maximum energy." *Nonindifferent Nature*, RW 3, pp. 356–357; FW 4, 221–22.

4. Out of respect for Eisensteinian terminology (and what it implies), and in spite of the rather unorthodox use of the term, I have stuck throughout to using "fragment" to designate what would normally be called a "shot."

5. The shot-breakdown of the sequence is on page 76. I have not found it necessary to provide a very detailed technical analysis, and have restricted myself to noting, for each fragment, its order in the sequence, its length (by the number of frames—at a projection speed of 18 to 20 frames per second), and an overall description of the movement in the frame (the camera does not move at all throughout the sequence).

6. Although it is not their primary intention, this is what comes out of the two texts by Ropars and Sorlin on the first 69 shots of *October*.

7. Lenin figures systematically throughout the film: his bust, for example, and its function (at once a *deus ex machina* and a moral conscience) in the sequence "satirizing the bureaucrats." Clearly, the agronomist is inscribed within this system, as much by his diegetic position as by his physical resemblance (slight as it is) to Lenin.

8. The "young Aryan blond" is a recurring figure throughout Eisenstein's films. He has been seen (by Dominique Fernandez) as the powerful return of a repressed homosexuality, and this is quite likely. In passing, I would like to suggest however, another possible determinant: Eisenstein's repression, until late on, of his Jewish origin, and the bad conscience of the Russian colonist

in the Baltic provinces, which marked his childhood, and which he touches upon in "Souvenirs d'enfance," and "Intellectual Cinema" in *Immoral Memories.*

9. This is all very well in a frame enlargement, but it raises the question of the validity of such considerations with respect to viewing the film in projection. We know that Eisenstein based his analysis of a sequence from *Nevsky* in "Vertical Montage" upon the possibility of such readings.

Personally, this idea has always perplexed me, and I am inclined to agree with Noel Burch's suggestion that "any film image obviously includes some elements that call attention to themselves more strongly than others do. . . . but we are nonetheless also aware of the compositional whole . . . and we are aware in particular of the actual rectangular frame" (*Theory of Film Practice,* p. 34).

Hence my analysis of Fragment 10 is something of an attempt to reconstitute the movement of the Eisensteinian mise-en-scène; although I am not sure whether the spectator can read the frame in the way in which I suggest, I am nonetheless convinced that such a reading (or something close to it) was intended by Eisenstein when he composed the shot.

10. Eisenstein himself takes up this notion in "The Filmic Fourth Dimension."

11. Consider this citation of Stalin's intervention at the 14th Congress of the Communist Party: "To transform our country from an agricultural into an industrial country, with the capacity to produce for itself the necessary apparatus, even the foundation, or base of our general line" (*History of the Communist Party* [Moscow, 1949, p. 305]). (The Congress took place in December 1925.)

12. This is the almost unanimous opinion of all the historians or observers of Eisenstein's life: Lebedev, Yurenev, Seton, Atasheva, etc. For my part, I do not see any clear contradiction between the line of the film and the general thrust of the 15th Congress (December 1927): "Now, the peasants march in step with the workers. For, in the provinces, the work impulse had won the peasantry over into supporting the kolkhoz. The majority of them made a clear commitment to the kolkhoz, and a decisive factor in this was the sovkhoz and the well-stocked tractor and machinery plants (SMT). Peasants came *en masse* to visit the sovkhoz and the SMT's; they were interested in how the tractors and other machinery worked, they expressed their enthusiasm, and, after holding a meeting, they decided to 'join the kolkhoz.' "

13. A point made by Jean Narboni in the debate on *Montage* (see Bibliography).

14. This way of making the characters stand out from the background is a staple among Russian films of the period. As Amengual notes, in his *Eisenstein,* the systematic use of back-lighting for this purpose is a stylistic feature, not only of Tisse, who was the photographer for four of Eisenstein's silent films, but also of Moskvin (see his incredible work on *The New Babylon*) who would subsequently work with Eisenstein on *Ivan the Terrible.*

15. Here is what Eisenstein wrote in 1945 about these "explosive sequences": "the gravitational center of the effect lies not so much in the explosion as in the process of compression which precedes the explosions. The explosion can happen at any time. Sometimes, it is at the pitch of the intensity of the preceding tensions, sometimes not, and sometimes it barely occurs at all." ("Sergei Eisenstein," RW 1, p. 95; FW 3, p. 70).

16. Shklovsky suggests yet another opposition, between the husbandmen and the crop farmers, an opposition which he equates with the mythical pair

Abel/Cain: from this point of view, the film would be the story of a recon- ciliation between secular enemies. . . . This hypothesis is attractive, and en- tirely consistent with the fact that, for Eisenstein, "two" always ends up being "one."

17. Alberti's "window on the world," taken up by Bazin in relation to the screen—frame-or-mask? problem (see "The Evolution of the Language of Cin- ema"). Also, Jacques Rivette's formula, "caméra à hauteur d'homme" ("man as the measure of the camera"), which is often taken to characterize the classical cinema.

18. Not to mention the obviously religious connotations of all of this. Martha as the suffering Mother (from Thomka's death), and somewhat antic- ipating the Mexican drawings (1930–31) which go out of their way to play up the Christ/bull relation. See the anthology *Meksikanskie risunki Eizenshteina*, Moscow 1969, whose drawings have been reproduced almost everywhere (*Ca- hiers du cinéma*, nos. 226–27; and in the books by Albéra and Fernandez). Otherwise, one could point to the shot in *The General Line* of the three bull's heads, an allusion to the pictorial theme of the crucifixion.

19. Martha is "on the side" of the cows, and this is hardly surprising since she works with cows (one could invoke here all sorts of likely justifications). But let us not forget that there is, at the level of the anecdote, something profoundly scandalous—for the same reason as the other transgression of the division man/beast represented by the old couple harnessed to the same plough earlier in the film.

20. Eisenstein says as much, implicitly: "White is the dominant tonality of *The General Line*: the whiteness of the sovkhoz, the clouds, the milk flowing in streams, the flowers. . . . Against the grey of the opening motifs—misery, against the black of crimes and atrocities, the whiteness always stands out, associated, as it is, with the theme of joy and new forms of work. It is intro- duced in the most intense scene: waiting for the first drop to come out of the separator. With this drop, the whiteness ushers in the theme of joy which is developed in the sequences about the sovhkoz, the rivers of milk, the herds, the poultry-yard" ("Not Colored, But in Color," 1940).

21. Sylvie Pierre, "Eléments pour une théorie du photogramme," *Cahiers du cinéma*, Nos. 226-27, p. 83. Sylvie Pierre also notes that without the support of the "first" and "second" meanings (those which Barthes describes respec- tively as the level of information and signification), it is doubtful that a third meaning could ever materialize. I am inclined to agree with such a point of view, and which, to my mind, is in accord with the Eisensteinian attitude that refuses to dissociate the "image" (*obraz: grosso modo*, the second meaning) from the "figurations" (the level of information), and which has the merit, moreover, of somewhat dampening the rather precipitous enthusiasm of those epigones of Barthes who are only too ready to see the "third meaning" ev- erywhere, thereby elevating it to the rank of a kind of "filmic essence," while forgetting Eisenstein and everything else.

22. By Christian Metz (*Essais sur la signification au cinéma*, p. 83). Amen- gual had also noted the "persistence of these tripartite formulations" without attaching any further significance to it either (see his *Eisenstein*, p. 66, note 1).

23. Seton sees this number as sacred, divine, christic, etc., while Fernandez links it to the emergence of the Oedipal triangle.

We know that Freud drew up a "catalogue" of symbols several times, in *The Interpretation of Dreams*, for example, where he designated the number 3 a symbol of the male organ. Clearly, this is not Freud at his best.

24. Throughout this passage, I make reference to Jean-Pierre Oudart's terminology, which distinguishes between an effect of reality (= conformity to figurative codes, especially that of perspective, and those which govern the figuration of shadows, reflections, etc.), and an effect of the real (a subjective and ideological consequence of the traditional Western pictorial system aimed at producing an existential judgment about figures that are supposed to have their referent in the real).

25. In the title of a famous 1928 article about kabuki, "Niezhdanny styk" ("The Unexpected [Meeting]"), the "meeting" in question is between kabuki and contrapuntal cinema; in either case, all the parameters of signification are given equal weight.

26. First of all, a vertical movement and from top to bottom (18-22), then a horizontal alternation (23-28), then an oblique alternation (29-34), then vertical again (35-38, with a sharp inversion of direction in the last fragment).

27. This is defined according to the correlations between the "real" lengths of the fragments (their "metric" lengths adjusted to a co-efficient that takes content into account). It should be noted that these *metric* relations are already rather simplified if one considers the average length of the fragments of each lexia: 45 frames for lexia 4, 24 for lexia 5, 36 for lexia 6, stripped of its two longest fragments, which makes 43 for the complete lexia 6.

28. A utopia which, as such, has its own iconography. It is not for nothing that the buildings and also some of the "framings" of the sovkoz allude to constructivist models and posters.

29. "In the second part of the film *Ivan the Terrible*, film director Sergei Eisenstein revealed his ignorance of historical fact by presenting . . . Ivan the Terrible himself, who had determination and character, as weak and indecisive, a little like Hamlet." This is the wording of the resolution of the Central Committee of the Party on 4 September 1946, condemning the second part of *Ivan* (and some other films).

30. This "other order" is at the same time marked by the extinction of Ivan's entire family (his wife, his mother, and later, the Staritskys) and by the appearance of homosexual ties, linking him with Basmanov and with the *oprichniki* in general.

31. Of course, many things have changed in the meantime. Ivan has made his retreat to Alexandrov; the people have come there to seek him out; he has had some nobles executed; he has set up his special corps of guards, the *Oprichniki*; he has sought in vain the help and love of Philip Kolychev . . .

32. This Ivan, and this Ivan alone, corresponds to the description of the character Eisenstein had already written in 1928: "Treated like a character out of Poe, Ivan the Terrible would be of no interest to the young Soviet worker; but the founder of the textile trade, the czar who strengthened Russia's economic situation, becomes infinitely more interesting for him. . . . The trader czar, now there we have something more concrete!" ("Soviet Cinema," an article published in English in "Voices of October," 1930—quoted from *Film Essays*).

The same trend of thought is to be found in the numerous articles written during the 1940s on cinema and history and on *Ivan the Terrible* (see "A Very Great Statesman," RW 1, p. 199; FW 1, p. 97; "A Film on the Russian Renaissance," RW 1, p. 189; FW 1, p. 87; "Problems of Soviet Historical Film," etc.).

33. See, in Nizhny's book, the vast erudition demonstrated by Eisenstein in discussing architecture in scenes involving Père Goriot, Dessalines, and Raskolnikov. It is striking that in each case his erudition is drawn upon only

in order to justify a particular solution to a specific problem of dramatic construction, to provide it with a foundation of historical validity. (Here again we see Eisenstein's dual aim—to construct expressive "global images," but without sacrificing the guarantee of the "authentic" referent.)

34. This is obviously another variation on the same double aim (see the preceding note). The same "image" is to be produced with different figurative means, film, drawing, and elsewhere, photographs (see the anecdote reported by Jay Leyda, cited by S. Pierre, according to which Eisenstein is purported to have wanted to illustrate his film with "synthetic" photos rather than stills).

35. This dismantling is particularly noticeable in the first sequence of the film, the coronation sequence. This is true with respect to the space, due to the absence of any general shot, which would have defined the respective positions of the characters, and to the fact that the shots are articulated solely in relation to facial expressions and lines of dialogue charged with meaning. It is also true with respect to the time, as suggested by the shots of the foreign ambassadors' "comments," for example, which literally suspend the ceremony (the music and the action stop in order to give them the time to make their statements, which are also very significant).

In a general way, of course, all of this is related to the passion for analysis which is very clearly manifested in Eisenstein's evaluation of the "Stanislavsky system," of which he retained only what suited him—the breaking down of each event into micro-actions. See "Montage 1937," p. 418 and ff., and the return to the same ideas in "Mise-en-jeu" and "Mise-en-geste," RW 4, pp. 717 ff.

36. Pascal Bonitzer, "Le Gros orteil," *Cahiers du cinéma*, no. 232, October 1971, pp. 14-23.

37. "A Close-Up View (by way of preface)," 1940, RW 5, p. 25; FW 1, p. 111); "A Close-Up View," RW 5, p. 290; FW 1, p. 263); "History of the Close-Up," (1946). In addition it would seem that a chapter on the close-up (a more theoretical one) is contained in Eisenstein's notes for the unpublished *Method*.

38. The reader should compare the work on *Crime and Punishment*, in particular, with what happens in shots 26/32/38 of our sequence, with respect to the foreground/background contrast and the movements towards the camera (or away from it).

39. Pascal Bonitzer, "Voici," *Cahiers du cinéma*, No. 273, Jan.-Feb. 1977, pp. 5-18.

40. His analysis of shot 47 does not seem to me to have completely avoided this "trap" of the still photo either. Deceived by the immobility of the photograph, Bonitzer calls Anastasia's look "radiant," where the film shows us a *terrorized* gaze (see Bonitzer, "Le Gros orteil").

41. "Here, with the most violent contrast of scale and color between the czar and the procession, the internal content of the scene unifies the czar and the people, the dramatic element (the head leaning forward) marking consent, and the concordance between the czar's profile and the contour of the procession's movement" ("Stereoscopic Films," 1947).

42. Sylvie Pierre, "Elements pour une théorie du photogramme," *Cahiers du cinéma*, no. 226-27, Jan.-Feb. 1971, pp. 75–83.

43. On several occasions Eisenstein mentions the virtues of this wide-angle lens (it was apparently the widest angle he could obtain under the technical conditions of the time and place). Each time he does so it is in order to point out its ability to "distort," "deform," or "fabricate" space. See, among other examples, "Stereoscopic Film" (1947). (The Soviet edition has three very

informative photographs three pages later); "History of the Close-Up," 1946 (RW 1, p. 504), and the statements reported by Nizhny about the work on *Crime and Punishment* in *Lessons with Eisenstein*, pp. 98-99 in particular. In an unfinished essay on color dating from 1946-47 and entitled "The Little Horse of Viatka," Eisenstein again lists the means of obtaining "dynamic" relationships with objects and makes special mention of perspective as a means of distorting space.

44. I will confine myself here to referring to what was said earlier in this essay, apropos of *The General Line*, on Barthes's concept of the "third meaning." Without the "first meaning" there can be no second meaning (and in Eisenstein, as we have seen, the first meaning is used to the maximum degree in order to produce the second one. Barthes himself was perfectly aware of this, as is shown by his statement, "Eisenstein's art is not polysemous, it chooses the meaning, imposes it, hammers it home. . . . the Eisensteinian meaning devastates ambiguity. How? By the addition of an aesthetic value, emphasis. Eisenstein's decorativism has an economic function: it proffers the truth") (trans. Stephen Heath in *Image/Music/Text* [New York: Hill and Wang, 1977], p. 56). In the same way, I repeat, without the first two meanings, it is difficult to imagine the emergence of the "third one." And above all, nothing authorizes us to think that, because of the presence of this third meaning, the anecdote would be reduced to the role of a "mere companion."

45. That is particularly clear in another moment of the film, the sequence of Ivan's coronation, very visibly articulated by words and looks, and in particular Ivan's looks, which comment and expand upon his "speech from the throne." Moreover, this moment greatly impressed the participants in the filming, as Kadochnikov's account reveals: "When these frames were filmed, Eisenstein, half-jokingly, gave the signal, 'Eyes right . . . eyes left.' Some superficial people, who had nothing to do with the film and who happened to be present during the shooting, made fun of this, saying, 'So that's Eisenstein's method of working with actors—'Eyes right, eyes left' " ("Interview," *Iskusstvo kino*, 1968, No. 1, pp. 133-38).

46. There are many anecdotes on this subject. In his *Notes of a Soviet Actor* (Moscow: 1957), Cherkasov tells of the extreme discomfort experienced by the actors during the filming of the sequence of Anastasia's lamentation. Kuznetsov (the actor who plays the role of Fyodor Basmanov and who did not get along with Eisenstein at all well) tells other stories on the same subject and gives a very intelligent description of Eisenstein's attitude toward the actors. "He showed us what had to be done, yes, and very adeptly. But that was concerned above all with the *line* of the movement, the line of the gesture. He felt the line, he could show it to us. But as for reproducing an actor's intonation or simply reading a monologue or playing a scene, those were things that Eisenstein couldn't do. My impression is that he had nothing of an actor about him."

47. See Kuznetsov's account (quoted in the preceding note) and especially the fragment from Eisenstein's memoirs specifically devoted to this clarity of the "inner vision." "I see what I am reading, or whatever goes through my mind, in extraordinarily sharp detail. A very large supply of visual impressions, and a very vivid visual memory, very probably goes along here with a very strong propensity for daydreaming, when you see in your mind's eye whatever you are thinking about or remembering, like in a film. . . . These impressions, which are above all sharply visual, demand forcefully, even painfully, to be reproduced" (untitled fragment, RW 1, p. 509).

48. The fact that what takes place at Ivan's desk can be heard clearly from Anastasia's bedside is even more clearly marked in the scenario: "In shouts

of fury, Ivan's wrath reaches Anastasia's ears. Anastasia wants to get up. To go to Ivan." (This is followed by a whole passage that does not appear in the film.)

49. Marie-Claire Ropars and Pierre Sorlin, *Octobre, écriture et idéologie,* (Paris: Editions Albatros, 1976).

50. On this point I can only refer the reader to texts in which this subject is discussed in detail, in particular the two "classics" on the topic, Raymond Bellour's analysis of a sequence from *The Birds,* and J.-P. Oudart's "La Suture."

51. This metaphor is not my invention. It appears explicitly in the scenario: "Seated above her, like a black bird, is Efrosinia Staritskaya."

52. These "themes" deliberately planned and defined by Eisenstein and Prokofiev, obviously do not function in reference to a supposed "content" of the music. Eisenstein emphasized on several occasions that they were the musical equivalent of those "global images" he was striving to produce with the picture image.

53. "We consider a film musical when the absence of music from the screen is read as a pause or a caesura—be that as long as an entire reel, so long as it is strictly intentional (not to say calculated), as a rhythmically calculated interruption of the sound, like strictly numbered measures of silence in the single overall system of the measures of sound" ("Color Cinema," 1948).

54. On this subject, see "Lesson on Music and Color in *Ivan the Terrible,*" in which Eisenstein insists, among other things, first on the necessity for a rhythmical, musical structure within each sequence and second, on the fact that the themes of the sequence can be carried, according to the moment, by any given expressive means, in particular by the music and the color. ("When the theme intersects with the character, the latter dons the appropriate color," etc., RW 3, p. 602; FW 1, p. 293).

55. Jean-Pierre Oudart, "Sur *Ivan le Terrible,*" *Cahiers du cinéma,* No. 218, March 1970, pp. 15-23.

56. This despite the many inaccuracies in his text, including even errors in factual details, which must after all be noted (clearly the result of the lack of analytical work). Example: in the sequence of "the mystery of the cathedral," Oudart is guilty of a serious misinterpretation when he identifies the little boy who wonders about the meaning of the playlet as Ivan's son, when clearly he is a child of the Staritsky clan (as is confirmed by the scenario) (Oudart, op. cit.).

57. When Ivan rushes into Anastasia's bedchamber, the scenario does in fact specify that "From the door, Malyuta is watching him. He speaks to Fedka Basmanov: 'Keep watch over the czar, do not leave him alone.'"

58. A conception very symptomatically summed up in these statements, repeated by the actor Mgebrov: "The image, we are the ones who make the image. We should show our feelings about him (the character)." That was Eisenstein's way of responding to the implied reproach that he was not sticking closely enough to the "historical sources." It is quite clear—he preferred to produce them himself.

59. Serge Daney, "Voir = 'supposé savoir,'" *Cahiers du cinéma,* No. 240, July-August 1972, pp. 7–9.

60. Since Basmanov is disguised in that sequence (in a disguise which is itself very symbolic and absolutely not naturalistic) as a Russian peasant girl, dressed in a sarafan and wearing a mask visibly inspired by the masks of the Chinese theater (see the description of this mask in the scenario, clearly imitating similar Chinese or Japanese poems).

61. The *Oprichniki* in general are represented under the same principle—plebeian ephebes. Fernandez provides an excellent contrast between this representation of the Oprichnina in the film and the historical reality. ("Dressed in black and carrying a dog's head and a broom on their saddles, symbols of their eagerness to smell out, to bite, to pursue the suspicious and the 'traitors,' they spread terror throughout the country, torturing men, raping women, slaughtering babies, poisoning lakes and rivers ... " [Dominique Fernandez, *Eisenstein* [Paris: Grasset, 1975]). However, Eisenstein's representation of them must still not have been sufficiently "idealized," since the official criticism of the film reproached it with having depicted "Ivan's progressive corps of body guards as a band of degenerates like the Ku Klux Klan" (Resolution of the Central Committee of the Party, 4 September 1946, cited by Marie Seton).

62. The expression is once again Fernandez's. I find it most appropriate. (Unfortunately, this time he draws conclusions from it which are purely conjectural.)

63. I must of course specify that this "third" level of the discourse could in no way be identified with Barthes's "third meaning." Symbolic character *typage* belongs by rights to the second level of meaning in the Barthesian terminology, i.e., the level of significations. However, it is certainly involved in the question of *signifiance* (which it supports, and on which it is supported, perhaps—but that would require a separate study, one which it would moreover be important to undertake.)

4. Montage in Question

1. Eisenstein's own expression in the chapter in *Immoral Memories* in which he recounts, somewhat tongue-in-cheek, the birth of "intellectual cinema," IM, p. 207.

2. See N. Lebedev, *Il cinema muto sovietico,* p. 275. Of all the quotations Lebedev brings to bear on his condemnation of "intellectual cinema," only one is absolutely clear on the question of "ideogram-shots": "Take the conceptual expression, 'a thin hand.' This must be shot so that the adjective 'thin' takes up one frame, and the substantive, 'hand,' another. The result would be such that the shot, for example, could not be read as 'white hand' " (p. 238). Now this is not taken from Eisenstein but from Shklovsky (in *The Count of Hamburg,* 1928). This is not to say that Eisenstein is not prone to such statements, and ambiguous ones at that—but that when he makes them, as we shall see, they are accompanied by particularly precise qualifications.

3. "For the content of the first part of the film, which is about the individualist tendency among the old peasantry, a tendency particularly manifest in the splitting-up of the larger holdings, which had been kept within the same family for generations, into much smaller and economically less viable parcels of land, I needed to have concrete details which would clearly express the idea of such divisions. Details that would be highly expressive and yet also be 'drawn from real life.' It would have been impossible to fabricate the details which we discovered in the everyday life of Penza province. In the dividing up of their property, the peasants there quite simply cut their *izbas* in half. These common living quarters were not broken up into pieces—each beam was sawn in half. In effect, the process of distribution 'by equal portions' was *literally* carried out, notwithstanding the economic absurdity of this practice. It is a fact, then, which is absolutely factual—what an unexpectedly concrete image! We were so attentive to the need for clarity when we shot this scene, that we failed to notice that this detail or image was *so* far removed from our

ordinary conceptual logic . . . and so the whole episode lost its 'typicality' . . . and became an autonomous element. Indeed, it was perceived as not having been drawn from everyday life; some doubted its authenticity . . . while others, worse still, thought that the scene had been conceived as an allegory" ("Montage 1937," RW 2, p. 427).

4. To such an extent that Mitry seriously proposes moving the "supplementary" significations over and placing them on side screens: "And so we can imagine some actions being pursued in accordance with concrete, dramatic events on the middle screen—the most important one—and on the side screen, dependent and juxtaposed images symbolically commenting on the main ones" (*S. M. Eisenstein*, p. 53).

5. One of the few critics to defend the case for consistency and continuity in Eisenstein's theoretical work is Marc Le Bot in his article in *Contre-champ*. Unfortunately, I wrote my first three chapters before I read Le Bot's work, which otherwise seems to me to be one of the few studies to successfully take up a point of view *within* the system or problematic of Eisenstein's work, rather than seek to judge its coherence according to some external criterion.

6. This denial appeared in the form of a letter to the editor in *Izvestiya*, 8 February 1937.

7. This desire to unify, under one common principle, a whole series of otherwise heterogeneous phenomena (from the "micro" to the "macro"), is nothing new for the Eisenstein of 1937. The same idea is given forcible expression in the famous "Dramaturgie der Film-Form." What is new, however, is the shift, by dint of this "unifying principle," from conflict to montage, and the concomitant upgrading of montage to the level of a general, or universal, principle.

8. "Indeed, it is a principle which, as we have seen, is not simply restricted to covering all the internal elements of cinematographic practice: the actor, the role, the frame, the montage, the whole object. It is a principle which encompasses the whole of art, well beyond the limits of cinema alone. Indeed, its scope reaches beyond the limits of art itself" ("Montage 1937," RW 2, p. 423).

9. See Pietro Montani, *L'ideologia che nasce dalla forma*, p. 18 in particular, and Marc Le Bot, "Serge Eisenstein, Théoricien de l'art moderne," *Contre-champ*, 3, unpaginated.

This affinity between intellectual montage and the montage of attractions is quite apparent, moreover, in those comments of Eisenstein about cine-attraction in which the theme of de-anecdotalization (which is so important to all the work on *Capital*) is already prominent. "There is nothing interesting about either the pained attempts of the old actor to look like Beideman, or the tears of his fiancée. What is interesting is the *ancien régime* of the Peter and Paul Fortress, presented in the full light of its methods," etc. ("Montage of Cine-Attractions," FW 1, p. 136).

10. These notes were published in Russian in *Iskusstvo kino*, 1973, no. 1, and subsequently translated into German (*Schriften* 3), Italian (*Cinema Nuovo*, 226, Nov/Dec. 1973), and, only partially, into French (*Ecran 74*, 31, December 1974). I have used the translations liberally, especially the French (by Luda and Jean Schnitzer), and, to avoid giving the full references each time, I shall give only the date of the note cited.

11. This idea runs through several of Eisenstein's other texts from the same period. Aside from the one already cited (note 9), see "Literature and Cinema" (RW 5, especially p. 526) where Eisenstein praises various authors, particularly Joyce and Fedorchenko, in whom he sees "an associative, non-

causal movement from theme to theme" which he claims as one of the models of intellectual cinema.

12. "First of all, a normal reaction, which develops into resistance against the acceptance of the alogical—a moment that must be transcended and transformed into acceptance, an attitude that is no longer tied to any context—and that runs very deeply indeed" (note from 23 November 1927).

13. "Of course, all of this is possible even in the absence of such a chain. . . . However, one concerted 'little step backwards' always adds to the overall structural sharpness" (6 April 1928).

14. There is no doubt that Eisenstein's attitude here has been directly influenced by Joyce's *Ulysses*: as much by the idea of a "chain" of events drawn from everyday life as by the emphatic contrast between the trivial character of these events and the "noble" character (ideologico-political for Eisenstein, cosmic for Joyce) of the subject.

15. This is something which Eisenstein repeatedly repudiates, and always quite vehemently: "And above all, no silk manufacturers entertaining bishops! Fie!" (8 April 1928).

16. I shall only mention one, that of the "baby box": "In one of the streets next to the orphanage, the Athenians placed a box into which mothers could throw their children. The children landed on a mattress, and every two hours, the box was emptied and the contents taken off to the orphanage. . . . Excellent, dazzlingly clear material, which pertains as much to 'oppression' as to 'cutting irony.' Bourgeois culture and philanthropy" (22 April 1928).

17. Let it be said in passing that this is what militates against any belief in the absolute opposition between an intellectual cinema, which is supposed to make the spectator *think*, and the montage of the thirties and forties, which, in aiming at pathos, or ecstasy, has left all of that behind. Intellectual montage no more implies the exclusion of emotion (even pathos) than ecstasy implies the exclusion of montage.

18. Eisenstein returns to this repeatedly in the "Notes on *Capital*," but he also takes pride in the "emotional" success of the "intellectual attractions" of *October*. In his speech at the 1935 congress, for example, he applauds himself, in retrospect, for having achieved an "emotionalization of thinking," and ten years later, in *Immoral Memories*, he repeats this: "It was possible on the stage to construct an emotionally effective 'montage of attractions' . . . so it must be possible to achieve effective montage of *intellectual attractions*. . . . God help me! Haven't we just succeeded in doing this with one of the most abstract philosophical themes? And with great emotional effect on the public, to boot: the audience laughed" (IM, p. 207).

19. This relation is more redolent of scenes in Sade, where one always finds a "metteur-en-scène," who organizes the pleasures, supervises the climaxes, and also comments on the various stages: "and now we are about to do such and such, etc."

20. *The Third Studio* is the title of a collection of essays by Viktor Shklovsky, ed. and trans. by Richard Sheldon (Ann Arbor: Ardis, 1977).

21. I cannot help thinking of the kind of haiku through which Barthes tries to account for the inscription of "the third meaning" in a frame enlargement:

> Mouth drawn, eyes shut squinting,
> Headscarf low over forehead,
> She weeps.
>
> (*Image/Music/Text*, p. 62)

In both cases (in the frame enlargement, in terms of the obtuse meaning, and in the montage chain, in terms of the obvious meaning) one finds the same process at work, which I would say is more *subtractive* than additive: it subtracts elements from figuration pure and simple.

22. The play on words here is somewhat lost in English ("means" having nothing to do with "immediate") whereas there is an obvious connection in Russian.

23. This, in particular, is one of the conclusions to be drawn from the emphasis in "The Filmic Fourth Dimension" which Eisenstein places upon providing, at the end of a series of thematically unified montage fragments, a *guiding-shot* which helps the spectator to choose unequivocally between different possible readings (a signal which can itself be an autonomous fragment, the function of which will then depend upon its position in the chain).

24. They were translated in 1942 by Jay Leyda for *The Film Sense* from versions which had been slightly revised by Eisenstein for the English edition.

25. "It is a long time since those heady days when montage was vying for sovereignty within the state of cinematographic expression" ("Montage 1937", RW 2, p. 331).

26. One of his perennial projects was to edit a history of the Soviet cinema. In "Through Theater to Cinema" (1934), for example, he describes this history in terms of three five-year periods.

27. Two Russian words used by Eisenstein, *izobrazhenie* and *obraz*, along with all their derivatives (*obraznost'*, especially) are familiar terms, and not neologisms. The translator's problems are rather delicate, however, since Eisenstein invests them with a very particular connotation which has little to do with their ordinary meanings. *Izobrazhenie* has frequently been translated into French as "representation," a term which has taken on a particular resonance within theoretical work on the cinematographic apparatus, and so I have chosen to translate it instead as *figuration*. As for *obraz*, it seems best to stick to the usual term, "global image," (although it does not render fully the play between the two words, which have the same root). *Obraznost'*, which the dictionary renders as "picturesque," is used by Eisenstein to describe the fact that such and such element is a global image. In order to avoid constant recourse to such periphrasis, and since it is an original concept anyway, I have chosen to translate it as *imaginicity*—a term whose inelegance will serve, I hope, to prevent any further confusion.

28. In "The Function of Metaphor in Eisenstein's *October*," trans. Sister Mary Christopher Baseheart, *Film Criticism* 2, no. 2-3 (Winter-Spring 1978).

Even more serious misreadings of the idea of "global image" have been offered, and by some of our best critics. Of Eisenstein's statement in "Reflections of a Filmmaker" (probably from "Montage 1937") concerning a "total image composed of fragmentary elements," Pascal Bonitzer states: "even Eisenstein . . . was seduced by the idea that film could eventually contrive a 'total image' capable of absorbing all heterogeneity" (" 'Réalité de la dénotation"). He relapses into this idea in a more recent text: "Their lacunary staging [he is referring to Straub, Duras, and Antonioni] can never be contained in a 'total image,' as Eisenstein attempted to do" ("Décadrages"). It is quite untrue to say that the notion of global image is about a *scenic* "reabsorption" of all heterogenous fragments (which is what Bonitzer claims). I am not mentioning this to chastise Bonitzer for any critical shortcomings but to point out the considerable confusion surrounding this crucial Eisensteinian concept.

29. "Montage 1937," RW 2, p. 332. In all subsequent citations from the notes on montage I have given only the page numbers (from RW 2).

30. Two very different examples: the discussion of "signifying zones" in the mise-en-scène of the Dessalines episode ("But if the position is really good

... it would pay to think over how to make the spy's arrival at that spot both possible and natural"—see Nizhny, p. 93); and second, the remarks on the "inorganicity" of shots from *Potemkin* inserted into an initial montage in *The General Line:* that it worked very well from a strictly metaphysical point of view (in both cases, there was a painful waiting scene)—but the absence of even the slightest trace of verisimilitude was unacceptable ("Pathos," FW 2, p. 114).

31. "We must distinguish clearly here between the concept of *spatial imaginicity*, which we have discovered and seen at work, and figurative *symbolism within the space.* The two are habitually confused by those whose emotional conscience is stirred only from the perspective of the global image, when confronted with the space which they are trying to construct" ("Organicism and Imaginicity," 1934—RW 4, p. 668).

32. "I am constitutionally inclined towards generalization. But is it that generalization that the Marxist doctrine of realism teaches us to understand? No. For in my work, generalization destroys the individual. Instead of being derived from the concrete and the particular, generalization trails off into detached abstraction" (Seton, p. 373). Eisenstein returns to this "penchant for improper generalization" many times, especially in the autobiographical fragments. It is on the basis of this distinction between good and bad generalization, for example, that he criticizes Griffith's *Intolerance,* which was "still a *drama of comparisons* rather than a *unique and powerful generalizing* idea . . . the formal shock of the attempt to forge them into a single image of Intolerance was only the reflection of a thematic and ideological error" ("Dickens, Griffith, and the Film Today," 1942).

33. See in the text written on the day of his death: "There is a widespread, but, to my mind, erroneous, opinion about utilizing the expressive medium of the cinema, which holds that a film is good when one does not hear the music, when one does not notice the labor of the cinematographer, when the mastery of the director goes unacknowledged. . . . What this point of view conventionalizes [*ériger en principe*] is the inability to control all the expressive means that contribute to the organically unified filmic oeuvre" ("Color Cinema"). This "celebration" of the figurative and signifying elements has been analyzed by Pierre Baudry in the case of *Nevsky.*

34. We should note that Eisenstein even includes the work of the actor: "The actor's role is exactly the same—to express, in two, three or four character-traits, those fundamental elements which, when combined, will present the total image conceived by the author, the director, and the actor himself" ("Montage 1938").

35. "The link between these two levels [sound and vision], the common language of synchronization, is, of course, movement. Plekhanov has said that all phenomena ultimately bear upon movement. It is movement which will reveal to us the full range of levels of internal synchronization. It is movement which will awaken us in a concrete way to the *meaning* of unification and its *method*" ("Vertical Montage," Part 1).

36. "The types of montage in semantic order:
   a) montage parallel to the linear development of the action (elementary montage of information);
   b) montage parallel to the development of several actions (parallel montage);
   c) montage parallel to sensation (montage of elementary comparisons);
   d) montage parallel to sensation and signification (montage of images);
   e) montage parallel to representations (montage constructions of the idea)" ("Course Outline," 1936).

37. "A consciously creative attitude toward the representata begins at the point when the independent coexistence of its various elements is broken up, and in its place is constructed a causal correlation of those elements, governed by this attitude, which is, in turn, itself determined by the world-view of the auteur. This is also the moment at which the mastery of the means of montage is established as the means of filmic expressivity" ("Color Cinema," 1948).

38. In an unfinished text about color, "The Little Horse of Viatka," Eisenstein suggests that the "dynamic" relation of color to its object must be the same, in principle, that obtains in the audio-visual counterpoint, in temporal (*Zeitlupe*) and spatial (wide-angle) distortions—and . . . in the "attractions!"

39. See this scenario, published by Ivor Montagu, *With Eisenstein in Hollywood* (for the "interior monologues," see pp. 286–87, 290, 293–94).

Clyde Griffiths' monologues are actually quite "exterior" inasmuch as they often resemble *character soliloquies* (as in theater, the novel, or film)—Ivan's soliloquy, for example ("By what right, Ivan, do you judge? etc."), at the beginning of the second part of the sequence commented on above. Although many critics (Aristarco, among others), have seen this soliloquy in terms of the theory of "interior monologue," it seems to me that it has little to do with a theory that looks to "the language of thinking" for a *model*, and not a *content*.

40. These ideas receive expression in a different version of the article "Pantagruel Is Born," according to Armand Panigel, who published an extract from it in his French version of *Film Form/The Film Sense*, containing two paragraphs which do not appear in RW (although Panigel provides no source)—and in which one finds this assimilation of the dissolve to the extinction of mental images, and of overprinting to the simultaneous presence of several representations within a single thought, etc. (See *Le Film; sa forme, son sens*, Paris, 1976, pp. 95-96).

41. Eisenstein is probably referring to Luria's experiments, when, in his 1935 speech, he talks of a patient whose only way of designating objects is through verbs which designate actions that can be carried out with the help of these objects.

42. Marie-Claire Ropars, "The Function of Metaphor in Eisenstein's *October*" (nonetheless I do not agree with her conclusion, which makes the global image into a "perfectly independent" element of the figured elements— p. 126— a reading which, as I suggested earlier, seems to contradict what Eisenstein expressly states about the "dialectical" relation between image and figuration).

43. Aside from the Soviet critics, the experts in this morbid game are the Italians; there are numerous examples in the debates from the Fiesole colloquium (published by P. Mechini and R. Salvadori); one can also mention the very symptomatic article by Liborio Termine, "Materialismo storico nell' opera di Ejzenstejn," in which he shows that "la concezione estetica del regista sovietico si cal[a] nel materialismo storico e non solo in quello dialettico."

44. R. Hébraud's *Hors-cadre Eisenstein*, a book which raises, in a very pertinent way, the question of possible approaches to Eisenstein; either a "return to Eisenstein" as the "beginning of film theory," or a "revival of Eisenstein" as "one way (among others) of transforming at least the filmic instruments [?] from the perspective of contemporary film theory." I cannot, however, go along with Hébraud's definition of the notion of the "filmic" that Eisenstein is supposed to have theoretically endorsed.

A BIBLIOGRAPHY
OF EISENSTEIN'S WRITINGS

This bibliography is the most complete ever published in English; it includes every text known to date, with the exception of his letters (of which only a small number have been published), interviews not written by him, and film and theater scripts.

Texts by Eisenstein are given here in chronological order, and dated as precisely as possible (dates given before the titles are dates of writing). For each text, I give a translation of the original title (all texts are in Russian except when otherwise indicated), and the place and date of first publication. [Titles of existing English translations are included when they differ significantly from those Jacques Aumont gives.—Translators] In addition to this, I give, whenever possible, the reference to existing English translations. For texts that have not been translated into English, letters in parentheses indicate the existence of this text in the following sources:

R: *Izbrannye proizvedeniya* (Selected Works in Russian, Moscow, Iskusstvo, 1964–71)

F: *Oeuvres* (Works in French, 6 vols., Paris, 1974–85)

G: *Schriften* (Writings in German, 4 vols., Munich, 1973–83)

I: *Opere scelte* (Selected Works in Italian, Venice, 1981–82)

An asterisk after the entry means that an English translation will appear in *Volume I: 1922–34, Eisenstein: Selected Writings*, Richard Taylor, general editor, to be published by the British Film Institute.

1922   The Eighth Art. On Expressionism, America, and Naturally Chaplin (with S. Yutkevich), *Echo*, no. 2, 1922. (G)*

1923   Montage of Attractions, *Lef*, no. 3, 1923. E: *The Film Sense* (excerpt) (R, F, G)*

Expressive Movement, first publication in English: *Millennium Film Journal*, Spring 1979 (with S. Tretyakov)

1924   The Devil's Nest, *Kinogazeta*, 11.11.24 (G)

S. Eisenstein on the Filmmaker's Rights, *Zrelishcha*, 72 1924 (G)

On "Mr. West," *Zrelishcha*, nos. 83–84, 1924

1925   Eisenstein on His Work and Projects, *Kinogazeta*, 1.20.25 (G)

A Letter to the Editors, *Kinonedelya*, 2, 1925 (G)

A Letter to the Editors, *Kinogazeta*, 2.17.25 (G)

A Letter to the Editors, *Kinonedelya*, 10, 1925 (G)

Is Film Criticism Necessary? *Novyi zritel'*, 3.31.25 (G)

On the Problem of the Materialist Approach to Form, *Kinozhurnal A.R.K.*, 4–5, 1925. E: Sitney, *Avant-Garde Film*, New York, 1978

The Method of Filming "1905," *Kinogazeta*, 7.7.25 (G)

"1905," *Vechernyaya Moskva*, 7.28.25 (G)

"1905," *Komsomolskaya pravda*, 8.5.25 (G)

The Method for Making a Workers' Film, *Kino*, 8.11.25 (R, F, G)*

Montage of Cine-Attractions, in Belenson, *Kino segodya*, Moscow, 1925 (F)*

1926   What They Have to Say about "Potemkin," *Sovetskii ekran*, no. 2, 1926 (G)*

What They Said about "Potemkin," *Vechernyaya Moskva*, 2.1.26 (G)

Potemkin's Way through German Censorship, *Sovetskoe kino*, 3, 1926 (G)

On Cinema in Germany (with E. Tisse), *Sovetskoe kino*, 3, 1926

How Strange—On Khokhlova, *Kino*, 3.20.26 (R)*

The Decay of Film Industry in Germany, *Vechernyaya Moskva*, 4.26.26

German Cinema, *Vestnik rabotnikov iskusstv*, 10, 1926*

S. Eisenstein on S. Eisenstein, *Berliner Tageblatt*, 6.7.26. (in German); E: translated as A Personal Statement in *Film Essays**

Five Ages, *Pravda*, 7.6.26*

The Way of Soviet Film, *Rabochaya Moskva*, 7.15.26

(6.22) On Balázs's Position, *Kino*, 7.20.26 (R, F, G)

Béla Forgets the Scissors, *Kino*, 8.10.26 (R, F, G)*

"General Line," *Kino*, 8.10.26

The Two Skulls of Alexander the Great, *Novyi zritel'*, 35, 1926 (R, F, G)*

Constantza, Kleiman, & Levina, eds., *Bronenosets "Potemkin*," Moscow, 1968 (F, G)*

Eisenstein, An Interview, *Dial*, New York, April (in English)

1927   Letter to the Editors, *Novyi zritel'*, 2, 1927

"General Line," *Sovetskoe kino*, 2, 1927

Eisenstein, Creator of "Potemkin," *The American Hebrew*, New York, 1.28.27 (in English)

"General Line," *Kino*, 3.12.27

From February to October, *Smena* (Leningrad), 3.15.27 (G)

The Triumphal March of Russian Film, *Das Neue Deutschland*, 1–2, 1927 (in German)

Literary Material for "October," *Chitatel' i pisatel'*, 2, 1927 (G)

Film and National Defense, *Sovetskoe kino*, 7, 1927

What Filmmakers Say, *Komsomolskaya pravda*, 9.21.27

Art As Weapon, *Das Neue Russland*, 9–10, 1927

The Future of Soviet Film, *Krasnaya panorama*, 40, 1927 (in German) (R, G)*

Fair Retribution, *Krasnaya gazeta*, 10.20.27

Mass Movies, *The Nation*, New York, 11.9.27 (in English)

S. M. Eisenstein on "October," *October* (pamphlet), Moscow, 1927 (G)

"October" on the Screen, *Sovetskii ekran*, 45, 1927

Why "October" Is Late, *Kino*, 12.20.27 (G)

Give Us a State Plan, *Kinofront*, 13–14, 1927 (G)*

How to Film Marx's "Das Kapital," *Iskusstvo kino*, 1, 1973 (G)

1928   What We Await from the Party's Conference on Film Questions, *Sovetskii ekran*, 1, 1928

Literature and Film, *Na literaturnom postu*, 1, 1928 (R)*

For a Special Section, *Kinofront*, 1, 1928

"General Line," *Komsomolskaya pravda*, 2.3.28

The Battle for "October," *Komsomolskaya pravda*, 3.7.28 (R, F, G)*

How We Filmed "October," *Vechernyaya Moskva*, 3.8.28 (with G. Alexandrov)

Our "October," *Kino*, 3.13.28 (G)*

Our "October," Beyond Acted and Non-Acted, *Kino*, 3.20.28 (R,F,G)*

"October," *Daily Worker*, New York, 11.3.28 (fragment of script, in English)

For a Working Class Blockbuster, *Revolyutsiya i kul'tura*, 3–4, 1928*

The Future of Film, *Die Literarische Welt*, March 1928 (in German)

For Soviet Film, *Na literaturnom postu*, 4, 1928*

We Are Waiting, *Komsomolskaya pravda*, 4.1.28*

The Creation of Our Film on October, *Das Neue Russland*, 4–5, 1928 (in German)

The Season in Moscow: Eisenstein and Lunacharsky (Interview), *The Nation*, New York, 6.27.28 (in English)

The Future of Sound Film, *Sovetskii ekran*, 32, 1928. E: *New York Herald Tribune* 9.21.28; *New York Times*, 10.7.28; *Close-up*, 10.28; translated as A Statement on the Sound-Film in *Film Form**

Interview with Theodore Dreiser, *Dreiser Looks At Russia*, New York, 1928 (in English)

Conversation with Eisenstein, *Die Weltbühne*, 32, 1928 (G) (in German)

Theatrical Junk and the New Weapons of Culture, *Sovetskii ekran*, 34, 1928

An Unexpected Juncture, *Zhizn' iskusstva*, Leningrad, 34, 1928. E: translated as The Unexpected in *Film Form*

Emile Zola and Cinema, *Voprosy literatury*, 1, 1928

How We Are Filming "General Line," *Vechernyaya Moskva*, 10.5.28

Why Soviet Film Is Becoming Catastrophically Dull, *Sovetskii ekran*, 44, 1928

The Twelfth Year, *Sovetskii ekran*, 45, 1928 (with G. Alexandrov)*

The New Clientele of Architect Le Corbusier, *Sovetskii ekran*, 46, 1928

Letter to the Editors, *Izvestiya*, 11.11.28

"General Line," *Gudok*, 11.21.28

One, Two, Three—We Are Alarmists, *Kino*, 11.27.28 (with G. Alexandrov)

The Trade of Teacher-Scholar at GTK, *Sovetskii ekran*, 48, 1928*

"General Line," *Izvestiya*, 12.6.28 (with G. Alexandrov)

My First Film, *Sovetskii ekran*, 50, 1928 (R, F, G)

A Komsomol in Dristalovka, Please! *Kul'turnyi pokhod*, 1928 (R)

The Soviet Film, *Voices of October*, New York, 1930 (in English) (also in *Film Essays*)

1929   (1.12) An Experiment Intelligible to the Millions, *Sovetskii ekran*, 6, 1929 (with G. Alexandrov) (R, F)*

Off-Frame, in N. Kaufman, *Japanese Cinema*, Moscow, 1929. E: translated as The Cinematographic Principle and the Ideogram in *Film Form*

"General Line," *Komsomolskaya pravda*, 2.3.29 (with G. Alexandrov)

On "General Line," *Kino*, 2.5.29

Days of Enthusiasm, *Rabochaya Moskva*, 2.22.29 (with G. Alexandrov) (R, F)*

Father Matvei, *Sovetskii ekran*, 7, 1929

(3.4) Prospects, *Iskusstvo*, 1–2, 1929. E: translated as Perspectives in *Film Essays*

Without Actors, *Ogonek*, 10, 1929. E: *Cinema*, New York, June 1930

GTK-VUZ, *Kino*, 3.12.29

Three Years, *Literaturnaya gazeta*, 7.1.29 (with G. Alexandrov)

(4.9) Dramaturgie der Film-Form, in D. Prokop, *Materialien zur Theorie des Films*, Munich, 1971 (in German). E: *Close-Up*, September 1931; translated as A Dialectic Approach to Film Form in *Film Form*

On the Film School, *Rabis*, 32, 1929

(July–Sept.) The Filmic Fourth Dimension, Part I, *Kino*, 8.27.29. E: *Close-Up*, March 1930; Part II, *Close-Up*, April 1930; both parts in *Film Form**

Sound Techniques in Russia, *Lichtbildbühne*, Berlin, 8.23.29 (in German)

Silent Film Is about to Die, *Der Film*, Berlin, no. 17, 9.1.29 (in German)

The Film of Tomorrow, *Vossische Zeitung*, Berlin, 9.15.29. E: *New York Herald Tribune*, 12.22.29

Letter to the Editors, *Film Kurier*, Berlin, 10.17.29 (in German)

A Salute to the Workers of Hamburg, *Hamburger Volkszeitung*, 10.19.29 (in German) (with Tisse)

Conversation with Eisenstein, Director of "Potemkin" (by Béla Balázs), *Arbeiter-Bühne*, Berlin, 10.29 (in German)

Germany, Country of the Strongest Energy, *Der Tagliche Spezialdienst*, 10.23.29 (in German)

Sound Film in Our Country, *Rabis*, 38, 1929

On the Form of Film Scripts, *Bulletin* of the Office for Cinema at the Commercial Representation of USSR in Germany, 1–2, 1929 (R, F)

The Form of Film Script, *Literaturnaya gazeta*, 12.9.29

A Script? No—A Cinematographic Novel, *Preface* to the German translation of the script of "General Line" (in German). E: *New York Times*, 3.30.29 (excerpt)

Preface to the Russian translation of Guido Seeber's *Der Trickfilm*. E: translated as The New Language of Cinema in *Film Essays*

Revolution in the World of Make-Believe: Eisenstein, Russian Master of the Screen, Sets Forth His Theories, *Boston Evening Transcript*, 3.1.30 (in English)

Season's Greetings to the Artists of German Film, *Film Kurier* and *Lichtbildbühne* 1.1.30 (in German) (with Tisse)

1930   (2.17) The Principles of the New Russian Film, *Revue du cinéma*, Paris, April 1930 (in French) (R, G) E (summary): *Close-Up*, April 1930*

The Gendarmes at the Sorbonne, *Kino*, 3.10.30

Interview, *Het Volk*, Amsterdam, 1, 1930. E: *New York Times*, 2.16.30

Filmic Art and Training, *Close-Up*, 3, 1930 (in English)

Eisenstein Explains Some Things That Make Sovkino (conversation with Harry Allan Potamkin), *The Daily Worker*, New York, 5.24.30 (in English)

Our Films Must Have Noise and Dialogue, *Za kommunisticheskoe prosveshchenie*, August 1930

(8.21) Lecture at the Academy of Cinematographic Sciences and Arts in Hollywood (in English) (R)

The Future of the Film, *Close-Up*, August 1930 (in English)

(9.17) The Dynamic Square, Lecture at the Academy of Cinematographic Sciences. . . , *Close-Up*, March–June 1931, also in *Film Essays* (in English)*

1931   Letter from Mexico to the GIK, *Kino*, 9.1.31

The Way to the Screen, *VGIK*, 3, 1.21.63 (R)

"An American Tragedy," *Proletarskoe kino*, 9, 1931

Prometheus (An Experiment), first publication in French in *Cahiers du cinéma*, no. 307

Notes for the Epilogue of "Que Viva Mexico!" *Sight and Sound*, Autumn 1958 (in English)

(10.23) Eisenstein Is Shooting in Mexico, *Film Kurier*, Berlin, 11.16.31 (in German)

Eisenstein's New Film: Russian Director at Work on "Que Viva Mexico!" *New York Times*, 11.29.31

A Mexican Film and Marxist Theory, *New Republic*, 12.9.31 (in English)

Siqueiros, *Catalogue* of a Siqueiros Exhibition in Mexico (in Spanish)

1932   Thinks Hollywood Gagged To Death: Afraid of New Things, *Los Angeles Times*, 4.26.32 (in English)

Eisenstein without Sound Film (interview with Lotte Eisner), *Film Kurier*, Berlin, 4.28.32 (in German)

"Que Viva Mexico!" *Arts Weekly*, 4.30.32 (in English)

Eisenstein's Monster, *Time*, 5.2.32 (in English)

The Final Cut: in Moscow, *Vechernyaya Moskva*, 5.9.32

Eisenstein Is Back In Moscow, *Komsomolskaya pravda*, 5.10.32

A Contribution to the Cause of Socialism, *Za bolshevistskii fil'm*, 6.16.32

The Most Amusing, *Sovetskoe iskusstvo*, 7.9.32

Eisenstein's Plans, *Living Age*, Boston, July 1932 (in English)

Overtake and Surpass, *Proletarskoe kino*, 15–16, 1932. E: *International Literature*, July, 1933

Help Yourself! *Proletarskoe kino*, 17–18, 1932. E: *Close-Up*, Dec. 1932 & March–June 1933; translated as A Course in Treatment in *Film Form**

October and Art, *Soviet Culture Review*, 7–9, 1932 (in English)

In the Front Line, *Kino*, 9.6.32

Die erste Kolonne marschiert, *Kino*, 9.18.32 (only the title is in German)

(9.23) Our Land Is Plentiful—But It Lacks Order (R)

To a Founder of Culture, *Kino*, 9.24.32

A Detective Job, *Kino*, 10.18.32

"The People Remain Silent," *Kino*, 10.24.32

On the Other Side, *Vechernyaya gazeta*, Leningrad, 10.26.32

In the Interests of Form, *Kino*, 11.12.32 (R, F)*

(Dec.) What Lenin Brought Me, *Iskusstvo kino*, 4, 1964 (R, G)

1933   Through the Revolution to Art, through Art to the Revolution, *Sovetskoe kino*, 1–2*

Pantagruel Is Born, *Kino*, 2.4.33 (R, F)

"Kino" Rings Proud, *Kino*, 2.16.33

Every Man to His Place, *Kino*, 3.10.33

Death to the "Blambs," *Kino*, 3.28.33

Georges Méliès's Morale, *Sovetskoe kino*, 3–4, 1933

Introduction, *Za bol'shevistskii fil'm*, 4.15.33
The Schoolmates' Day Out, *Kino*, 6.22 & 6.28.33*
Adventures in a Health Resort, *Tvorchestvo*, 11, 1971
Literature and Film, *Voprosy literatury*, 1, 1968
The Granite of Cine-Science, *Sovetskoe kino*, 5–6, 7 & 9, 1933
A Difficult Bridesmaid, *Literaturnaya gazeta* 6.29.33. E: Film Art, London, Spring 1934
Moscow, *Sovetskoe iskusstvo*, 7.20.33
Moscow through the Ages, *Literaturnaya gazeta*, 7.11.33 (R, F)
Eisenstein Aims at Simplicity (interview with Marie Seton), *Film Art*, London, Summer 1933 (in English)
Film and the Classics, *Literaturnaya gazeta*, 12.23.33*
Regissura—A Treatise on Mise-en-Scène; fragmentary publication (R, G)
Director and Dialectics, *Put' k ekranu*, 3.13.62

1934   For High Ideals, For Cinematic Culture, *Kino*, 1.22.34
I Owe Everything to the Party, *Rabis*, 1, 1934
The American Workers' League of Cinema and Photography, *Kino*, 2.10.34, (with P. Atasheva & E. Tisse)
Torito, first publication in Russian Selected Works (R, F)
(3.9) On Fascism, German Cinema, and Real Life: An Open Letter to Doctor Goebbels, German Minister of Propaganda, *Literaturnaya gazeta*, 3.22.34. E: *Film Art*, London, Winter 1934; *New York Times*, 12.30.34*
Eh! On the Purity of Cinematic Language, *Sovetskoe kino*, 5, 1934. E: translated as Film Language in *Film Form**
Matchless, *Literaturnaya gazeta*, 6.18.34
Siko, *Kino*, 6.28.34
(June) Organicism and "Imaginicity," first publication in Selected Works (R)
Metro, Moscow, Literature, *Pravda*, 8.17.34
Why I Don't Make Films Any More, *Vechernyaya krasnaya gazeta*, Leningrad, 8.22.34
The End of the Mansard Roof, *Izvestiya*, 8.19.34
(9.22) Theater and Film, *Almanakh iskusstva kino*, 8, 1971
(Sept.) The Second of Three, *Sovetskoe kino*, 11–12, 1934. E: translated as Through Theater to Cinema in *Film Form**
With Cinema as a Weapon, *Komsomolskaya pravda*, 11.7.34
At Last! *Literaturnaya gazeta*, 11.18.34. E: *New Theater*, Jan. 1935*
(11.30) A Priori, first publication in Selected Works (R)
To Crush the Enemy, *Komsomolskaya pravda*, 12.4.34
The Komsomols in the Cinema, Odessa, *Kommunist*, 12.5.23 (in Ukrainian)
Paul Robeson, *Pravda*, 12.23.34
Lessons in Mise-en-scène at the VGIK, E: V. Nizhny, *Lessons with Eisenstein*

1935   GTK—GIK—VGIK: Past—Present—Future, *Sovetskoe kino*, 1–2, 1935. E: *Film Essays*
The Most Important, *Izvestiya*, 1.6.35 (R)
In the Sixteenth Year, *Komsomolskaya pravda*, 1.11.35
(1.8) Intervention at the Conference of Soviet Film Workers, *Za bol'shoe kino-iskusstvo*, 1935. E: translated as Film Form: New Problems in *Film Form* (with a few additional pages of introduction)

(1.11) The Truth of Our Time, *Pravda*, 1.12.35
(1.13) Final Speech at the 1935 Conference . . . , *Literaturnaya gazeta*,
1.15.35. E: *Film Form*
We Know What We Have to Do, *Kino*, 1.15.35
At the Time of the 15th Anniversary, *Za kommunisticheskoe pros-
veshchenie*, 1.15.35
(2.3) Lecture at Lenfilm, *Iskusstvo kino*, 4, 1968
"Bezhin Meadow," *Komsomolskaya pravda*, 2.5.35
"The Peasants," *Izvestiya*, 2.11.35 (R)
Film Is a Powerful Tool, *Radioprogramma*, 2.18.35
(Feb.) "The Greedy Ones," first publication in Selected Works (R)
The Theater of Mei Lan-fang, *Komsomolskaya pravda*, 3.11.3. E:
International Literature, 5, 1935
(March) To the Enchanter from the Pear Garden, *Mei-Lan-Fang and
Chinese Theater*, Moscow: VOKS, 1935. E: *Theater Arts Monthly*,
Oct. 1935
Letter to the Pioneers, *Znamya Triekhgorkii*, 4.8.35
The April Decree of the C.C. of the C.P. Is the Basis for the Devel-
opment of Artistic Creation, *Kino*, 4.22.35
Eisenstein's New Film, *International Literature*, 5, 1935 (in English)
From Screen To Life, *Komsomolskaya pravda*, 6.27.35 (R, F)
He Is Ours! *Kino*, 9.5.35 (R)
I Appeal to Socialist Emulation, *Za bol'shevistskii fil'm*, 9.9.35
We Can! *Za bol'shevistskii fil'm*, 9.9.35 (R)
(11.5) Essay on an Essayist, first publication in Selected Works (R)
A Reasonable Measure, *Kino*, 11.17.35 (R)
We'll Keep Our Word, *Kino*, 11.23.35 (R)
The Artistic Year, *Sovetskoe iskusstvo*, 12.29.35
Wolves and Sheep, *Selected Essays*, Moscow, 1956. E: *Notes of a
Film Director*

1936   An Answer to the Survey "In 1936," *Izvestiya*, 1.1.36
By Way of an Intervention, *Kino*, 3.11.36
It Will Be a Film on Heroic Childhood, *Za kollektivizatsiyu*, 3.18.36
"Bezhin Meadow," *Krestyanskaya gazeta*, 3.31.36
Program for Teaching the Theory and Practice of Film Directing,
Iskusstvo kino, 4, 1936. E: Nizhny, *Lessons with Eisenstein*
In One's Heart of Hearts—and Aloud, *Kino*, 5.6.36
The Greatest Creative Honesty, *Kino*, 6.22.35. E: *Notes of A Film
Director*
A Brilliant Scenario for the Future, *Kino*, 6.17.36
Letter to the Editors, *Kino*, 8.17.36
To Chastise the Murderers, *Sovetskoe iskusstvo*, 8.23.36
Paul Robeson, *Rabochaya Moskva*, 12.20.36 (R)
Foreword to V. Nilsen, *Cinema as a Graphic Art*, London, 1936;
Theater Arts Monthly, May 1938 (in English)

1937   The Errors of the Film "Bezhin Meadow," *Sovetskoe iskusstvo*, 4.17.37.
E: *International Literature*, 7, 1937
Why Is "Bezhin Meadow" a Failure? *Vechernyaya Moskva*, 4.25.37
(Summer) Montage, first publication in Selected Works (R)
(9.29) El Greco and Cinema, *Voprosy iskusstva*, 7, 1963
(11.7) Preface to "Montage," first publication in Selected Works (R)
An Image of Immense Historic Truthfulness and of Great Realism,
Za bol'shevistskii fil'm, 12.27.37 (R)

The Epic in Soviet Film, *International Literature*, 10, 1937 (in English)

Bolsheviks Laugh, *Selected Essays*, 1956. E: translated as A Few Thoughts about Soviet Comedy in *Notes of a Film Director*

An Excerpt from the History of the Creation of "Alexander Nevsky," first publication in Selected Works (R, F)

Ermolova, first publication in Selected Works (R)

1938   "The Land of Soviets"—to the Land of Soviets, *Kino*, 2.17.38 (R)

"Alexander Nevsky," *Literaturnaya gazeta*, 4.26.38 (with Pavlenko) (R)

The Film "Alexander Nevsky," *Krasnyi Oktiabr'*, Syrzan, 6.28.38 (with D. Vasiliev)

(March–May) Montage 1938, *Iskusstvo kino*, 1, 1939. E: *The Film Sense; Notes of a Film Director*

Alexander Nevsky and the German Collapse, *Izvestiya*, 7.12.38

Once Again on National-Heroic Theater, *Teatr*, 7, 1938 (R)

Answer to Survey: "What Are Film Directors Doing?" *Proletarskaya pravda*, Kalinin, 8.26.38

We Are Ready for Any Task, *Za bol'shevistskii fil'm*, 11.11.38

How We Made "Alexander Nevsky," *Trud*, 11.11.38

Patriotism Is Our Theme, *Kino*, 11.11.38. E: *International Literature*, 2, 1939; *Daily Worker*, 4.1.39

"Alexander Nevsky," *Sovetskoe iskusstvo*, 11.12.38

"Alexander Nevsky," *Gudok*, 11.14.38

A Film on the Patriotism of the Great Russian People, *Krasnaya gazeta*, Leningrad, 11.29.38

Notes of a Film Director, *Ogonek*, 22, 1938

"Perekop," *Kino*, 12.2.38

Us and Them, *Kino*, 12.5.38 (R, F)

A Merry Companion, *Vechernyaya Moskva*, 12.7.38

His Life Is an Exploit, *Sovetskoe iskusstvo*, 12.16.38 (R)

In Enthusiasm Lies the Basis of Creation, *Young Masters of Art*, Moscow, 1938 (R)

Director of "Alexander Nevsky" Describes How the Film Was Made, *Moscow News*, 12.5.38 (in English); *Daily Worker*, 3.19.39

(12.24) The Enigma of "Nevsky," first publication in Selected Works (R)

On the Film-Novel "We, the Russian People," *Selected Essays*, 1956 (R)

A Year of Progress for Soviet Cinema, *Kurortnaya gazeta*, Sochy, 12.31.38

1939   The Right Principle, *Kino*, 1.5.39

"Alexander Nevsky," *Historical Soviet Film*, Moscow, 1939. E: *International Literature*, 1, 1939

To Glorify Our Fatherland, *Sovetskoe iskusstvo*, 2.4.39

(Jan.) On the Structure of Things, *Iskusstvo kino*, 6, 1939. E: translated as The Structure of the Film in *Film Form*

We Shall Prove Worthy of the High Award, *Za bol'shevistskii fil'm*, 2.8.39

We Serve the People, *Izvestiya*, 2.11.39

Before the Shooting of a Film on Frunze, *Kino*, 2.23.39 (R, F)

(Feb.) The Birth of an Actor, first publication in Selected Works (R)

Autobiography, first publication in Selected Works (R)

A Proud Joy, *Za bol'shevistskii fil'm*, 3.23.39

Lenin in Our Hearts, *Izvestiya*, 4.6.39 (R)

Hello, Charlie!, *Izvestiya*, 4.17.39. E: *Notes of A Film Director*

Speech at the Meeting of Moscow Studios Intellectuals, *Kino*, 4.23.39

Foreword, *Soviet Films 1938–39*, Moscow, 1939 (in English)

Greatness of Soviet Aviation, *Vechernyaya Moskva*, 5.1.39

25 and 15, *Kino*, 5.23.39. E: *Notes of a Film Director*

The Soviet Screen, Pamphlet for the Soviet Pavilion at the New York World's Fair, 1939 (in English)

Autobiographical Notes, *Kul'tura i zhizn'*, 5, 1958. E: *Culture And Life*, Moscow, 1958

A Film on the Fergana Canal, *Pravda*, 8.13.39 (R, F)

(Aug.) The Fergana Canal, *Iskusstvo kino*, 9, 1939 (F)

We Don't Recognize the Region, *Pravda*, 9.2.39

(Aug.–Sept.) My Theme Is Patriotism, first publication in Selected Works (R, F)

(Sep.) Encounters with Millionaires, *Literaturnaya Rossiya*, 11.7.68 (F)

(10.13) Pushkin and Cinema, *Iskusstvo kino*, 4, 1955. E: translated as Lessons from Literature in *Film Essays*

1940   Pride, *Iskusstvo kino*, 1–2, 1940. E: translated as Achievement in *Film Form*

Frenzied Artists, *Sovetskoe foto*, 1, 1940 (R)

The Fatherland Embraces Its Valiant Sons, *Literaturnaya gazeta*, 1.30.40

Birth of a Master, *Iskusstvo kino*, 1–2, 1940. E: translated as The Birth of an Artist in *Notes of a Film Director*

Twenty, *Twenty Years of Soviet Films*, Moscow, 1940 (R)

Even—Odd, first publication in French in *Cinématisme*, Bruxelles, 1980

Not Colored, But in Color, *Kino*, 5.29.40. E: *Notes of a Film Director*

The Splitting of the Unique, first publication in French, *Cinématisme*, 1980

(5.15) The Inexhaustible Object, *Nedelya*, 4.29.61

Once Again on the Structure of Things, *Iskusstvo kino*, 6, 1940. E: translated as More Thoughts on Structure in *Film Essays*

Poor Salieri! first publication in Selected Works (R, F)

A Great Joy, *Trudovaya gazeta*, Riga, 8.24.40

Before the Premiere of "Die Walküre," *Vechernyaya Moskva*, 9.21.40

Vertical Montage, *Iskusstvo kino*, 9, 1940; 12, 1940; 1, 1941. E: translated as Synchronization of Senses, Color and Meaning, and Form and Content in *Film Sense*

(2.15) We Are Twenty, *Soviet Cinema 1919–1939*, Moscow, 1940 (R)

Soviet Historical Film, *Pravda*, 2.8.40

Problems of Soviet Historical Film, *Soviet Historical Film*, Moscow, 1940 (R)

(March–Oct.) The Embodiment of a Myth, *Teatr*, 10, 1940. E: *Film Essays* (abridged)

(March) Notes on "Boris Godunov," *Iskusstvo kino*, 3, 1959 (excerpt)

Creative Encounter with Wagner, *Ogonek*, 29, 1940. E: *Sunday Worker*, New York, 4.20.40

(Apr.–Jun.) Notes on Mayakovsky, *Iskusstvo kino*, 1, 1958 (R, F)

What Film Studios Are Working On, *Izvestiya*, 11.27.40

A Salute to Armenia on the Victory of Socialism, *Kommunist*, 11.26.40
Eisenstein Makes His Debut in Opera: Noted Film Director Discusses His Work on "The Valkyrie," *Moscow News*, 11.20.40 (in English)
To the Editors of "International Literature": A Communication, *International Literature*, Nov.–Dec. 1940 (in English)
On Color in "The Poet's Love," first publication in Selected Works (R, F, I). E: *Quarterly Review of Film Studies*, Spring 1978
Preface to Kuleshov's *The Foundations of Film Directing, Sovetskii ekran*, 23, 1940 (Kuleshov's book was published in 1941)
An Eye for an Eye, first publication in Selected Works (R, F)
In Close-Up, first publication in Selected Works (R, F)
By Way of a Postface, first publication in Selected Works (R)
Beyond the Stars, first publication in Works in French (F)
Notes on Pushkin, *Voprosy literatury*, 10, 1971
(Nov.–Dec.) The Psychology of Art, *Psikhologiya protsessov khudozhestvennogo tvorchestva*, Leningrad, 1980

1941   For a Fruitful Work, *Za bol'shevistskii fil'm*, 1.1.41
Our Creative Tasks, *Za bol'shevistskii fil'm*, 2.12.41
On the "Mysteries" of Film Technique, *Illustrirovannaya gazeta*, 3.2.41
Memorable Days, *Izvestiya*, 3.18.41
Forward! *Za bol'shevistskii fil'm*, 3.21.41
Let's Prove Worthy of the [Government's] Trust, *Kino*, 3.21.41
A Film on Ivan the Terrible, *Izvestiya*, 4.30.41
(4.1) Young People of America! first publication in Selected Works (R)
(5.1) We've Met Each Other, first publication in Selected Works (R, F)
Three Directors, *Iskusstvo kino*, 5, 1941
Let's Strengthen the Military Power of Our Country, *Za bol'shevistskii fil'm*, 6.3.41
Heirs and Builders of World Culture, *Pravda*, 4.30.41
Fascism Must and Shall Be Destroyed, *Defense of Civilization against Fascist Barbarism*, Moscow, 1941 (in English)
Notes on Young Film Directors, *Pravda*, 6.16.41
A Film That Falsifies History, *Internatsional'naya literatura*, 5, 1941
"The Great Dictator," *Kino*, 6.27.41. E: translated as The Dictator in *Notes of a Film Director*
Organization and Discipline, *Za bol'shevistskii fil'm*, 7.1.41
To Brother Jews of the Whole World, Pamphlet *Brother Jews of the Whole World*, Moscow, 1941 (in English)
Fascist Bestiality on the Screen, *Krasnyi voin*, 7.11.41
Crush and Destroy the Vile Invaders, *Krasnyi flot*, 7.18.41
Hitler Is Caught in Pincers, *Kino*, 7.18.41
(9.11 & 18) On the Composition of Short Films, *Voprosy kinodrama*, 6, 1974
Cinema against Fascism, *Pravda*, 10.8.41
(9.21–5.8.43) Notebooks on "Ivan the Terrible," *Voprosy kinodramaturgii*, 4, 1962 (excerpt in R)
"Ivan the Terrible": A Film on Russian Renaissance of the 16th Century, *Literatura i iskusstvo*, 7.4.42 (R, F)

1942   (Feb.–Nov.) Notebooks on "Ivan the Terrible," *Voprosy kinodramaturgii*, 4, 1962 (R, excerpt)

(4.19) Notes for a Lecture on Mayakovsky, in A. Fevralsky, *Mayakovsky and Soviet Literature*, Moscow, 1964. E: *Artforum*, New York, Jan. 1973

Ten Years Ago, *Literatura i iskusstvo*, 5.1.42

"Ivan the Terrible," *Trud*, 8.20.42

Our Friends from Overseas, *Literatura i iskusstvo*, 8.15.42

(8.21–22) American Films Reflect Fighting Qualities of American People, *Bulletin* of the Soviet Embassy in Washington, 1942 (in English)

(Oct.) Preface to "The Film Sense," unpublished as such; large excerpts in *Nonindifferent Nature* (R, F, I)

(10.17) Posthumous Memories, first publication in Selected Works (R, F)

Valya Kadochnikov, first publication in Selected Works (R, F)

(11.11) Notes on Prokofiev's Music, *Voprosy kino-iskusstva*, 10, 1967 (excerpt)

(Nov.) PRKFV, first publication in Selected Essays, 1956. E: first version, in I. Nestyev, *Sergej Prokofiev: His Musical Life*, New York, 1946; final version: *Notes of a Film Director*

1943   Dickens, Griffith, and Us, *Amerikanskaya kinematografiya: Griffith*, Moscow, 1944. Longer version (1946) first published in *Selected Essays*. E: translated as Dickens, Griffith and the Film Today in *Film Form*

(Oct.) A Few Words on My Drawings, *Mosfilm*, 1, 1959. E: *"Ivan the Terrible,"* London, 1963; *Notes of a Film Director* (abridged)

(Autumn) Charlie the Kid, *Charles Spencer Chaplin*, Moscow, 1945. E: *Film Essays, Notes of a Film Director*

The Letter That Was Never Sent, *Iskusstvo kino*, 1, 1958

Diderot Spoke of Cinema, first publication in French, *Europe*, May 1984.

Notebooks on "Ivan the Terrible," *Voprosy kinodramaturgii*, 4, 1962 (R, excerpt)

(1943–1947) *Method*; only short excerpts of this projected book have been published so far—notably "Unity," *Voprosy kinodramaturgii*, 4, 1962 (F)

On Detective Films, *Priklychencheskii fil'm*, Moscow, 1980

1944   The Show Is Moving and Touching, *Kazakhstanskaya pravda*, 8.6.44

(11.21) Twenty Years Ago, *Bronenosets "Potemkin,"* Moscow, 1969 (F)

Sergei Eisenstein, first publication in Selected Works (R, F)

On Myself, *Selected Essays*, 1956 (R, F)

1945   Our Work on the Film, *Izvestiya*, 2.4.45

How We Made the Film, *Vechernyaya Moskva*, 2.15.45

How We Shot "Ivan the Terrible," *Bulletin* of VOKS, Feb. 1945. E: *Film Chronicle*, Feb. 1945; translated as Notes from a Director's Laboratory in *Film Form*

France Liberated! *Sovetskoe iskusstvo*, 4.19.45 (R)

The "Twelve Apostles," *Iskusstvo kino*, 4, 1950. E: *Notes of a Film Director*

Resurrection, *Literaturnaya gazeta*, 6.23.45

Rodin and Rilke, first publication in French, *Cinématisme*, 1980

(Spring–Summer) Nonindifferent Nature, first publication in Selected Works (R, F, I)

A Very Great Statesman, *Ogonek*, 9–10, 1945 (R, F)

(Sept.) Peace and the Atomic Bomb, *Iskusstvo kino*, 12, 1965

In Close-Up, *Iskusstvo Kino*, 1, 1945. E: *Film Essays*

Comrade Léon, first publication in Selected Works. E: *Immoral Memories*

Mr. Lincoln by Mr. Ford, *Iskusstvo kino*, 4, 1960. E: *Film Essays*

"You Won't Forget This," first publication in Selected Works (R)

How I Became A Film Director, *How I Became A Film Director*, Moscow, 1946. E: *Notes of a Film Director*

It Has Been Accomplished! first publication in Selected Works (R)

The Voltairean Disease, first publication in Selected Works. E: *Immoral Memories*

The Day of the Dead in Mexico, first publication in Selected Works (R, F)

A Few Words on Graphic and Audiovisual Composition, first publication in French, *Cinématisme*, 1980

1946   (May–Nov.) Memories, first publication in Selected Works. E: *Immoral Memories*

(5.10) The People of a Film, first complete publication in Selected Works (R, F). E: Y. Barna, *Eisenstein*, London, 1972 (excerpts)

(June) First Letter on Color, first publication in Selected Works (R, F, I)

A Word from the Author, first version: *Film Form*; second version: *Selected Essays*, 1956. E: *Notes of a Film Director*

On "Ivan the Terrible," *Kul'tura i zhizn'*, 10.20.46. E: M. Seton, *Eisenstein*, London, 1952

(10.14) True Ways of Invention, *Selected Essays*, 1956. E: *Notes of A Film Director*

(10.14) Planning, first publication in Selected Works (R)

(11.46-4.47) From an Unpublished Essay on Color, first publication in Selected Works (R, I)

(12.25) Problems of Composition (Final Lesson), *Voprosy dramaturgii*, 1, 1954. E: *Film Essays*

On Ivan Pyriev, first publication in Selected Works (R, F)

(1946–47) Pathos, first publication in Selected Works (R, F, I). E: *Oppositions*, Winter 1977 (excerpts)

1947   (March) Excerpts from a Lesson on Music and Color in "Ivan the Terrible," first publication in Selected Works (R, F, I)

(March) Judith, first publication in Selected Works (R, F)

(March) On Three-Dimensional Film, first complete publication in Selected Works. E: translated as Stereoscopic Films in *Notes of a Film Director* (abridged) (R, I)

(7.1) The Incomparable Galina Sergeevna Ulanova, first publication in Selected Works (R)

Purveyors of Spiritual Poison, *Kul'tura i zhizn'*, 7.31.47. E: *Sight And Sound*, Autumn 1947

(9.30) Genealogy of Color in "Moscow 800," *Mosfilm*, 2, 1961 (R, I)

(10.24) Thirty Years of Soviet Cinema and the Traditions of Russian Culture, *Iskusstvo kino*, 5, 1949 (R)

(11.7) The Spectator-Creator, *Ogonek*, 26, 1948 (R)

(11.19) A Lesson on the Psychology of Art, *Psikhologiya protsessov khudozhestvennogo tvorchestva*, Leningrad, 1980

To the Soviet Militia-Man, *Na boevom postu*, 11.12.47

(Nov.) Unified (Reflections on the History of Soviet Cinema), first complete publication in Selected Works (R)

Postface To "Que Viva Mexico!" *Iskusstvo kino*, 5, 1957. E: M. Seton, *Sergei Eisenstein, A Biography*

Dedication (To Battleship "Potemkin"), first complete publication in Selected Works (R)

Always Forward! *Iskusstvo kino*, 1, 1952. E: *Notes of a Film Director* (abridged)

The Only One, first publication in Selected Works (R)

1948   (Jan.) "Mise-en-jeu" and "Mise-en-geste," first publication in Selected Works (R)

(1.21), On Color, first complete publication in *Kino i vremia*, Moscow, 1980

(2. 10–11) Color Film (A Letter to Kuleshov), *Selected Essays*, 1956. E: *Notes of a Film Director*

(Eisenstein died during the writing of this last text.)

INDEX

Absent One, 38
Abstraction, 101, 175–76, 184
Accent, 134–35, 186–87
Actors, 28, 33, 185, 193–94, 221 n.34; in the circus, 20; movements and gestures of, 123, 128, 215 nn.45, 46
Affairs: in Eisenstein's life, 200 n.3
Aggressiveness: and attraction, 42, 47
Agitprop, 45, 49
Agronomist (in *General Line*,) 75, 83, 84
Albéra, François, 51, 207 nn. 25, 26
Alberti, 212 n.17
Alexander Nevsky, 13, 18, 31, 33, 60, 170; completion deadline, 202 n.17; studio used for, 165
Alexander III, statue of: in *October*, 131–32
Alternating (rhythmic) montage, 105, 157, 213 n.26; in *General Line*, 88, 97; in *Ivan*, 130, 134–35
Amengual, 43, 145, 149, 188, 195, 211 n.14
American Tragedy, An, 190, 222 n.39
Analogy, 32, 126, 129
Anastasia (in *Ivan*), 115–19, 127–30, 135, 137–39, 142–44
Anecdotes: in films, 16–17, 160–62, 175; in work journals, 161, 219 n.16
Anti-naturalism, 42, 115–16, 128, 165, 167, 175–76
Anxiety: in *General Line*, 87, 88, 92
Archetypes: and symbolic *typage*, 142
Architecture, 208–209 n.35, 213–14 n.33; as referent in *Ivan*, 117–18, 120, 131
ARRK, 152
Art, 28, 44–45, 48–49
Articulation, 171, 187
Artist-engineer, 5, 7
Aryan blond: in Eisenstein's films, 85, 210–11 n.8
Association, 43–44, 47, 48, 166–69, 190; in *General Line*, 93–94; and intellectual montage, 158, 160–61, 163
Atheism, 3–4
Athenians: baby box anecdote about, 219 n.16
Atasheva, Pera, 5
Attraction, 28, 41–51, 58, 63; definition of, 47; intellectual attraction, 44, 147, 156, 165

Audio-visual counterpoint, 28, 68, 172, 184–85, 187
Authenticity, 165
Authorial status, 12–13, 202 n.22
Autonomy, 53, 126; of attraction, 42, 43–44, 47, 48, 206 n.20
Avant-garde cinema, 35–37
Axis matches, 133, 135

Baby box: anecdote about, 219 n.16
Balázs, Béla, 147–48, 149, 194
Barbaro, Umberto, 146
Barricade: representation of, 176–78
Barthes, Roland, 10, 104, 200–201 n.16; on meanings, 99–100, 212 n.21, 215 n.44, 219–20 n.21
Basmanov (in *Ivan*), 115–17, 128, 139–40, 143–44, 213 n.30, 215 n.60
Bathos, 208 n.29
Battleship Potemkin. See Potemkin
Bazin, André, 30, 90, 92, 145, 147, 212 n.17
"Béla Forgets the Scissors," 147
Bezhin Meadow, 17, 24, 52, 85, 153, 165; interior monologue in, 44, 64, 191; self-criticism of, 178, 179
Bird of prey: Efrosinia as, 135, 216 n.51
Blackness, 128–29
Bonitzer, Pascal, 122, 124–25, 214 n.40, 220 n.28; on close-ups, 38, 204–205 n.8
Bordwell, David, 152
Bounds. *See* Leaps
Bourgeoisie, 20, 21, 58, 178–79
Braking, 90, 98, 102
Brecht, 21, 140
Brewster, Ben, 191
Bricolage, 150
Building to be built: representation of, 197, 198
Burch, Noel, 32, 134

Cadre. *See* Frame
Calculus, 7
Calligraphy, 19–20
Camera, 92, 123, 154
Capital (Marx), 161, 163
Capital (proposed film), 150, 159–69

students as, 8; understanding of meaning, 126
Spontaneity, 26, 39
Stalin, 13; and *General Line,* 88, 211 n.11
Stalinism, 13, 66–67, 71, 107; Eisenstein and, 21–22, 23; and unity, 60, 65, 69
Stanislavsky system, 33, 193
Statesman: Ivan as, 116, 117
Stereotypes, 4, 85
Still photographs: and errors of analysis, 125, 214 n.40
Stimuli (excitants), 32–33, 53, 54, 63, 189; role in attraction, 45–46, 47; role in intellectual montage, 159, 160, 163
Strauch, Maxim, 200 n.4, 203 n.26
Stream of consciousness, 190
Strike, 46, 48, 53, 54, 149; intellectual montage in, 158, 160, 164
Studio: shooting in, 165
Styk (join; junction; link), 104–106, 125, 174, 213 n.25
Subjectivism, 64
Subliminal code, 104
Suspense, 140
Symbolic, the: Freud's conception of, 5
Symbolic *typage,* 142–44, 217 n.63
Symbolism, 148, 149–50, 161, 179, 195–96, 218 n.4; in *General Line,* 87, 94, 95, 105; and imaginicity, 221 n.31; in *Ivan,* 115, 139, 142
Synecdoche, 97, 158, 181–82, 184
Syntagm, 35–36, 69, 97–98, 130, 168
Syntax, 34–35, 158–59

Teaching. *See* VGIK courses
Tension, 47, 90, 94
Theater, 37, 42, 119–20, 132, 181
Thematization: code subliminal to, 104
Theme, 43–44, 47, 93, 141, 207 n.27
Theory of Film Practice (Burch), 32
Third meaning, 99–100, 212 n.21, 215 n.44, 219–20 n.21
Thought, figures of. *See* Figures of thought
Thought, laws of, 63, 190, 192
Thought and language (Vygotsky), 191
Three, 102–103, 212 n.23
"Through Theater to Cinema," 220 n.26
Time, 87, 132, 158, 180
Tisse, 211 n.14
Tonal montage, 32, 105

Tones, 33
"Torito," 44
Transcendence: and ecstasy, 59–60
Transparency: attraction as escape from, 42
Tretyakov, 207 n.26
Triangles, 103, 104
Trick: as attraction, 42
Trotsky: and agitprop, 45
28 mm. lens. *See* Wide-angle lens
Typage, 141–44

Ulysses (Joyce), 164, 219 n.14
Uninterrupted montage, 30
Unity, 60, 65, 66–68, 69–70, 188, 194; of mental image, 193; of narration, 130; of opposites, 124, 125, 179; of space, 87
Univocality, 168
Utopia: depiction in *General Line,* 106–107, 213 n.28

Vasiliev, Sergei, 57
Verticality, 31–34, 36, 56, 87, 168, 207 n.27
"Vertical Montage," 29, 31, 170
Vertical montage, 135. *See also* Organic montage
Vertov, 30, 34
VGIK courses, 7–8, 33, 90, 154, 201 nn.11, 12; "Course Outline," 182, 221 n.36; on *Crime and Punishment,* 123; on mise-en-scène, 119–20, 121
Violence, 17, 98
Vision, 16
Vygotsky, 191, 192

Whiteness, 3, 128–29, 212 n.20
Wide-angle lens, 39, 126, 133–34, 214–15 n.43
Wolf-Man, 93
Woman: symbolization of, 142–43
Women: and Eisenstein, 4–5, 15, 201 n.8
Working class: effect of films on, 46, 206 n.19
Writing (écriture), 123, 124, 134, 141, 148–49
Writing (Eisenstein's), 1, 9–12, 151

Yazyk, 34
Yin-and-yang, 20
Yutkevich, 52